Dr B. R. Ambedkar's Vision of Nation-Building

Dr B. R. Ambedkar's Vision of Nation-Building

Professor Kanta Kataria

KALPAZ

First Published, 2017

Published by

Kalpaz Publications
C-30, Satyawati Nagar,
Delhi – 110052
E-mail: kalpaz@hotmail.com
Ph.: 9212142040

Printed at: G. Print Process, Delhi

Cataloging in Publication Data—DK
Courtesy: D.K. Agencies (P) Ltd. <docinfo@dkagencies.com>

Kataria, Kanta, author.
Dr B.R. Ambedkar's vision of nation-building / Professor Kanta Kataria.
pages cm
Includes bibliographical references.
ISBN 9789351282778

1. Ambedkar, B. R. (Bhimrao Ramji), 1891-1956—Political and social views. 2. India—Politics and government—20th century. 3. India—Social conditions—20th century. I. Title.

DS481.A43K38 2017 DDC 954.035 23

Contents

Foreword

An eminent scholar of political science, Professor Kanta Kataria specializes in modern Indian social and political thought, particularly that of Dr B. R. Ambedkar. Her earlier work on the 'Relevance of Ambedkar's Ideology', published by Rawat Publications, Jaipur, in the year 2015, is an outstanding one, fully appreciated and recognized by the scholars in the said field. Her present research work, titled: 'B. R. Ambedkar's Vision of Nation-Building'; sponsored by the University Grants Commission., New Delhi, is another scholarly output, demonstrating her interest, worth and ability in understanding and grasping the dimensions of Dr Ambedkar's political and social ideas. She has clearly shown that most of the traditional researchers on Ambedkar have emphasized that the abolition of untouchability, the making of the Indian Constitution and conversion to Buddhism, were his significant contributions. While agreeing to this view point, Professor Kanta Kataria, in addition, asserts that there is need to evaluate Ambedkar in totality in order to know his more significant and more lasting contribution, which resides in his vision of nation-building. She argues that the ultimate aim of Ambedkar's ideology is to build a vibrant and integral nation.

Dr Ambedkar held the view that India is not a nation, because of the lack of social and psychological unity among the people, but it can become a nation provided proper processes of social amalgamation are put in motion. What are the hindrances to the path of nation-building? What are the requisites for making India a healthy and a virile nation? The present work of Professor Kanta Kataria provides a proper answer to these two fundamental questions relating to nation-building in the context of Ambedkar's ideology.

Professor Kanta Kataria states that the idea of nation-building occupies a central place in Dr Ambedkar's ideology. His is an integral rather than a piecemeal approach towards nation-building. She highlights a number of impediments, propounded by Ambedkar, that cripple the task of nation-building, such as, the existence of *Varna* and caste systems, the notion of infallibility of the *Vedas*, the lack of social and psychological unity among the people, the nature of Hindu religion which is based on rules, outdated religious notions, graded inequality and the like. Simultaneously, she mentions a number of the Ambedkarian components that are necessary for nation-building, such as, the recognition of the importance of Man and the supremacy of reason; abolition of untouchability root and branch; the acceleration of social and economic democracy; constitutional and peaceful methods of social change; creation of a new society based on liberty, equality, fraternity and social justice; the promotion of education, human rights and human dignity; the safeguarding of minority interests; individual development and social emancipation; revolt against orthodoxy and traditional taboos; creation of a true religion based on principles; the primacy of the country against narrow creeds of the political parties; and the like. Infact, social justice and equality of rights are the basic pillars on which Ambedkar would like to erect his nation-building edifice over the ruins of *Varna* ideology of injustice, inequality and privilege. No nation-building is possible, according to Ambedkar, unless we wipe out and annihilate the spirit of the *Varna* system and its ally the graded inequality, which have dislocated the limbs of the social order. Infact, Ambedkar is deeply wounded by the wickedness of graded inequality, and if it prevails exclusively and in full, the task of nation-building is bound to be a hollow one.

Though diehards may think that Dr Ambedkar's vision of nation-building is strange and unpleasant; the caste-Hindus may denigrate Ambedkar's new ideas of nation-building; Professor Kanta Kataria has boldly supported Dr Ambedkar's vison of nation-building and characterizes it as an original, sublime and of very high quality. She has categorically stated that Ambedkar's model of nation-building alone can usher in social change in the direction of strengthening social solidarity and social cohesion; and ultimately may be helpful in developing a viable, healthy and just social order.

Professor Kanta Kataria thinks that Ambedkar had a great passion for analysis and a hatred of woolly thinking. She argues that Ambedkar's vision of nation-building is highly pragmatic; it is not an utopian exercise. She asserts that Ambedkar is neither a paradise dreamer nor a propounder of false ideas about nation-building; because of his remarkable capability to distinguish between illusion and reality. She frankly says that Ambedkar is clear and exact; he is direct, vigorous and even rebellious; he expresses in the briefest possible way the fundamentals of nation-building. His vision of nation-building reflects an equilpibrium of thought and action.

Professor Kanta Kataria, in my opinion, has spent a lot of time studying Ambedkar and possesses a lot of wide knowledge about him. It seems to me that there is an explosion of scholarly interest in her study of Ambedkar. Her approach has been a holistic one, wherein she has shown a great capability in conjoining the scattered parts of Ambedkar's thought on nation-building, and putting it into a coherent whole. Her knowledge, information and understanding of Dr Ambedkar's thought is deep and profound, which is clearly evident in this magnificent work. Written in a lucid style, with decorative quotes at appropriate places and a careful analysis of facts, the present work of Professor Kanta Kataria is illuminative and seminal, depicting Dr Ambedkar's vision of nation-building clearly and precisely. The work opens to us new avenues, or a way of making progress towards the ideal of a strong nation.

I would like to congratulate Professor Kanta Kataria for producing an impressive and brilliant work on Ambedkar as nation-builder. Written in almost flawless and ornamental English, her work will be of great use and benefit to the researchers and students who wish to understand Dr Ambedkar's vision of nation-building in its true perspective.

Professor L. S. Rathore

Preface

Dr B.R. Ambedkar was a notable 'thinker-activist' in modern India. The Hindu social order of the period was highly exploitative in character which denied equality and freedom to millions of untouchables or depressed classes. The caste Hindus considered them as a polluted class and, therefore, kept them isolated and alienated from the main stream of society. Even the treatment given to them was worst than slaves. They had no opportunities for advancement and the caste Hindus regarded them as a degraded class, meant to serve them. It was at such a stage in modern Indian history that Ambedkar appeared on the scene and heralded a new era of liberation for this helpless mass of humanity. Unmindful of formidable difficulties that stood in his way, Ambedkar carried on his task of liberating the downtrodden, with a lot of courage, fortitude and determination. After a prolonged struggle, Ambedkar achieved a remarkable success, at the time of framing the Constitution of Free India, when untouchability was abolished and its practice in any form forbidden. This marked the beginning of a great social revolution in modern India.

Apart from his role in the framing of the Constitution and the abolition of untouchability, the ultimate aim of Ambedkar's social revolution has been the nation-building. The important element of his nation-building are: Man, social change, fraternity and psychological unity amongst the people.

In Ambedkar's ideology of nation building the primary focus is on Man, not God. To him, Man is the measure of all things. He exalts the dignity of Man. He regards the Hindu scriptures – the Vedas, Smritis, and Shrutis– as essentially retrograde, because they are meant to block the advancement of the millions of men belonging to depressed classes. He discards all the outdated traditions rooted in the Hindu social order, because they derive their inspiration from the said scriptures, thereby deny the dignity to Man. No nation-building is possible unless the dignity of Man is restored, and he is liberated from the bondages of social ills and obnoxious tradition.

Ambedkar has been an ardent champion of social change. His ideology of social change is replete with realism and vision. His concept of social change is meant to promote the transformation of society on the lines of liberty, equality, fraternity and social justice. His efforts towards the abolition of untouchablity, the initiation of Hindu Code Bill, the empowerment of women, and the quest for a just society, are a few instances that demonstrate Ambedkar's vision of nation-building. Social change, he argues, must happen in a harmonious, peaceful and constitutional ways; and not through violent or revolutionary methods. Such a social change, he believes, would be lasting and useful towards building a cohesive and viable nation.

The essence of Ambedkar's nation-building lies in fraternity. Neither the just society nor the nation-building is possible in the absence of fraternity. The cultivation of fraternity or the feelings of brotherhood among the citizens of all castes and creeds is vital for the growth and development of a strong nation.

Though Ambedkar is an earnest nation-builder, this aspect of his contribution has received scant attention from the writers on him. Analysing the hindrances in the path of nation-building, Ambedkar frankly states that in a social and psychological sense India is not a nation. Realising the significance of nation-building, he offers useful models towards the attainment of the ideal. To promote social and psychological feelings of oneness, he recommends the annihilation of Chaturvarna, the caste system and the sanctity of the Hindu scriptures. He believes that political democracy alone is not enough to bind the individuals in a bond of unity; it must be supplemented with social and economic democracy. Both social transformation and liberation of Man are essential for the creation of a strong nation.

Place: Jodhpur **Professor Kanta Kataria**
Dated :: ....

Acknowledgements

At the outset, I must express my sense of gratefulness to the University Grants Commission (UGC) for the sanction of a major research project, titled: 'Man, Social Change and Fraternity: Ambedkar's Model of Nation Building'. The financial assistance provided by the UGC has been of immense help towards the completion of this project.

I am greatly indebted to Professor L.S. Rathore, Emeritus Professor of Political Science and former Vice Chancellor, J.N. Vyas University, Jodhpur, for helping me sincerely at various stages during the course of the preparation of this research project. I am also thankful to Professor P.S. Bhati, Emeritus Professor of Political Science and former Head of Department of Political Science, J.N. Vyas University, Jodhpur, for providing valuable suggestions relating to the theme of the project. To Professor Poonam Bawa, the former Head of the Department of Political Science; and Professor H.S. Rathore, the present Head of the Department of Political Science, J.N.Vyas University, Jodhpur, I am equally thankful for extending all possible co-operation towards the completion of my project.

And lastly, I am deeply indebted to my husband, Dr M.L. Kataria, and to all family members, who have constantly encouraged me towards the pursuit of scholarly activities.

Professor Kanta Kataria

Introduction

B.R. Ambedkar was an eminent and most celebrated 'realist thinker' in the social and political history of modern India. An outstanding scholar, a creative iconoclast, a great constitutionalist, an able administrator, Ambedkar was, above all, one of the greatest nation-builders of modern India. He was both a social rebel and a mighty exponent of social change. As social rebel, he revolted against the evils of graded inequality and the oppressive features of the Hindu social order. As an advocate of social change; he struggled to break the centuries old shackles of the Hindu society in order to liberate the untouchables. His struggle for social change aimed towards the creation of a new, integrated society, based on human rights, liberty, equality, fraternity and social justice, through non-violent and peaceful means. The ultimate aim of social change, according to Ambedkar, is the building up of a healthy nation. Nation-building is the crux of Ambedkar's ideology.

Apart from the liberation of the untouchables, the goal of Ambedkar's ideology has been national unity and fraternal relationship amongst the countrymen, and the method is constitutional rule of law and justice. His vision of nation-building is both negative and positive. Negative speaking, he discards the notions of infallibility of the Vedas, the caste system, the *varna* system and graded inequality, and regards them as great obstacles in the path of nation-building. Positively speaking, he visualises a new, vibrant society – the key features of which are liberty, equality, fraternity and social justice. So Ambedkar destroys what is undesirable, and builds the seminal ideas which are desirable for nation-building.

Ambedkar's vision of nation-building in neither fanciful nor imaginative; it is based on realism, facts and reason. Neither it is abstract nor theoretical; it is replete with pragmatism, if looked in the context of Indian situation, where pluralism, diversity and heterogeneity are widespread. It is derived from his struggles, experience, observation and knowledge. It is a coherent concept founded on well-organised ideas and thoughts, and logical arguments. A brief description of the various components that constitute his vision of nation-building are given below.

The first component is the primacy of Man. Man and his dignity occupy the central place in his vision of nation-building. Man is placed above God; he is supreme. Man is his own lord. Man must solve his problems here and now.

The second component is the principle of rationality. No nation-building is possible unless Man recognises the supremacy of reason. All sorts of problems requiring social change must be judged from the angle of rationality. Man and rationality, thus, form the central components in Ambedkar's vision of nation-building.

The third component is social change. Social transformation is essential in order to wipe off the ills of the *varna* system and graded inequality from the Hindu society. Social change, Ambedkar says, is necessary for the realisation of the values of political idealism enshrined in our Constitution, and in the rejection of prevailing social idealism of *Sanatani* attitude, which is obstructing the path of nation-building. At the same time, Ambedkar pleads that social change should not come through revolutionary and violent methods, but through constitutional and peaceful means. The constitutional methods are better for achieving economic and social objectives. Such methods are more suitable for building a sense of social cohesion and nationhood.

The fourth component is the creation of a casteless society. Ambedkar believes that the caste structure is a formidable obstacle towards the creation of a strong nation. Caste in the hand of the orthodox has been a powerful weapon for killing all reform. He writes:

> 'The effect of caste on the ethics of the Hindus is simply deplorable. Caste has killed public spirit. Caste has destroyed the sense of public charity. Caste has made public opinion impossible.'

The worst thing is that the Hindus have committed treason against their country in the interests of their caste. No just society is possible, unless the caste is abolished. Ambedkar, therefore, pleads for change in social order by doing away with caste. To uproot caste and to create a casteless society, argues Ambedkar, is a national cause. It is not possible to build anything on the foundations of caste. He says:

> 'You cannot build up a nation; you cannot build up a morality. Anything that you will build up on the foundations of caste will crack, and will never be a whole.'

As such, casteless society is an essential requirement for nation-building. A casteless society alone can infuse energy and strength in the decadent structure of the Hindu society. No healthy nation-building is possible unless caste is abolished, and a new, homogeneous casteless society is created.

The fifth component is the cultivation of the feelings of unity of the country. The unity of the country, Ambedkar regards, as the ultimate goal. He had not the slightest doubt in his mind as to the future evolution and the ultimate shape of the social, political and economic structure of India. He was quite convinced that given time and circumstances nothing in the world will prevent this unity of the country. He even hoped that despite the agitation of the Muslim League for the partition of India some day enough light would dawn upon them and they (Muslim League) too will begin to think that a United India will be better even for them.

The sixth component is protection of the interests of minorities. Ambedkar regards that for nation-building it is essential to provide safeguards to minorities. It is wrong for the majority to deny the existence of minorities. It is equally wrong for the minorities to perpetuate themselves. The diehards should not develop a kind of fanaticism against minority protection. The minorities are an explosive force, if they erupt, they can blow up the whole fabric of the state. The majority should not discriminate against minorities. Whether the minorities will continue or vanish will depend upon the habit of the majority. Thus, the safeguards to minorities are necessary for nation-building.

The seventh component relates to linguistic states. While Ambedkar acknowledges the danger to the unity of India inherent in the creation of linguistic states with their pride in race, language and literature developing into mentalities of being separate nations, he expresses certain definite political advantages in the reconstitution of states on linguistic basis. He favours formation of unilingual states as against multi-lingual states. The unilingual states can foster the fellow-feeling which is the foundation of a stable state. The multi-lingual states are harmful, because they encourage faction fights for leadership and discrimination in administration. While supporting the cause of unilingual states, Ambedkar mentions the condition that the official language shall be Hindi and until India becomes fit for this purpose, English shall continue. He asserts that the Indians must accept this; and if they do not, linguistic states may easily become a peril, or a hindrance in the path of nation-building.

The eighth component is economic and social democracy. Ambedkar believes that the creation of political democracy is not enough. It must be supplemented by economic democracy and social democracy. Any constitution which merely prescribes the form of the political structure of the society, leaving the economic structure untouched, is not a complete document. He, therefore, pleads for state socialism and economic equality. Similarly, he argues in favour of social democracy. He writes:

> 'Political democracy cannot last unless there lies at the base of it social democracy… it means a way of life which recognises liberty, equality and fraternity as the principles of life.'

The main thrust of Ambedkar's argument is that the creation of political democracy alone is not enough for nation-building. Political democracy must be accompanied by economic democracy and social democracy, failing which nation-building is a distant dream.

The ninth component is social justice, reducing social cleavages and promoting social amalgamation. Ambedkar regards social justice as essential for social equality and the resurgence of Indian society. It is the philosophy of good life and a harmonious whole. It is a prime social ethic and an instrument of social transformation. It can reduce social cleavages. Social cleavages sap the vitality of the society and create divisions which are injurious for nation-building. Social justice not only minimises social cleavages, it also accelerates social amalgamation. It is helpful towards the creation of *Samata Samaj* or an ideal society. Social justice, therefore, is the central plank of nation-building.

The tenth component is fraternity. Ambedkar lays great emphasis on the principle of fraternity. Fraternity means a sense of common brotherhood of all Indians. It gives unity and solidarity to social life. It is the cultivation of fellow feeling. It is the cornerstone of the whole democratic civilisation. It helps to sustain the moral order among men. It strengthens socialites and gives to each individual a stronger personal interest in sustaining the welfare of others. It can hasten the dissolution of castes. If we wish to become a nation in reality, the answer lies in fraternity. Without fraternity, the principles of equality and liberty are difficult of realisation. Ambedkar writes:

> 'I would like to hold fraternity as supreme, because in the event of liberty and equality being disobeyed the very fraternity itself would prove to be the protector indeed.'

The eleventh component relates to a true religion. Ambedkar rejects a religion of rules and wishes that its place be taken by a religion of principles. He states that the Hindu religion is a religion of rules – of habitual ways of doing things according to prescription. Its mass of sacrificial, social, political and sanitary rules are contained in the *vedas* and the *smritis*. These rules are nothing but a multitude of commands and prohibitions. They are at best 'legalised class-ethics.' They have promoted graded inequality, oppression and servility in society. While condemning a religion of rules, Ambedkar writes:

> 'I have, therefore, no hesitation in saying that such a religion must be destroyed and I say, there is nothing irreligious in working for the destruction of such a religion.'

Instead of a religion of rules, Ambedkar upholds a religion of principles. Religion must be based on intellectual or spiritual principles; such principles alone are truly universal, applicable to all races, to all countries, to all times. A true religion must be based on the principles of liberty, equality and fraternity. A religion based on principles alone can promote nation-building. It can create a new life, a new society and a new nation.

The last component is empowerment of women. Ambedkar is a great exponent of women's dignity and their empowerment. In this context, he vehemently attacks *Manusmriti* which has shown contempt for women, degrades them as slaves, denies them the right of education and the right to property. He therefore made efforts to free women from the age-old thralldom by reforming the Hindu social laws created by Manu. His Hindu Code Bill introduced in the Constituent Assembly is justly regarded as a landmark towards women's empowerment. Defending the Hindu Code Bill in the Constituent Assembly, Ambedkar said:

> 'And all I am asking this House is: if you want to maintain the Hindu system, Hindu culture and Hindu society, do not hesitate to repair where repair is necessary. This Bill asks for nothing more than to repair those parts of the Hindu system which have become dilapidated.'

Thus, Ambedkar pleads that orthodox elements who are unwilling to change pose a great threat to nation-building. The empowerment of women and giving them an independent status is necessary for building a strong nation.

Ambedkar's vision of nation-building has great relevance for us. On the one hand, it consists of destroying the social laws and practices that weaken nation-building; namely, untouchability in practice, sanctity of the Vedas, the *varna* system and the caste. On the other, it stands for developing reforming tendencies for the promotion of nation-building; namely, social change, social justice, social democracy, social amalgamation and social harmony. It advocates a mental revolution in the psychology of the people in order to create a sense of oneness and unity amongst the people. All the dead wood, outdated traditions, ignoble practices and social deformities of the past that have nestled in us must be expunged from our memories; instead, new principles, new ideas, new values and new reforms must be introduced in the decadent Hindu society in order to build a viable nation.

Professor Kanta Kataria

CHAPTER–1

Dr B. R. Ambedkar: Life and Mission

Among all the social and political thinkers of modern India, Dr B.R. Ambedkar (1891-1956) occupies a distinctive and unique position. He was both a social rebel and the harbinger of human rights and social change. He wanted to bring a complete transformation in social, economic and political life of the Indian society. He had experienced that the millions of depressed people were deprived of even basic human rights. He fought relentlessly for these rights till his last breath and succeeded in securing them. Social justice was the cornerstone of his struggle. He was undoubtedly one of the illustrious figures who played a historic part in the annals of modern India. He was one of those who helped to accelerate the process of social change in the country, a process in the case of which hundreds of thousands, even millions, had been enabled to look forward to a better and happier life.[1]

At the time in India, there existed a traditional social set-up which was dominated by caste Hindus; and the multitude of the depressed were held under the graded inequality, and that too for centuries together. It was like a pond of stagnant water. Ambedkar emerged as a promising leader to break the centuries old shackles and to liberate the untouchables from the age-old bondage of the Hindu society. The Hindu society of the period was based on the laws of Manu which ordained the lowest status to the depressed classes. The untouchables were the dumb victims of the Hindu social order who were made to suffer silently. The humiliations, indignities and atrocities heaped on them were appalling. For them Ambedkar appeared as a saviour.

Indian society of the period was a gradation of castes forming an ascending scale of reverence and descending scale of contempt, where there was no scope for the establishment of egalitarian society. In Ambedkar, the depressed classes found a pragmatic, political, intellectual and spiritual leader. He boldly proclaimed the ideals of liberty, equality and fraternity and regarded them as fundamentals for the creation of a new society. He was, in short, a believer of an integrated society through the Constitution and the peaceful means. He was a great social reformer because he laid emphasis on all-round development of the Indian society. He fought for social justice throughout his life, and guided the humanity to create homogenous society. Because of his outstanding contribution towards the creation of a vibrant and just society, Ambedkar is regarded as one of the greatest nation-builders of modern India.

Ambedkar brought a new awakening and a sense of social significance and confidence among the deprived, dispossessed and depressed sections of the society. His untiring crusade against 'cruel caste regime' and graded inequality greatly enraged the orthodox and caste-Hindus. However, that did not deter Ambedkar from his noble goal of liberating his fellowmen from slavery and misery. He was, indeed, a symbol of revolt against all the oppressive features of Hindu society. As far back as in 1936 Mahatma Gandhi remarked, "Dr Ambedkar is not the man to allow himself to be forgotten."[2]

Ambedkar proved beyond any shadow of doubt that a person from the lowest rung of the society, if given an opportunity, can even surpass the most meritorious of the privileged class. He was a profound scholar, a valiant crusader, an enlightened parliamentarian, an able administrator, and above all, a great visionary.

Ambedkar was a nationalist and patriot to the core. He was determined to defend Indian independence to the last drop of his blood. Although an indomitable fighter, he never deviated from the democratic norms. He was opposed to civil disobedience and other unconstitutional methods. He regarded democracy as a form and method of government whereby revolutionary changes in the economic and social life of the people could be brought about without bloodshed.

He never threw his lot with those who adopted violent and unconstitutional means. He regarded unconstitutional means 'the grammar of anarchy.'

Ambedkar believed that 'the country is greater than the man.' He emphasised on social unity for strengthening the roots of democracy in India. He warned the countryman:

> 'Democracy in this country is like a summer sapling. Without social unity, the roots of sapling cannot be strengthened. If social unity is not achieved this summer sapling of democracy, will be rooted out with gust of summer wind.'[3]

Ambedkar, thus, gave a clarion call to the Indians to learn that the democracy would remain a top-dressing on Indian soil, which is essentially undemocratic because of the lack of social democracy. He advised the countrymen to cultivate good relations between man and man based on fraternity. He, thus, envisaged the cohesive social order based on equality and justice. He recognised that the most vital need of the day was to create amongst the people the sense of a common nationality.

Ambedkar was a 'creative iconoclast'. He was a designated as 'constitution maker and an institutions breaker.' He was not an abstract thinker. He always lived in the world of action. He was one of the very few Indians, who had done yeomen services to restructure the society on the egalitarian and humanitarian principles. He was in fact a harbinger of new social order in India. He was designated as 'the jewel of Nehru Cabinet.' Among his contemporaries, he was perhaps the most highly learned man in public life. He was posthumously conferred 'Bharat Ratna,' the highest civilian award under Indian Constitution, for the outstanding role he played as a maker of modern India.

Ambedkar had realised that, thousands years old mental twist of the caste Hindus would be impossible to untwist. Hence, he resolved to renounce Hinduism. He fulfilled his Yeola pledge of 1935 by embracing Buddhism in 1956 at Nagpur along with his five lakh faithful followers. After the conversion, Dr Ambedkar remarked:

> 'I am overjoyed, I am excited. I feel I have been liberated from the hell.'[4]

Why did Ambedkar accept Buddhism? He accepted Buddhism because it was built on the foundations of liberty, equality, fraternity, morality and professes scientific, rational and humanistic outlook. The principal aim of Buddhism is to emancipate suffering humanity. He undertook the stupendous task of reviving and spreading the gospel of the Lord Buddha. He exhorted the downtrodden to take refuge in Buddha and propagate *Dhamma*. He had chosen Buddhism because that was the least harmful way for the country. After embracing Buddhism, he said:

> 'It is the greatest benefit I am conferring on the country by embracing Buddhism, as Buddhism is a part and parcel of Bhartiya culture. I have taken care that conversion will not harm the traditions, the culture and history of this land.'[5]

Thus, Ambedkar demonstrated that he was a hardcore nationalist and patriot.

All in all, as a maker of modern India, Ambedkar had played the revolutionary role in the eradication of untouchability, establishing the parliamentary democracy, reconstruction of the society based on the triple gem – liberty, equality and fraternity, and revival of Buddhism in India.

Ambedkar's Early Life

Bhimrao Ambedkar was born at Mhow (in Madhya Pradesh near Indore) on 14th April, 1891 in a Mahar family. His father, Ramji Sakpal, was a junior Commissioned Officer (Subedar Major) in the Army. Ramji Sakpal was a deeply religious man, who regularly read *Mahabharata* and *Ramayana*. The daily vespers at Ramji Sakpal's house had an impact on Ambedkar. The devotional readings at home made Ambedkar a deeply religious man in his life. Even after he could rationalise the meaning of religion, later on, with his mature mind, his rationalism convinced him that religion is a must for one's life. He had once said, 'Without religion society will perish.'

Ramji Sakpal's devotional songs had taught some values to his son, Bhimrao, who was his fourteenth child. Ramji Sakpal was convinced and inculcated into the minds of his children that though Karna and Droncharya were of humble origin, by sheer dint of hard work and dedication one could like them rise to great heights. This deep-rooted conviction that was put into the heart of child Ambedkar was perhaps the beginning of the success story of Bhimrao, who resolved to acquire recognition by learning. His surname as he entered the school in 1900 was 'Ambedvekar', but his kind Brahmin teacher, who was fond of him, changed his name 'Ambedkar'. Excepting the love shown by his Brahmin teacher, Bhimrao experienced nothing but humiliation by his class fellows, his school peon and others.

Some of the humiliations that Ambedkar faced while at school, could be cited. Once in the school, he rushed to drink water and the peon of the school probably a degree higher in caste than Ambedkar called him to cup his palms together to enable the peon to pour water. In the school, he was asked to squat on the floor while children of the higher caste parents would be seated on the bench. Once when the teacher asked Ambedkar to write something on the black-board, other students did not allow him to go near the board, as the other side of the board contained tiffin's of the higher-caste children. He was also not allowed to take Sanskrit as the second language owing to the restrictions imposed by the Hindu religion. He was stoned and reprimanded for drawing water from a public well. This emotional suffering led Ambedkar not to despair but to question 'Why'. This 'why' eventually – over the years – offered him the answer and made him to find a solution 'How'.[6]

Horrified Incidents

Ambedkar himself stated a few incidents in his life which had left deep impression on his mind. He wrote:

> 'I was born at Mhow, Indore, where my father was employed in the army. He held the rank of Subedar at that time. Since we lived in the cantonment we had little to do with the world outside the military area. I had no experience of 'untouchability'. When my father retired from service on pension, we shifted to Satara to live there. My mother had passed away when I was barely five years old. Famine broke out in Goregaon, in the district of Satara, and to combat this, the government started 'Famine Relief Employment'. My father was appointed as a pay-master to disburse wages to the workers in the labour camp. He had to join the labour camp at

Goregaon and we, the four children, were left behind at Satara. For nearly four to five years, we had to live only on rice. It was only after coming to Satara that we began to experience what untouchability was.'[7]

The first thing which struck Ambedkar most was that no barber was prepared to cut his hair. This disturbed him. His elder sister who was still alive used to cut his hair sitting on platform outside their house. Ambedkar could not understand why inspite of the presence of so many barbers, no barber was prepared to cut his hair.

The second incident also related to that period. Whilst his father was at Goregaon, he used to send them letters. In one letter he invited the children to visit Goregaon. The idea that they would be travelling by train to Goregaon thrilled Ambedkar very much because he had never seen a train before. With the money sent by their father they got new clothes stitched and Ambedkar, his brother, his sister's daughter all set off for Goregaon. They had sent a letter beforehand but, unfortunately, due to the carelessness or a mistake on the part of their servant, it had not reached their father. They were certain that their father would send a servant to receive them at the railway station. On their alighting from the train they were distressed to find the servant nowhere in sight. Soon everybody departed and there were no passengers, excepting them, left on the platform. They waited in vain for some three-quarters of an hour. The Station Master enquired who they were meeting, what caste they belonged to, and where they wanted to go. They told him that they belonged to the Mahar caste. This gave him a shock and he retreated some five steps backwards. But seeing them well-dressed, he presumed that they belonged to some well-to-do family. He assured them that he would try to set a cart for them. But owing to their being members of the Mahar caste, no bullock-cart driver was willing to drive them. Evening was approaching and till 6 or 7 p.m., they did not succeed in getting a cart. Finally a cart-man agreed to take them in his cart. But he made it clear at the outset that he would not drive the cart for them.

Ambedkar had lived in the military area and driving a cart was not difficult for him. As soon as they agreed to this condition, he came with his cart and they, all the children, started for Goregaon. At a short distance outside the village they came across a brook. The cart driver asked them to eat their food there for no water was available elsewhere on the way. Accordingly, they got down from the cart and ate their food. The water was murky and mixed with dung. In the meantime, the cart driver also returned after having his dinner.

As the evening grew darker, the driver quietly boarded the cart and sat beside them. It became so dark soon, that, neither any flickering lamp nor any human being was visible for miles. Fear, darkness, and loneliness made them cry. It was well past mid-might and they were frightened. So scared were they that they thought they would never reach Goregaon. When they reached a *Naka* (toll post) they jumped out of the cart. They made enquiries from the toll-collector whether they could get anything to eat in the vicinity. Ambedkar spoke to him in Persian. He knew how to speak in Persian and had no difficulty in speaking to him. He replied in a very curt manner and pointed towards the hills. Somehow, they spent the night near the ravine and early in the morning, they set off again on their journey to Goregaon. At last, they reached Goregaon on the following day in the afternoon, utterly exhausted and almost half-dead.

The third incident related to the period when Ambedkar served in Baroda State. With a scholarship granted by Baroda State, he had gone for education abroad. After returning from England, in accord with the terms of the agreement, he came to serve under the Baroda *Durbar*. He could not get a house to live in at Baroda. Neither a Hindu nor any Muslim was prepared to rent out a house to him in the city of Baroda. Failing to get a house in any locality, he decided to get accommodation in a Parsi *Dharamsala*. After having stayed in America and England, Ambedkar had developed a fair complexion and an impressive personality. Giving himself a Parsi name, 'Adalji Sorabji', he began to live in the Parsi *Dharamsala*. The Parsi manager agreed to accommodate him at ₹ 2 per diem. But soon the people got wind of the fact that His Highness the Maharaja Gaikwad of Baroda had appointed a Mahar boy as an officer in his *Durbar*, his living in the Parsi *Dharamsala* under an assumed name gave rise to suspicion and his secret was soon out.

On the second day of his stay, when Ambedkar was just leaving for his office, a mob of some fifteen or twenty Parsis, armed with

Lathis (sticks) accosted him, threatening to kill him and demanded who he was, Ambedkar replied, 'I am a Hindu'. But they were not satisfied with his answer. Exasperated, they began to shower abuses on him and bade him to vacate the room immediately. Ambedkar's presence of mind and knowledge gave him the strength to face the situation boldly. Politely he asked for permission to stay for eight hours more. Throughout the day, he searched for a house to live in, but miserably failed to get any place to hide his head. He approached his friends but all turned him down on some plea or the other, expressing their inability to accommodate him. Ambedkar was utterly disappointed and exhausted. What to do next? He just could not decide. Frustrated and exhausted, he quietly set down at one place, with tears flowing out of his eyes. Seeing no hope of getting a house, and no alternative but to quit, he tendered his resignation and left for Bombay by the night train.

Like these horrified incidents of his life, had left deep impression on his mind. He felt that there was no sense in living in a society which was devoid of humanity; instead it casted insults and humiliations. He thought that any person with an iota of self-respect and decency would not like to remain in this satanic (Hindu) religion. Only those who loved to be slaves could remain in this religion.

Education and Career

After retirement from Mhow, Ramji Sakpal had moved to Satara. At Satara, Ambedkar was admitted in Maratha High School. After a few months, the family shifted to Bombay, where Ambedkar was sent to Elphinstone High School, a leading institution of Bombay. Whether Ambedkar was in school or in colony, he had to face the grim social situation of the underdogs. While facing the intolerable insults and social ills implicated by the upper caste Hindus, Ambedkar passed matriculation examination through Elphinstone High School in 1907. He being the first ever boy amongst his community to do so, the Mahar Community organised a function to felicitate him, presided by the well-known scholar and social reformer of those days, namely S.K. Bole. Bole had authored a book on the life of Buddha and Ambedkar was presented with that book. At that period, no one could dream that 'Buddhism' would subsequently create a lasting impression on Ambedkar.

Soon after passing the matriculation examination, Ambedkar was married to Rami, a daughter of a porter at Dapoli. It was, then very difficult for Ambedkar to prosecute his studies, but his father encouraged the young boy for higher studies. He joined Elphinstone Degree College, Bombay, and he passed the Intermediate examination in 1910, though he lost one year due to ill-health. At this stage, his father told Ambedkar that he was helpless to support him for further studies. Fortunately, the Maharaja of Baroda sanctioned a scholarship to Ambedkar for graduation. Ambedkar passed his B.A. examination in 1912. In February, 1913, his father expired.

Ambedkar was again granted a scholarship by the Maharaja of Baroda for higher studies in the U.S.A. He was admitted into Columbia University, from where he did M.A. in 1915 and Ph.D. in 1916. In Columbia University, Ambedkar had studied under John Dewey, a renowned pragmatic humanist. He left America in June 1916 and came to London for higher studies in Law and Economics. He took admission into London School of Economics and Political Science for M.Sc. and into Grays Inn for Barrister-at-Law. He was awarded the degree of M.Sc. in June 1921 and then, D.Sc. in January 1923. Afterwards, he was called to bar.

Before completing his studies in London, Ambedkar served as a Professor of Political Economy in Sydeham College of Commerce and Economics of Bombay during the year 1918. He also became the Principal of Government Law College, Bombay, in 1928.

Ambedkar started a weekly, *Mookanayak* (Leader of the Dumb) in 1920, after his return from first visit abroad. It was meant to voice the woes of the depressed classes of India. In the editorial of the first number, on January 31, he wrote: 'The existing newspapers look after the interests of certain castes. They do not pay heed to the interest of other castes… This country is the home of inequality. Devoid of power and knowledge, the non-Brahmins and the depressed classes cannot make any progress….poverty, inequality and ignorance have swept away the depressed society.' Shahu Maharaj of Kolhapur donated one thousand rupees to this weekly. But this weekly could not last long.

Ambedkar's leadership of the untouchables at large began only from 1923 (after his second visit abroad). He was instrumental in founding the *Bahishkrit Hitakarini Sabha* (Association for the Welfare of the Depressed Classes) on 20 July, 1924. Sir Chimanlal Setalvad was its first President and Ambedkar was Chairman of the Managing Committee. The objects of the Sabha were: 'To spread education, improve economic conditions and represent the grievances of the depressed classes'. Through this Sabha, Ambedkar wanted to light the fire of self-help and self-respect among the untouchables and wished to bring all untouchables under one banner.

In April 1927, Ambedkar had started *Bahishkrit Bharat,* a fortnightly paper in Marathi. In that he once wrote in the editorial that had Tilak been born among the untouchables, he would not have raised during the national movement the slogan 'Swaraj is my birthright', but a slogan like: 'Annihilation of untouchability is my birthright.' In that fortnightly, Ambedkar emphasised that 'lost rights are never regained by begging, but by relentless struggle. Goats are used for sacrificial offerings and not lions.'

Dr Ambedkar was nominated to the new Bombay Legislative Council in the year 1927, wherein he vigorously fought for the rights of the untouchables.

Ambedkar had established several educational institutions like schools and hostels for the education of the poor boys and girls. He established Siddharth College in Bombay. He also established 'People's Education Society' in 1945, which is, at present running about fifteen major educational institutions in Maharashtra. In fact, he had a great passion for the educational development of the needy and depressed classes.

In 1930-31, at the first and second Round Table Conferences held in London, Ambedkar represented the case of untouchables, carefully and intelligently. He roared like a lion at the Round Table Conference causing flutter in the political circles of India and England. The power in Britain were made to see reason and understand the dire necessity to ameliorate the conditions of the depressed classes who for centuries were mercilessly thrown into the quagmire of social segregation, political deprivation, economic destitution and perpetual subjugation. Ambedkar's pursuit of his theory of separate electorate was opposed tooth and nail by Mahatma Gandhi at the second Round Table Conference. With a great vigour Ambedkar impressed upon the

Conference to recognise the fact that depressed classes were not a part of Hindu society and hence deserved separate electorates and due share in power for their political advancement. He strongly pleaded for urgent settlement of the problem of depressed classes, as he felt that it was a part of the general political settlement, which must not be left to the shifting sands of sympathy and the goodwill of the rulers of the future. He pleaded for parity and not charity.[8]

The Communal Award declared by J. Ramsay MacDonald, the then Prime Minister of Great Britain, conceded separate electorates to the depressed classes, was the crowning glory of the splendid and stupendous work done by Dr Ambedkar at the Round Table Conference.[9] On account of his magnificent, learned and unparalleled contribution to the Round Table Conference in the spheres of social, political and constitutional reforms, Dr Ambedkar was "acclaimed as the uncrowned king of the depressed classes." But opposition and fast unto death by Mahatma Gandhi led to Poona Pact. The crux of the Poona Pact was that the separate electorates which were granted by the Communal Award were ultimately withdrawn and the method of joint electorates was introduced with the principle of reservation of certain seats for depressed classes in the Central as well as the Provincial Assemblies. The Poona Pact was the result of an agreement generously and graciously agreed by Ambedkar to save the life of Mahatma Gandhi, although he knew that it was no splendid gesture on the part of caste Hindus.

Subsequently events favoured Ambedkar and he was appointed the Labour Member of Viceroy's Executive Council in 1942. Afterwards, when India became an independent country, Pandit Jawaharlal Nehru invited Dr Ambedkar to join his Cabinet. Then, Ambedkar became the first Law Minister of India in 1947. Another significant event happened when Dr Ambedkar was nominated as the Chairman of the Drafting Committee for the Constitution of free India in August 1947. His contribution towards the framing of the new Constitution was unique.

The advent of Dr Ambedkar on the political horizon at the time when the transfer of power was on cards gave fillip and encouragement to the depressed classes of India to advance their cause with greater vigour for legitimate and adequate share in power. Despite innumerable hurdles, political setbacks and socio-cultural shackles, Dr Ambedkar waged a relentless war against his adversaries in Hindu social order for social equality, human dignity and politico-economic empowerment.

The Hindu reform which Ambedkar dreamed through the Hindu Code Bill met with a stiff resistance from the Hindu orthodoxy. Ambedkar realised that, thousands years old mental twist of the caste Hindus would be impossible to untwist. Hence, he resolved to renounce Hinduism. He fulfilled his Yeola pledge of 1935 by embracing Buddhism in 1956 at Nagpur along with his five lakh faithful followers.

Ambedkar expired on December 4, 1956. He was posthumously conferred 'Bharat Ratna', the highest civilian award under Indian Constitution, for the outstanding role he played as a maker of modern India.

Influences on Ambedkar

Ambedkar's life, ideas and ideals were the projection of various influences. The diverse influences that shaped his ideology of social change and nation-building could be briefly stated.

The first and foremost influence was that of Ramji Sakpal, the father of Ambedkar who was a religious man. Ambedkar made a deep study of the various religions and developed a firm belief in the necessity of religion. He held that religion had a direct connection with heart and laws with reason. His interest in religion, approach towards social and political problems, reading habits, etc. could be traced back to his father. Ramji Sakpal once said:

> 'Bhima (Ambedkar) you are going to learn a lot. You are going to be a great and learned man. You are going to get great fame and make the name of your family shine in the world.'[10]

The second was the influence of John Dewey, who was the teacher of Ambedkar at Columbia University. His philosophy of instrumentalism led Ambedkar towards critical analysis of the concrete problems facing humanity. Dewey's pragmatic approach convinced him that any philosophy, which sought after a way out from the troubles in which humanity had landed, be dynamic and pragmatic. Dewey's realistic ideas cast a deep impression on Ambedkar. His realistic ideas stated that before passing judgment on any scheme of politics, it is essential that one must consider the ground plans. The ground plan means the social structure of a community to which the political plan is sought to be applied. Dewey's ideas provided the basis for a systematic analysis of problems relating to politics, economics, sociology, religion and history. Ambedkar derived from Dewey that the problems of society called for an integral rather than a piecemeal approach.[11] Thus, Ambedkar was influenced by Dewey's pragmatic and integral approaches.

The third influence was that of Jyotirao Phule, who was a great social reformer of the nineteenth century. His ideas of abolition of untouchability, of *sati*, of child marriage and upliftment of women greatly influenced Ambedkar. Ambedkar appreciated Phule's efforts towards the promotion of education among women and the depressed classes. He believed that with the dissemination of knowledge light would come to them. In short, Ambedkar was very much influenced by Phule on social and political reforms.

The fourth influence was that of Lord Buddha. It is said that there were three *Gurus* (teachers) of Ambedkar – the two being Jyotirao Phuley and Kabir, the third was Buddha, the founder of Buddhism. Ambedkar was very much influenced by Buddha. He had a great faith in Buddha's doctrines of egalitarianism and humanism. The concepts of liberty, equality and fraternity were borrowed by Ambedkar from Buddha. Buddha's influence on Ambedkar was as follows:

> 'Buddha's emphasis on the recognition of the mind as the centre of everything and that mind is the fountain of all the good and evil that arises within and befalls us from without, led Ambedkar to affirm that the cleaning of the mind is the essence of religion. The untouchability was not a by-product of blood or race inferiority. He ceaselessly strove to raise the mental stature of the downtrodden masses by encouraging them to have faith and hope in their creative potentialities. He laid great emphasis on the individual as the centre of all doctrines and activities. Ambedkar appreciated Buddha's belief in man's capacity to work out his salvation without extraneous aid.'[12]

The fifth was M.G. Ranade who also influenced Ambedkar. Ranade gave precedence to social and economic reforms over political reform. Ambedkar accepted the wisdom of Ranade and he stressed that social reform in order to be lasting must precede political reform. Ambedkar accepted the wisdom of Ranade and he stressed that social reform in order to be lasting must precede political reform.

The sixth was J. S. Mill, whose writings impressed upon Ambedkar about the importance of individual's initiative and personal responsibility. Mill's ideas of freedom of thought and individual liberty exercised a great influence upon Ambedkar.

And lastly, Karl Marx also influenced Ambedkar. He critically appreciated the theory of class struggle. He was aware of the ruthless exploitation of the poor going on all over the world. But he differed from Marx on the point that the suffering was not only due to economic exploitation but also due to social exploitation. He also thought that the establishment of state socialism was possible avoiding the pitfalls of dictatorship, which was advocated by Karl Marx.

Thus, it could be stated that:

> 'Ambedkar's philosophical thought grows and develops through intellectual craving and an eternal search for knowledge, while, action follows through his incredible industry and unflinching aim for individual development and social emancipation...His political philosophy grows out of his unbending struggle for the freedom of servile humanity… He during his life time, with a strong faith in revolt against orthodoxy and traditionalism, developed a sort of philosophy, which gives us some definite trend of thought and action in the political history of our nation.'[13]

Ambedkar's Works

Ambedkar was a great thinker and a prolific writer. He had written so many books on different fields, like economics, political science, religions, etc. His books on the problems of the depressed classes are of permanent value. Some of his important books are as follows:

(i) Buddha and His Dhamma, (1957).

(ii) Who were the Shudra, How they came to be the fourth Varna in the Indo-Aryan Society? (1946).

(iii) Who were the Untouchables and why they became untouchables, (1948).

(iv) What Congress and Gandhi have done to the Untouchables? (1945)

(v) States and Minorities, (1947).

(vi) Mr Gandhi and the Emancipation of the Untouchables.

(vii) Annihilation of Caste, (1935).

(viii) Castes in India, their genesis, mechanism and development.

(ix) The Evolution of the Provincial Finance in British India, (1925).

(x) The Problem of the Rupee, (1923), and

(xi) Pakistan or Partition of India, etc.

Mahad Satyagraha

Ambedkar struggled throughout his life for securing human rights. A momentous event in his life was the Mahad *satyagraha* (1927). That event was a march on Mahad. It had its origin in the important resolution of the Bombay Legislative Council moved by S.K. Bole and adopted by the Bombay Government. In pursuance of the Bole resolution passed in 1923 and reaffirmed with a slight change in 1926, the Mahad Municipality had thrown open the Chawdar Tank to the untouchables. However, the resolution of the municipality remained a mere gesture in that the untouchables had not exercised their right owing to the hostility of the caste Hindus.

It was, therefore, decided by the Kolaba District Depressed Classes to hold a conference at Mahad on March 19 and 20, 1927. The aim of Mahad *satyagraha* was to unfurl 'the banner of equality' and to smash the 'steel frames of the caste system?' This Conference was the first public attempt to assert their civic rights. It was a great event that opened an epoch in the history of Hindustan. It was an event which changed both Ambedkar's personal life and the current of social and national reorganisation.

Under the leadership of Ambedkar, the downtrodden, the dehumanised and dumb millions opened a new chapter in the annals of India. They not only voiced their age-long grievances but also took on themselves energetically to mitigate them. They now summoned up courage and showed the right spirit in standing boldly and shaking off the dust from their feet and faces.

Ambedkar took water from the tank and drank it, followed by the vast multitude of men, who vindicated their right. But soon 'the caste Hindus retaliated and riots occurred'. Ambedkar's heart grew indignant and launched a *satyagraha* struggle (December, 1927) for the vindication of his people's rights. He said to his critics that mere spread of education and exposition of the scriptures would not be able to root out the age-long disease. The disease, he said, was deep-rooted and merely dressing it with bandages of knowledge or ingenuous schemes would not cure it. Deadly diseases required drastic remedies.

Ambedkar launched the *satyagraha* movement at Mahad on 25 December, 1927, where *Manusmriti* was consigned to flames as a symbolic protest against the unjust social order. He criticised the graded inequality which was the fundamental principle of the Hindu social order. This pernicious principle was eating into the vitals of the society. His *satyagraha* was meant to end the special privileges enjoyed by the caste Hindus. He said that if Bal Gangadhar Tilak would have born as an untouchable, he would not have declared 'Swaraj is my birthright' but, would have proclaimed that restoration of human dignity and eradication of untouchability as his primary duty. He further claimed, had Lenin born in India, he would have first fought to eradicate untouchability and then would have taken up the programme of revolution.[14]

The importance of Mahad struggle lay in the fact that it enkindled the flame of self-respect and self-elevation among the depressed classes. Smarting under the insults and humiliations inflicted upon them at Mahad, they applied their minds to self-improvement and self-culture as never before.

Kalaram Temple Entry Agitation

Another important social struggle that Ambedkar launched was the entry movement to Kalaram temple at Nasik. It was launched on March 2, 1930, that is, ten days before the famous Dandi March of Gandhi.

On the said date, a conference was held under the presidentship of Ambedkar to consider the situation and adopt ways and means for launching the *satyagraha.* He put forward a thought-provoking speech about the entry to Kalaram temple. He said that the depressed classes were about to enter the temple, but the entry would not solve the whole problem, because the problem was comprehensive. It was political, social, religious, economic, educational, etc. The issue of Kalaram temple entry was an appeal to the Hindu mind. The high caste Hindus had deprived the untouchables from the temple for ages. Whether the same Hindus were willing to grant the depressed classes humanitarian rights would be the question raised from this temple entry *satyagraha*? Whether the Hindu mind was willing to accept the depressed as human beings, this was the question to be tested through this *satyagraha*? Ambedkar said that the high caste Hindu had looked down upon the untouchables and treated them even worse than cats and dogs. He wished to know whether those very Hindus would give the depressed the status of man or not. The *satyagraha* was meant to provide answer to these questions. The *satyagraha* was one of the efforts for bringing about a change of heart among the caste Hindus.

Ambedkar said that the real problem of the depressed was not going to be solved by the entry into the Kalaram temple. It would not bring about any radical change in the life of the depressed. But this was a test to judge the high caste Hindu mind. He stated:

> "Whether the Hindu mind is willing to accept the elevated aspirations of the new era that 'man must be treated as man; he must be given humanitarian rights; human dignity should be established' is going to be tested. In order to achieve this goal, we have launched this *satyagraha*."[15]

The historic struggle thus commenced on the morning of March 3, 1930. About 8000 *satyagrahis* sang *Bhajans* and peacefully sought entry into the temple, the doors of which were closed. The *satyagraha* movement continued for about a month. Then April 9 dawned. It was the day of the chariot procession of the image of Rama. A compromise was patched up between the caste Hindus and the untouchables. It was decided that strong men from both sides should draw the chariot. Thousands of people assembled at noon near the main gate of the temple to see the sight. Ambedkar, with his choice gymnasts, stood near the gate. What happened next is reproduced here in the words of Ambedkar himself:

> 'But before they could touch the chariot, they were engaged in broils by the riotous element of the caste Hindus, and the caste Hindus ran away with the chariot, as secretly planned, through a street, narrow, thorny and inconvenient on either side, and the mouth of which was guarded by the armed police. A daring Bhandari youth by name Kadrekar broke the cordon of the armed police who were awaiting orders to fire, and in a movement crowd of untouchables pursued the chariot amidst showers of stones and captured it. Dangerously wounded Kadrekar fell down in a pool of blood.'[16]

Ambedkar was protected by his men and as the umbrellas that protected his person were shattered, he too, received minor injuries. There was free fighting between groups of untouchables and caste Hindus all over the city.

The *satyagraha* provoked considerable ill-feeling in the minds of the orthodox Hindus throughout the district. As a result of this tension children of the untouchables were thrown out of schools, roads were closed to them, and necessaries of life were denied to them in the market because they claimed equal rights with all other Hindus. Untouchables in several villages were maltreated. Despite these sufferings, the struggle at Nasik was continued. Attempts made to persuade both the parties to reach a compromise proved futile. So firm was the resolve of the depressed classes that orthodox Hindus kept the famous temple closed for a whole year and the agitation continued till October, 1935.

In one of his letters dated the March 3rd, 1934, Ambedkar made it clear as to why he started the Kalaram temple entry *satyagraha*. He wrote:

> 'I did not launch the temple entry movement because I wanted the depressed classes to become worshippers of idols which they were prevented from worshipping, or because I believed that temple entry would make them equal members in and an integral part of the Hindu society… I started temple entry *satyagraha* only because I felt that was the best way of energising the depressed

classes and making them conscious of their position. As I believe I have achieved that purpose, I have no more use for temple entry. I want the depressed classes to concentrate their energy and resources on politics and education and I hope that they will realise the importance of both.'[17]

The year 1935 was a decisive year in the religious history of India. Convinced that Hindu religion could not be reformed, Ambedkar in that year declared that though he was born a Hindu, he will not die a Hindu. From then he started his search for an alternate religion.

Liberal-Minded High Caste Hindus

The study of Ambedkar towards the abolition of untouchability would be incomplete, if we fail to mention some enlightened individuals belonging to the higher strata within the Hindu caste system, who were advocating upliftment of the social conditions of the untouchables. Some of them even stood for the eradication of untouchability.

As early as 1920, Mahatma Gandhi declared; 'untouchability cannot be given a secondary place in the programme. Without the removal of that taint, Swaraj is a meaningless term.'

There were scores of liberal-minded high caste Hindus who sincerely tried for the upliftment of the untouchables. In Maharashtra, Vithal Ramji Shinde, Rao Sahib Ranga Rao, G.G. Agarkar, Shivram Kamble, etc. were the pioneers who worked for the upliftment of the untouchables by opening schools for them in the beginning of the twentieth century. There were different leaders at different places who worked for the upliftment of the untouchables. It is not possible to mention their names.

Two prominent persons who did a lot for the upliftment of the untouchables were Maharaja Sayaji Rao Gaekwad of Baroda and Maharaja Shahu of Kolhapur. Ambedkar would not have become even a graduate, had not the Maharaja of Baroda granted him a scholarship for his graduate studies; he could not have dreamt going abroad for his M.A. and Ph.D. He would not have, later on, become a Barrister and a proven scholar of Economics, had the Maharaja of Kolhapur and his friend Naval Bhattenha did not help him financially.[18]

It is unfortunate that Maharaja Sayaji Rao Gaekwad of Baroda's contribution to the cause of alleviating the distress of untouchables have not been given due attention. He was, in fact, the most significant ruler who had established schools for the untouchables in 1833, which by 1891 became ten schools, and in 1911, there were 242 untouchables serving in the State of Baroda. He was the same benevolent ruler who instituted scholarships for untouchables, and the chief beneficiary of which was Ambedkar. Further, it must be noted that the first All-India Depressed Castes Conference which was held in March 1918 was presided over by this Maharaja Sayaji Rao Gaekwad of Baroda, who had made an appeal to the 'conscience of the country for removing the blot of untouchability.' Thus, the Maharaja of Baroda was the real person who had initiated the cause of the upliftment of the untouchables.

Another great ruler of the period was Maharaja Shahu Chatrapai of Kolhapur, whose contribution to the cause of the upliftment of untouchables was equally significant. It was his patronage that enabled Ambedkar to go to London to complete his post-doctoral studies (D.Sc.) in Economics and to qualify as a Barrister. Further, the Maharaja of Kolhapur had established one free hostel for the untouchable class in an effort to raise them to a level of the Brahmins. This Maharaja was the one who presided over two conferences of the Depressed Classes at Nagpur in 1918 and Kolhapur in 1920. He was the first who saw in Ambedkar, 'the potential for becoming an all India leader.' The Maharaja had told the untouchables attending the conference:

> 'You have found a Saviour in Ambedkar….I am confident that he will break your shackles. Not only that, a time will come so whispers my conscience that Ambedkar will shine as a front rank leader of All-India…..'

The Maharaja's words proved prophetic! In fact, the Nagpur Conference of 1918 had laid the foundation of Ambedkar's future work.

Apart from other high caste Hindus who worked for the upliftment of the untouchables, the names of two aforesaid Maharajas of Baroda and Kolhapur stand out most prominently. The intentions of the Maharaja of Baroda and Maharaja of Kolhapur did not go in vain. The struggle for the emancipation of untouchability, later on, reached a culmination and fruition through the untiring and brilliant leadership of Dr Ambedkar, who combined action and struggle in his approach.

Ambedkar as Nation-Builder

This book titled Dr B.R. Ambedkar's Vision of Nation Building, analyses and constructs Ambedkar's ideas towards nation-building. He did not write sitting in an ivory tower as most of the academicians do, but his ideology evolved out of his active life. The following are some of his main ideas which have a direct relationship for nation building.

Primarily, Ambedkar is a rationalist who gives importance to Man. Man is the measure of all things. Man is something more than god. He did not believe in god. He said, 'you must abolish your slavery yourself. Do not depend for its abolition, upon god or superman.' He did not teach the people to adopt wrong means to end their miseries of life. He had strong faith in his mission. He stated that 'man is mortal. Everyone is to die some day or other. But one must resolve to lay down one's life enriching the noble ideal of self-respect and in bettering human life.'[19] Thus, Man and supremacy of reason are central in Ambedkar's theory of nation-building. His faith in reason and rationality was unshakeable. He believed that all rational rules should replace the supernatural. Consciousness is created by reason. Reason is the only means of knowing reality. Theology and morality should be based on reason. Rational men ought to be free to pursue their interests, and customs that have been erected to block their path should be altered or destroyed so as to permit them greater liberty. Morality should be founded not on scriptures and theology, but on rationality. The orthodox scriptures, metaphysics, theology and supernatural sanctions should be swept away as they are antagonistic to reason. In Ambedkar, reason is triumphant. He exalts reason and believes that social order should be guided by it. Irrationalism is a great hindrance in the path of social change. No social transformation can take place in the absence of rationality. Thus, Ambedkar's concept of man and rationality are central in the task of nation building.

An important aspect of Ambedkar's ideology of social change relates to his concept of man and society. He discards the traditional view of four-fold Varnas which is contained in Hindu scriptures. He develops his own view of man and society which perhaps is a new and novel one in the Indian context. His basic ideas regarding man and society are reflected in his concept of social humanism. The two main features of social humanism are 'Samata Samaj'and 'Samatagrahi'. The former is his concept of society and the latter the concept of man. Ambedkar believes that for the liberation of society these two concepts must be interlinked.

Ambedkar regards education as a significant instrument of social change and nation-building. He said:

> 'If you give education to the lower strata of the Indian society which is interested in blowing up the caste system, the caste system will be blown up… Giving education to those who want to blow up caste system will improve prospect of democracy in India and put democracy in safer hands.'[20]

It is, therefore, essential to educate the poor masses and develop in them a genuine sense of political consciousness and constitutional temper. Their education means social revolution and social revolution would lead to better nation-building.

Ambedkar held the view that nation-building is possible through democracy. He said:

> 'Democracy is not merely a form of government. It is primarily a mode of associated living of conjoined communicated experience. It is essentially an attitude of respect and reverence towards fellowmen.'[21]

His concept of democracy aims towards social transformation. For social transformation the people should cultivate democracy as a state of mind, a style of social life, which may assure them work and security, proper facilities for education and human rights for all.

For Ambedkar, political democracy is not enough. Political democracy is meaningless, unless it is accompanied by economic equality and social democracy. No political democracy can be a success in the absence of social democracy. The eradication of caste and social inequalities is necessary for building the durable foundations of political democracy.

Ambedkar is concerned for social unity and nation-building. He warned the countrymen saying, "I have hopes that my countrymen will some day learn that the country is greater than the man." He emphasises on social unity for strengthening the roots of nation-building and of democracy in India. He warns the people to cultivate good relations between man and man based on fraternity, which is the cornerstone of all progress. His is a glorious call for ushering in India a social and economic democracy. He envisages the cohesive social order based on equality and justice i.e. social, economic and political. He advocates egalitarian and humanitarian principles for the restructuring of society. He said that the most vital need of the day is, to create amongst the people the sense of common nationality. He is, therefore, regarded as a 'creative iconoclast'; and a 'harbinger of new social order' in India. The key feature of the new social order is social justice.

According to Ambedkar, the legislative, persuasive and peaceful methods are the best means for the social and economic change. He believes that radical social change can be brought about in a peaceful way through the medium of parliamentary democracy. He said:

> 'Democracy is a form and method of government whereby revolutionary changes in the social and economic life of the people are brought about without bloodshed.'[22]

Thus, according to Ambedkar, social change and nation-building is possible through the parliamentary form. Further, in his opinion, the downtrodden cannot make any progress without sharing political power. He holds that political power is the key to all social progress.

Ambedkar's ideology has great relevance for social solidarity and nation-building. He fought relentlessly against the exploitative tendencies of an antique society and struggled to build a just society based on the ideals of liberty, equality, fraternity and social justice. He realised that the *Varna*, caste and untouchability were the greatest evils of Hindu society. Unless these evils were rooted out, there would be no just social order in India. It would be relevant here to repeat the words written by one of the biographers of Ambedkar:

> 'What did Ambedkar achieve for the untouchables? The story of the past life of the scheduled castes was pitch dark...it was for the first time in the history of the past twenty-five hundred years that the sun of a better future arose on their horizon. Ambedkar, the son of their soil, their kith and kin, focused the world's attention

on their civic, social and political rights and liberties; made untouchability a burning topic of the day, raised it to an international importance, and gave it a global publicity. His ceaseless hard struggle and his merciless hammer forced an opening for them; and inaugurated an era of light and liberty. He awakened in them a sense of human dignity, a feeling of self-respect and a burning hatred of untouchability that was worse than slavery. He pulled them out of slough and exorcized despondency and despair from their minds. He infused courage and the new life into their demoralised and dehumanised cells. He gave them their soul and reimbued them with a spirit which ennobled them to voice their grievance and to stand up for justice, equality and liberty. Before the rise of their leadership they were treated worse than animals. His heroic struggle raised them to political equality with other communities in India.'[23]

This is the greatest social revolution that Ambedkar ushered in. He fought relentlessly against the eradication of untouchability, and finally succeeded in its abolition. This is the most significant social change brought about by Ambedkar, and it has strengthened the roots of nation-building. The ending of untouchability was his mission, and he fulfilled it.

Another significant contribution of Ambedkar was the revival of Buddhism in India. He held that Buddhism was his ancestral faith which was based on purely secular outlook and humanistic morality. His conversion to Buddhism was a historic event. His attraction towards Buddhism was on account of three principles in combination which no other religion evinces. Buddhism teaches *Prajna* (understanding as against superstition and supernaturalism), *Karuna* (love) and *Samata* (equality). That is what a man needs for a good and happy life.

Man is a Central Figure

The whole ideology of Ambedkar revolves around Man. He regards man as the maker of history and a catalyst for social change. Man is capable of accelerating social change; or on the contrary he can also clog the wheels of social change. In short, Ambedkar never denied the central place of man in promoting social change.

In his address titled, 'Ranada, Gandhi and Jinnah,' delivered in 1940, Ambedkar discussed the role of man as a maker of history or an instrument of social change. According to him, the theory of Buckle that the history is created by geography and physics, and that of Karl Marx that it is the result of economic forces, both speak the half-truth only, because they do not give any place to man. Disagreeing with Buckle and Marx, Ambedkar asserts that man is a factor in the making of history and social change, and that environmental forces alone are not the makers of historical growth.

Ambedkar stated that history is the biography of great men, because if great men were not the makers of history, there is no reason why we should take more notice of them than we do of cinema stars. There are those who assert that however great a man may be, he is a creature of Time: Time called him forth, Time did everything, he did nothing. Those who hold this view, in Ambedkar judgement, wrongly interpret history.

There have been three different views on the causes of historical changes. The first is the Augustinian theory of history, according to which history is only an unfolding of a divine plan in which mankind is to continue through war and suffering until that divine plan is completed at the Day of Judgment. The second is the view of Buckle who held that history is made by geography and physics. The third is the view of Karl Marx who said that history is the result of economic forces. These views, according to Ambedkar, do not represent the whole truth. He writes:

> 'None of these three would admit that history is the biography of great men. Indeed they deny man any place in the making of history. No one except theologians accepts the Augustinian theory of history. As to Buckle and Marx, while there is truth in what they say, their views do not represent the whole truth. They are quite wrong in holding that impersonal forces are everything and that man is no factor in the making of history. That impersonal forces are a determining factor cannot be denied. But that the effect of impersonal forces depends on man must also be admitted. Flint may not exist everywhere. But where it does exist, it needs man to strike flint against flint to make fire. Seeds may not be found everywhere. But where they do exist, it needs man to

> ground it to powder and make it a delectable and nutritious paste and thereby lay the foundation of agriculture. There are many areas devoid of metals. But where they do exist, it needs a man to make instruments and machines which are the basis of civilisation and culture.'[24]

Take the case of social forces. Various tragic situations arise. One such situation is of the typed described by Thayer in his biography of Theodore Roosevelt when he says:

> 'There comes a time in every sect, party or institution when it stops growing, its arteries harden, its young men see no visions, its old men dream no dreams; it lives on the past and desperately tries to perpetuate the past. In politics when this process of petrification is reached we call it Bourbonism and the sure sign of the Bourbon is that, being unconscious that he is the victim of sclerosis he sees no reason for seeking a cure. Unable to adjust himself to changed and new conditions he falls back into the past as an old man drops into his worn-out arm-chair.'[25]

The other kind of situation is not one of decay but of destruction. The posibilities of it are always present whenever there is a crisis. The old ways, old habits, and old thought fail to lift society and lead it on. Unless new ones are found there is no possibility of survival. No society has a smooth sailing. There are periods of decay and possibilities of destruction through which every society has to pass. Some survive, some are destroyd, and some undergo stagnation and decay. Why does this happen? What is the reason that some survive? Ambedkar quotes Carlyle with approval. Carlyle puts it in his characteristic way:

> 'No time need have gone to ruin, could it have found a great enough, a man wise and good enough. Wisdom to discern truly what the Time wanted, valour to lead it on to the right road thither, these are the salvation of any Time.'[26]

This seemed to Ambedkar quite a conclusive answer to those who denied man any place in the making of history. The crisis can be met by the discovery of a new way. Where there is no new way found, society goes under. Time may suggest possible new ways. But to step on the right one is not the work of Time. It is the work of man.

Man therefore, says Ambedkar, is a factor in the making of history and social change.

The role of man in the making of history cannot be denied. In the ushering in of social change or social revolution or social transformation or nation-building the role of man is undeniably great. He is always a central figure or an active component in the shaping of social change. Instead of castes and clases and status by birth, Ambedkar in his ideology gave a pre-eminent place to Man. Man alone occupies the most central or dominant place in his ideology.[27]

In short, Ambedkar's concepts of man and rationality; annihilation of caste and Varna System; '*Samata samaj*' and '*Samatagrahi*'; education and political power; emancipation of untouchables and abolition of untouchability; liberty and equality; fraternity and social justice; political, economic and social democracy; and the revival of Buddhism, have been significant landmarks towards the social change and social transformation of society, and also towards the promotion of social unity, social solidarity and nation-building. In the removal of socio-economic disparities and inequalities, and accelerating a social revolution, Ambedkar did not adopt a doctrinaire approach, he refused to yield blindly to abstract notions, and, in fact, adopted a realistic and pragmatic approach towards nation-building.

References

1. M.G. Chitkara, *Dr Ambedkar and Social Justice* (New Delhi, APH Publishing Corporation), 2002, p. 192.
2. Op. cit., *Dr Babasaheb Ambedkar Writings and Speeches*, Vol. 17, Part One, p. xxii.
3. *Ibid.,* p. xxiii.
4. *Ibid.,* p. xx.
5. *Ibid.,* p. xx.
6. Ramesh Chandra and Dr Sangh Mittra: *The Ambedkar Era* (New Delhi, Commonwealth Publisher, 2003), pp.1, 3.
7. *Dr Babasaheb Ambedkar Writings and Speeches*, Vol. 3, p. 108.
8. *Dr Babasaheb Ambedkar Writing and Speeches*, Vol. 17, Part One, p. xix.
9. *Ibid.*
10. op. cit., K. S. Bharthi: *Foundation of Ambedkar Thought* (Nagpur, Datta Son Publication, 1910), p. 41.

11. Chandrakant D. Shivakeri: *Dr B. R. Ambedkar's Political Philosophy*, (New Delhi, Amol Publication, 2004), p. 44.
12. K. S. Bharthi, op.cit, p. 58.
13. Chandrakant D. Shivakeri, p. 49.
14. *Dr Babasaheb Ambedkar Writings and Speeches*, Vol. 17, Part One, p. xviii.
15. *Ibid.,* p. 182.
16. *Ibid.,* p. 184.
17. *Ibid.,* p. 202.
18. Ramesh Chandra and Dr Sangh Mittra: *The Ambedkar Era* (New Delhi, Commonwealth Publisher, 2003), p. 9.
19. Dr Dhananjay Keer : *Dr Ambedkar Life and Mission* (Bombay, Popular Prakashan, 1962), p. 127.
20. Op. cit. *Ibid,* p. 488.
21. Op. cit. K. S. Bharthi, p. 138.
22. Op. cit. *Ibid,* p. 140.
23. Op. cit. Dhananjay Keer, p. 233.
24. *Dr Babasaheb Ambedkar Writings and Speeches*, Vol. 1, p. 212.
25. Op. cit. Vol. 1, pp. 212-213.
26. Op. cit., Vol. 1, p. 213.
27. Kanta Kataria : *Relevance of Ambedkar's Ideology*, (Jaipur, Rawat Publications, 2015), p. 238.

Chapter–2

On the Hindu Social Order

Ambedkar was critical of Hindu religion because it is constituted on a class concept. Hindu religion does not teach how an individual should behave with another individual. There is no place for an individual in Hindu society. As such, the Hindu religion did not appeal to Ambedkar's conscience. It did not appeal to his self-respect. The Hindu religion, he asserted, is devoid of sympathy, equality and liberty. Therefore, to get human treatment, he advocated conversion to Buddhism.

The Philosophy of Hinduism

Ambedkar believed that the philosophy of Hinduism neither satisfies the test of social utility nor does it satisfy the test of individual justice. It is a philosophy which dissects society in fragments, which dissociates work from interest, which disconnects intelligence from labour, which expropriates the rights of man to interests vital to life and which prevented society from mobilising resources for common action in the hour of danger. The reason why the philosophy of Hinduism does not answer the test either of utility or of justice is because the religious ideal of Hinduism for divine governance of human society is an ideal which falls into a separate class by itself. Ambedkar writes:

> 'It is an ideal in which the individual is not the centre. The centre of the ideal is neither individual nor society. It is class – the class

> of supermen called *Brahmins*. Those who will bear the dominant and devastating fact in mind will understand why the philosophy of Hinduism is not founded on individual justice or social utility. The philosophy of Hinduism is founded on a totally different principle. To the question what is right and what is good the answer which the philosophy of Hinduism gives is remarkable. It holds that to be right and good the act must serve the interest of this class of supermen, namely, the Brahmins.'[1]

Thus, the core of the philosophy of Hinduism is that it is the gospel of the superman and it teaches that what is right for the superman is only thing which is called morally right and morally good. Therefore, the philosophy of Hinduism does not satisfy the test of justice or of utility. Hinduism is not interested in the common man. It is not interested in society as a whole. Ambedkar says:

> 'The centre of its interest lies in a class and its philosophy is concerned in sustaining and supporting the rights of that class. That is why in the philosophy of Hinduism the interests of the common man as well as of society are denied, suppressed and sacrificed to the interests of this class of supermen.'[2]

In short, Ambedkar argues that the philosophy of Hinduism is such that it cannot be called the religion of humanity. That is why Hinduism, if it penetrates, does not vitrify the inmost life of ordinary humanity. Indeed if it does anything it paralyses it. There is in Hinduism no nourishment for ordinary human soul, no comfort for ordinary human sorrow, and no help for ordinary human weakness. Ambedkar writes:

> 'It leaves men in darkness face to face with the unthinking energies of nature which gives them birth to which after a few fruitless struggles they succumb. Not less cruel than the crudest irreligion, does it leave men divorced from all communions with God. Such is the philosophy of Hinduism. It is Superman's heaven and the common man's damnation.'[3]

Ambedkar believed that 'inequality is the soul of Hinduism.' The morality of Hinduism is only social. It is unmoral and unhuman to say the least. What is unmoral and unhuman easily becomes immoral, inhuman and infamous. This is what Hinduism has become, according to Ambedkar. He stated that those who doubt this or deny this preposition should examine the social composition of the Hindu society and ponder over the condition of some of the elements in it. Take the cases of tribes and untouchables.

The primitive tribes form a total of 25 million souls (before the independence). The Criminal tribes number 4.5 millions and the untouchables number 50 millions. This makes a grand total of 79.5 millions. Here, Ambedkar asks how these people could have remained in the state of moral, material, social and spiritual degradation surrounded as they have been by Hinduism. Hindus say that their civilisation is older than any civilisation, that Hinduism as a religion is superior to any other religion. If this is so, Ambedkar asks:

> 'How is that Hinduism failed to elevate these people, bring them enlightenment and hope; how is it that it failed even to reclaim them; how is it that it stood with folded hands when millions and millions were taking to life to shame and crime? What is the answer to this? The only answer is that Hinduism is overwhelmed with the fear of pollution. It has not got the power to purify. It has not the impulse to serve and that is because by its very nature it is unhuman and unmoral. It is a misnomer to call it religion. Its philosophy is opposed to very thing for which religion stands.'[4]

Ambedkar, thus, emphatically stated the Hindu religion is a misnomer and that its philosophy is deceptive and full of ineradicable evils. The philosophy of Hinduism is quite antithetical to social utility or individual justice. It is the gospel of the superman and is meant to protect and safeguard his interests. It promotes inequality; it is immoral, inhuman and infamous.

Hindu Social Order is not a Free One

Ambedkar examined the character of the Hindu social order and derived the conclusion that it is not a free social order. A free social order is that in which the individual is an end in himself and that the aim and object of society is the growth of the individual and the development of his personality. Society is not above the individual and if the individual has to subordinate himself to society, it is because such subordination is for his betterment and only to the extent necessary. Another essential element of a free social order is that the terms of associated life between members of society must be regarded by consideration founded on liberty, equality and fraternity. Ambedkar held the view that the Hindu social order is not a free one; it is a closed one because it does not admit the sacredness of human personality and the necessity of liberty, equality and fraternity for the development of personality.

The Hindu social order says Ambedkar does not recognise the individual, or his distinctiveness, or his moral responsibility. It does not recognize the individual as a centre of social purpose. For the Hindu social order is based primarily on class or *Varna* and not on individuals. Originally and formally the Hindu social order recognised four classes: (i) Brahmins, (ii) Kshatriyas, (iii) Vaishyas and (iv) Shudras. Subsequently it consists of five classes, the fifth being called the Panchamas or untouchables. The unit of Hindu society is not the individual Brahmin or the individual Kshatriya or the individual Vaishya or the individual Shudra or the individual Panchama. Even the family is not regarded by the Hindu social order as the unit of society except for the purpose of marriage and inheritance. Ambedkar writes:

> 'The unit of Hindu society is the class or Varna. In the Hindu social order, there is no room for individual merit and no consideration of individual justice. If the individual has a privilege it is not because it is due to him personally. The privilege goes with the class, and if he is found to enjoy it, it is because he belongs to that class. Contrawise, if an individual is suffering from a wrong, it is not because he by his conduct deserves it. The disability is the disability imposed upon the class and if he is found to be labouring under it, it is because he belongs to that class.'[5]

Chaturvarna is Wretched

Ambedkar asserts that the Hindu social order is based on Chaturvarna or the division of society into four classes which is utterly repellent. It is an ideal to which Ambedkar could not reconcile himself. He could not understand why the Hindu social order insists upon labelling men as Brahmin, Kshatriya, Vaishya and Shudra. He states that a learned man would be honoured without his being labelled a Brahmin. A soldier would be respected without his being designated a Kshatriya. If European society honour its soldiers and its servants without giving them permanent labels, why should Hindu society find it difficult to do so is a question, which the advocates of Chaturvarna have not cared to consider. He further states that there is another objection to the continuance of these labels. He writes:

> 'All reforms consist in a change in the notions, sentiments and mental attitudes of the people towards men and things. It is commn experience that certain names become associated with certain notions and sentiments, which determine a person's attitude towards men and things. The names, Brahmin, Kshatriya, Vaishya and Shudra, are names which are associated with a definite and fixed notion in the mind of every Hindu. That notion is that of a hierarchy based on birth. So long as these names continue, Hindu will continue to think of the *Brahmin, Kshatriya, Vaishya* and *Shudra* as hierarchical divisions or high and low, based on birth and act accordingly. The Hindu must be made to unlearn all this. But how can this happen if the old labels remain and continue to recall to his mind old notions. If new notions are to be inculcated in the minds of people it is necessary to give them new names. To continue the old name, is to make the reform futile.'[6]

Ambedkar thus pleads that the social divisions based on birth is a snare, and the labels of Brahmin, Kshatriya, Vaishya and Shudra are nothing but 'stinking labels.'

Further, Ambedkar argues that a system of social organisation based on Chaturvarna is impracticable and harmful; because here a man acquires status on account of his birth and not ability. A mere classification of people into four definite classes is worthless. This is neither possible nor desirable. In this respect, the ideal of Chaturvarna has a close affinity to the Platonic ideal. To Plato, men fall by nature into three classes. In some individuals, he believed mere appetites dominated. He assigned them to the labouring and trading classes. Others revealed to him that over and above appetites, they have a courageous disposition. He classed them as defenders in war and guardians of internal peace. Other showed a capacity to grasp the universal reason underlying things. He made them the law-givers of the people. Stating this close affinity between Chaturvarna and Platonic ideal, Ambedkar states:

> 'The criticism to which Plato's Republic is subject, is also the criticism which must apply to the system of *Chaturvarna*, in so far as it proceeds upon the possibility of an accurate classification of men into four distinct classes. The chief criticism against Plato is that his idea of lumping of individuals into a few sharply marked off classes is a very superficial view of man and his powers. Plato had no perception of the uniqueness of every individual...He had no recognition of the infinite diversity of active tendencies and combination of tendencies of which an individual is capable. To him, there were types of faculties or powers in the individual constitution. All this is demonstrably wrong.'[7]

Ambedkar upholds that modern science has shown that lumping together of individuals into a few sharply marked off classes is a superficial view of man not worthy of serious consideration. Since the qualities of individuals are so variable, any stratification by classes is worthless. Hence, 'Chaturvarna must fail for the very reason for which Plato's Republic must fail,' that it is not possible to pigeon men into holes, according to accurately classify people into four definite classes.

The whole concept of Chaturvarna, Ambedkar says, is 'absurd'. It has given rise to numerous social evils. It has completely disabled the lower classes and have made their life 'wretched'. Neither they could receive education, nor could rebel, nor could think of their salvation. They were condemned to be lowly and not knowing the way of escape and not having the means of escape, they became reconciled to eternal servitude, which they accepted as their inescapable fate. Chaturvarna, therefore, is a strong weapon in the hands of caste-Hindus, which has been continually used for centuries for the spoilation of the weak. Ambedkar states:

> 'There cannot be a more degrading system (than Chaturvarna) which deadens, paralyses and cripples the people, from helpful activity.'[8]

If one interprets Ambedkar's ideas on Chaturvarna, it would be clear that the existence of Chaturvarna is a negation of nation-building. So long as the four-fold classification of people exists in society, it is bound to have a baneful effect on a heatlthy nation-building. Chaturvarna, in practice, is antithetical to nation-building, because of its various debilities and viciousness, which have been logically exposed by Ambedkar.

Ambedkar believes that the task of nation-building cannot precede a step further without demolishing Chaturvarna, both in theory and practice. Surely, those who wish to retain Chaturvarna and simultaneously carry on nation-building are living in glass houses. There is no code of laws more infamous regarding social rights than the laws of Manu. Any instance from anywhere of social injustice must pale before it. Ambedkar writes:

> 'Why have the mass of people (untouchables) tolerated the social evils to which they have been subjected? There have been social revolutions in other countries of the world. Why have there not been social revolution in India is a question which has incessantly troubled me? There is only one answer, which I can give and it is that the lower classes of Hindus have been completely disabled for direct action on account of this wretched system of chaturvarna.'[9]

The untouchables, says Ambedkar, could not bear arms and without arms they could not rebel. They were all ploughmen or rather condemned to be ploughmen and they never were allowed to convert their ploughshare into swords. They had no bayonets and therefore everyone who chose could and did sit upon them. Further, on account of Chaturvarna they could receive no education. They could not think out or know the way to their salvation. They were condemned to be lowly and exploited.

Comparing the situation with Europe, Ambedkar writes that there in Europe, the strong have never contrived to make the weak helpless against exploitation so shamelessly as was the case in India among the Hindus. Social war between the strong and the weak had been far more violent in Europe than it has ever been in India. Yet the weak in Europe had his freedom of military service his physical weapon, in suffrage his political weapon and in education his moral weapon. These three weapons for emancipation were never withheld by the strong from the weak in Europe. All these weapons were, however, denied to the untouchables in India by Chaturvarna. Chaturvarna, therefore, is a dead weight upon the souls of the exploited masses. The reorganisation of the Hindu society on the basis of Chaturvarna is impossible because the *Varna* system is 'like a leaky pot or like a man running at the nose.' So long as Chaturvarna survives, the task of nation-building is a distant dream. Chaturvarna degrades the masses by denying them opportunity to acquire knowledge and, therefore, the task of nation-building is unimaginable.

Absence of Fraternity

There is complete absence of fraternity in the Hindu social order. Or it does not recognise fraternity. This is one of the basic weaknesses of the Hindu social order, according to Ambedkar. He says that the Hindus like the Christians and the Muslims do believe that men are created by God. But while the Christians and the Muslims accept this as the whole truth the Hindus believe that this is only part of the truth. According to them, the whole truth consists of two parts. The first part is that men are created by God. The second part is that God created different men from different parts of his divine body. The Hindus, asserts Ambedkar, regard the second part as more important and more fundamental than the first. He writes:

> 'The Hindu social order is based on the doctrine that men are created from the different parts of the divinity and therefore the view expressed by Paul or the Pilgrim Fathers have no place in it. The Brahmin is no brother to the Kshatriya because the former is born from the mouth of the divinity while the latter is from the arms. The Kshatriya is no brother to the Vaishya because the former is born from the arms and the latter from his thighs. As no one is a brother to the other, no one is the keeper of the other.'[10]

Ambedkar, therefore, states that the doctrine that the different classes were created from different parts of the Divine body has generated the belief that it must be divine will that they should remain separate and distinct. It is this belief which has created in the Hindu an instinct to be different, to be separate and to be distinct from the rest of his fellow Hindus.

Ambedkar further states that the most extensive and wild manifestation of this spirit of isolation and separation is of course the caste-system. The castes exist in plural number; originally there were four only; today it might be 3000. Further, the castes are divided into sub-castes. Their number is legion. The total population of the Brahmin castes is about a crore and a half. But there are 1886 sub-castes of Brahmin caste. In the Punjab alone, the Saraswat Brahmans are divided into 469 sub-castes. The Kayasthas of Punjab are divided into 890 sub-castes. The same is the case of other castes. One could go on giving figures to show this infinite process of splitting social life into fragments. The splitting process has made a social life quite impossible. The guiding principle of their behaviour towards one another is 'be separate', 'do not intermarry,' 'do not interdine' and 'do no touch.'

Ambedkar continues to say that there can be no fraternity in a social order based upon such sentiments. Far from working in a spirit of fraternity the mutual relations of the castes are fratricidal. This has given rise to class consciousness, class struggle and class war. The fratricidal spirit has destroyed the spirit of fraternity. Each caste is engaged in nothing but establishing for itself a status superior to that of another caste. All castes are infested with the spirit of hyper-commensality and hypergamy and there is no caste which is free from it. Ambedkar says:

> 'The Hindu social order is a ladder of castes placed one above the other together representing an ascending scale of hatred and a descending scale of contempt.'[11]

This spirit, asserts Ambedkar, has exhibited itself in the proverbs coined by one caste with the object of lampooning another caste. All in all, the spirit of fraternity is not recognised in the Hindu social order.

Equality is not Recognised

As stated above, the Hindu social order does not recognise fraternity; equally it does not recognise equality. Ambedkar tells us, 'that men are born equal is a doctrine which is repugnant to the Hindu social order'. Though it recognises that men are the children of

Prajapati, the Creator of the Universe, they are not equal on that account. For, they were created from the different parts of the body of *Prajapati*. The Brahmins were created from the mouth, the Kshatriyas from the arms, the Vaishyas from his thighs and Shudras from his feet. Therefore, Ambedkar says:

> 'The limbs from which they were created being of unequal value the men thus created are as unequal. In the biological sense, the Hindu social order does not bother to examine whether the doctrine is founded in a fact...The Hindu social order is indifferent to the doctrine as a fact. It is equally indifferent to it as an ethical principle...It is against equalitarian temper.'[12]

Ambedkar thus emphatically proclaims that the Hindu social order is not based on equality and fraternity.

Graded Inequality

The Hindu social order is reared on three principles. The first principle, according to Ambedkar, is the principle of graded inequality. The four classes are not on horizontal plane, different but equal. They are on vertical plane. Not only different but unequal in status, one standing above the other. The order of precedence among the classes is not merely conventional; it is spiritual, moral and legal. There is no sphere of life which is not regulated by this principle of graded inequality.

The second principle, according to Ambedkar, on which the Hindu social order is founded, is that of fixity of occupations for each class and continuance thereof by heredity. Every member must follow the trade assigned to the class to which he belongs. It leaves no scope for individual choice, individual inclination. An individual under the Hindu social order is bound to the profession of his ancestor. It is an inexorable law from which he cannot escape.

Ambedkar says that the third principle on which the Hindu social order is founded is the fixation of people within their respective classes. What is striking about the Hindu social order is its ban on free inter-change and inter-course between different classes of Hindu society. There is also a bar against inter-dining and inter-marriage.

Opposed to Liberty

Ambedkar states that the Hindu social order is not only opposed to equality and fraternity; it is also opposed to liberty. The freedom of speech exists, only for those who are in favour of the social order. This freedom is not the freedom of liberalism. Further, there is no room for liberty of action. The Hindu social order leaves no choice to the individual. It fixes his occupation. It fixes his status. All that remains for the individual to do is to conform himself to these regulations. The same can be said with regard to political liberty. Ambedkar writes:

> 'The Hindu social order does not recognise the necessity of a representative government composed of the representatives chosen by the people. Representative government rests on the belief that people must be governed by law and law can be made only by the representatives of the people. The Hindu social order recognises the first part of this thesis which says that people must be governed by law. But it denies the second part of the thesis which says that law can be made only by the representatives chosen by the people. The tenets of the Hindu social order is that the law by which people are to be governed is already made and is to be found in the Vedas. Nobody has a right to add to and subtract from it. That being so, a representative assembly of the people is unnecessary, Political liberty which is liberty to frame laws and to make and unmake government is futility for which there is no place in the Hindu social order.'[13]

Ambedkar sums up by saying that the Hindu social order is an order based on classes and not on individuals. It is an order in which classes are graded one above the other. It is an order in which the status and functions of the classes are determined and fixed. The Hindu social order is a rigid order. No matter what changes take place in the relative position of an individual his social status as a member of the class he is born in relation to another person belonging to another class shall in no way be affected. The first shall never become the last. The last shall never become the first.

Special Features

Having narrated the essentials of the Hindu social order, Ambedkar states that there are some unique features of it too. No study of the Hindu social order would be complete or accurate without mentioning its special features. He is of the opinion that the special features of the Hindu social order are three in number.

Of these three, he believes that the most striking is the worship of the superman. This superman is Brahmin because the *Manusmriti* gives him the first rank and the supremacy over all other classes. The Brahmin or the superman has been given certain privileges by *Manusmriti* in matters of law, marriage, learning, etc. The Brahmin is the lord of all classes. For example, in the matter of marriage in addition to his marrying a woman of his own class he (Brahmin) is entitled to enter into wedlock with a woman of any of the classes lower to him without being bound to the woman by the tie of marriage or conferring upon the children the right to his status or to his property.

Ambedkar states that a *Shudra* or the untouchable (also called the common man) is born to serve the Superman (Brahmin). In order to keep the Superman satisfied, happy and secure the Hindu social order takes special care to keep the common man in a state of perpetual degradation. The main job of *Shudra* is to serve the Brahmin.

The Common man (Shudra) is not permitted to acquire learning. Ambedkar gives citations from Manu and says that the Superman will not tolerate the *Shudra* to have the comfort of a high-sounding name. He must be contemptible both in fact and in name. Ambedkar writes:

> 'The Hindu social order is openly and avowedly devised and intended for the good of the Superman. In it everything is ordained for the Superman. The Superman is the Brahmin and the Common man is the *Shudra.* The Superman has rights and no duties. Everything is at the disposal of the Superman; everything must be ascribed in the interests of the Superman.'[14]

The counterpart of the same feature, states Ambedkar, is the degradation of the Common man. As against the Superman the Common man (*Shudra*) has no right to life, liberty, property or pursuit of happiness. He must be ready to sacrifice everything for the sustenance of the life and dignity of the Superman. Such sacrifice should be made willingly by the Common man. The Common man should respond to such call for sacrifice in the interest of the Superman as his supreme duty. The Superman has rights against the Common man but he has no duties towards the Common man.

The concept of Superman in the Hindu social order, according to Ambedkar, is a degraded and degenerate concept. It is an odious and loathsome concept. He believes that the most obnoxious thing in the Hindu social order is that it has fixed the social status of the lower orders for all generations to come. Their economic status is also fixed. It has denied education to the lower orders. There cannot be a rebellion by the lower orders against the Hindu social order because it denies the masses the right to use arms. There is no equal opportunity to the Common man. He has no freedom to acquire knowledge.

In addition to the role of the superman, there is yet another special feature of the Hindu social order and that is the *Chaturvarna* and its by-product the caste system, which Ambedkar considers harmful. He says that the ideal of *Chaturvarna* degenerated into an 'instrument of oppression and intolerance' and it developed 'inequality' and 'the spirit of exclusiveness.'[15] Similarly, out of caste system and untouchability many sorts of cruelty have grown.[16] About caste system, Ambedkar writes:

> 'The effect of caste on the ethics of the Hindus is simply deplorable. Caste has killed public spirit. Caste has destroyed the sense of public charity. Caste has made public opinion impossible. A Hindu's public life is his caste. Virtue has become caste-ridden and morality has become caste bound. There is no appreciation of the meritorious. There is no charity to the needy. Suffering as such calls for no response. There is charity but it begins with caste and ends with the caste. There is sympathy but not for men of other caste.'[17]

Riddles in Hinduism

Ambedkar believes that in the Hindu social order or in Hinduism there are many mysterious things which one cannot explain. These are the riddles in Hinduism. According to him, there are around 24 riddles in Hinduism. These riddles obstruct the path of inquiry and without inquiry there can be no knowledge. It is neither possible nor desirable to discuss all the riddles mentioned by Ambedkar. What he wished was a rational approach towards the social and religious problems of Hinduism! A few of the significant riddles are explained below.

Why one is a Hindu?

Ambedkar argues that there is a riddle in Hinduism and that is the difficulty of knowing why one is a Hindu; or who is a Hindu?

Ambedkar discusses a very fundamental problem, why one is a Hindu? A Hindu position is so embarrassing and so puzzling in the matter of his religion. Why is he not able to answer so simple a question which every Parsi, every Christian, and every Muslim can answer? According to Ambedkar, "Ask a Parsi why he calls himself a Parsi he will have no difficulty in answering the question. He will say he is Parsi because he is follower of Zoraster. Ask the same question to a Christian. He will say he is Christian because he believes in Jesus Christ. Put the same question to a Muslim. He will say he is a believer in Islam and that is why he is a Muslim."

If one ask the same question to a Hindu and there is no doubt that he will be completely bewildered and would not know what to say, as all Hindus do not worship one God. Some Hindus are monotheists, some are polytheist and some are pantheists. Polytheists among the Hindus do not confine their homage to the Hindu Gods. Thousands of Hindus go to the Christian Goddess. Thousands of Hindus go to a Muslim Pir. Even the beliefs, the customs, the costumes and marriage rituals often differ more widely from each other than do those of Christians and Muhammadans. Again if a Hindu says he is a Hindu because he believes in the caste system his answer cannot be accepted as satisfactory. As many Musalmans and many Christians observe caste if not in the matter of inter-dinning certainly in the matter of inter-marriage. Ambedkar writes that this brings us back to the old question who is a Hindu? What are the causes that have brought about this religious chaos?

Ambedkar says that this chaos is on account of the following reasons:

> 'A complex congeries of creeds and doctrines is Hinduism. It shelters within its portals monotheists, polytheists and pantheists; worshippers of the great Gods Shiva and Vishnu or of their female

> counterparts, as well as worshippers of the divine mothers or the spirits of trees, rocks and streams and the tutelary village deities; persons who propitiate their deity by all manner of bloody sacrifices, and persons who will not only kill no living creature but who must not even use the word 'cut'; those whose ritual consists mainly of prayers and hymns, and those who indulge in unspeakable orgies in the name of religion; and a host of more or less heterodox sectaries, many of whom deny the supremacy of the Brahmans, or at least have non-Brahmanical religious leaders.'[18]

It is therefore difficult for a Hindu to answer the basic question: Who is a Hindu? It is a great riddle in Hinduism: Ambedkar writes:

> 'Is it not a question for every Hindu to consider why in the matter of his own religion his position is so embarrassing and so puzzling? Why is he not able to answer so simple a question which every Parsi, every Christian, and every Muslim can answer? Is it not time that he should ask himself what are the causes that have brought about this religious chaos?'[19]

The existence of religious chaos is a riddle in Hinduism; and that is preventing a Hindu to answer the question 'who is a Hindu?'

The Riddle of the Vedas

The Vedas are the sacred books of the Hindus. There is hardly any Hindu who does not regard the Vedas as the most sacred book of his religion. Yet, says Ambedkar, there are several questions that arise in connection with them. What is their origin? Who is their author? What is their authority? What is their moral or spiritual value? These are some of the important riddles connected with the Vedas.

The first is the riddle about the origin of the Vedas. There is hardly any Hindu who can give a clear and a definite answer to this simple question. Ambedkar states that so many different but vague answers have been given by the Hindus of this simple question. One answer given by the Hindus about the origin of the Vedas is that they are *Sanatana* which means they are 'eternally pre-existing.' Another explanation of the origin of the Vedas is attributed to *Prajapati*, that is, the Vedas were produced by *Agni* (fire), *Vayu* (wind), and *Surya* (the sun). Further, the legends regarding the origin of the Vedas are also to be found in the *Upanishads*. The *Smritis* and *Puranas* also have to say about the origin of the Vedas. Some say that the Vedas are reproduced from memory.

There are thus, according to Ambedkar, eleven different explanations regarding the origin of Vedas - (1) as originating from the mystical sacrifice of *Purusha,* (2) as resting on *Skambha*, (3) as cut or scraped off from him, as being his hair and his mouth, (4) as springing from *Indra*, (5) as produced from Time, (6) as produced from *Agni, Vayu* and *Surya*, (7) as springing from Prajapati, and the Waters, (8) as being the breath of Brahma, (9) as being dug by the Gods out of the mind-ocean, (10) as being the hair of Prajapati's beard and (11) as being the offspring of Vach.[20]

The real question is, according to Ambedkar, who made the Vedas. The Vedas could not have coming to being *ex-nihilo*. They must have a beginning though they may have no end. Why don't the Brahmins say openly? Why this circumlocution? Ambedkar writes:

> 'This bewildering multiplicity of answers to a simple question is a riddle. The writers who have come forward to furnish these answers are all Brahmins. They belong to the same Vaidik school of thought. They alone were the guardians of the ancient religious lore. Why should such a coherent body of scholars have given such incoherent and chaotic answers to a very simple question?'[21]

The second riddle about the Vedas is: Who is the author of the Vedas? The belief of the Hindu or a Brahmin is that the Vedas are supernatural productions; or to use the technical term, the Vedas are *Apaurusheya*, i.e. made by a non-human agency.

Ambedkar refutes the above view. He asserts that Vedas are not the supernatural productions; the *Rishis* are the authors of the hymns contained in the Vedas. The *Rishis* themselves have treated the Vedas as a human and as a historical product. The hymns of *Rig-Veda* distinguish between ancient and modern *Rishis*. Ambedkar, therefore, states:

> 'Given this abundance of evidence to prove the human origin of the Vedas it is a riddle to find that the Brahmins should so strenuously propagate so extravagant view that the Vedas are of

> supernatural origin. What made the Brahmins propagate such a view?'[22]

The third riddle of the Vedas, according to Ambedkar is: What is the authority of the Vedas? With regard to this he says that there prevail two distinct dogmas amongst the Hindus. The first is that the Vedas are eternal. The second dogma is that the Vedas are not only sacred but they are also infallible. Ambedkar rejects both these dogmas and calls them 'absurd'. He states that 'given that the *Rishis* are the authors of the Vedas the dogma as to their eternal character is an absurdity.' He writes.

> 'The riddle is why did the Brahmins propound this doctrine of the eternity of the Vedas? Why did the Brahmins adopt such an absurd reasoning in support of their doctrine?'[23]

The dogma relating to the authority of the Vedas is that they are not only sacred but they are also infallible. This too, Ambedkar says, is 'absurd'. Given the nature and substance of the contents of the Vedas Ambedkar is astonished and said, 'Why the Brahmins claimed infallibility for such superstitious writings as the Vedas?' It seems to him that 'there was a deliberate attempt to invest the Vedas with an infallible authority which they did not at one time possess.' Discarding the dogma of the infallibility of the Vedas, Ambedkar writes:

> 'The Brahmins have propounded a most mischievous dogma and have spread it among the masses… it is the dogma of the infallibility of the Vedas. If the Hindu intellect has ceased to grow and if the Hindu civilisation and culture has become a stagnant and stinking pool, this dogma must be destroyed root and branch if India is to progress. The Vedas are a worthless set of books. There is no reason either to call them sacred or infallible. The Brahmins have invested it with sanctity and infallibility only because by a later interpolation of what is called the *Purusha Sukta*, the Vedas have made them the lords of the Earth. Nobody has had the courage to ask why these worthless books which contain nothing but invocation to tribal Gods to destroy the Enemies, loot their property and give it to their followers, (have been made sacred and infallible). But the time has come when the Hindu mind must be freed from the hold which the silly ideas

propagated by the Brahmins, have on them. Without this liberation, India has no future.'[24]

The fourth riddle of the Vedas, according to Ambedkar, is about their contents: have the Vedas any moral or spiritual value? Ambedkar, on the basis of evidences examined by him denies any spiritual value to the Vedas. He collects the quotations of Charvakas, Brahaspati and the various schools of philosophy such as the Nyaya, Vaishashikha, Purva and Uttar Mimamsa and proves that the Vedas contain the defects of falsehood, self-contradiction and tautology; and that the authors of the Vedas were 'buffoons, knaves and demons'. Nor does the Rigveda contain elevating examples of moral life. As to philosophy there is nothing of it in the Rigveda. Similarly, Ambedkar states that Atharva-Veda is nothing but a collection of sorcery, black-magic and medicine. He holds that the Vedas may be useful as a source of information regarding the social life of the Aryans. As a picture of primitive life it is full of curiosity but there is nothing elevating. There are more vices and few virtues. He concludes:

> 'Enough has been extracted from the Vedas to show that they contain nothing that can be said to be spiritually or morally elevating. Neither the subject-matter nor contents of the Vedas justify the infallibility with which they have been invested. Why then the Brahmins struggle so hard to clothe them with sanctity and infallibility?'[25]

The Riddle of Four Varnas

Ambedkar states that there is the riddle regarding the origin of the four *Varnas* or *Chaturvarna*. According to *Chaturvarna* society is permanently divided into four classes, namely (1) Brahmins, (2) Kshatriyas, (3) Vaishyas and (4) Shudra. The four classes in point of their mutual status are linked together in an order of graded inequality. The Brahmins are at the head and above all others. The Kshatriyas are below the Brahmins but above the Vaishyas and the Shudras. The Vaishyas below the Brahmins and the Kshatriyas but above the Shudras and the Shudras below all. Further, the occupations of the four classes are fixed. The occupation of the Brahmins is to acquire learning and to teach. The occupation of the Kshatriyas is to fight, that of the Vaishyas to trade and that of the Shudras to serve as menials to the other three classes above him. This is called by the Hindus the *Varna Vevastha*. It the very soul of Hinduism. Ambedkar points out that the Brahmins have not been able to explain the origin of the four Varnas, and a lot of confusion and contradiction prevail in the Hindu scriptures.

Ambedkar states that Rigveda and Manu talk of four Varnas, whereas the version is different in other Hindu scriptures. There is no unanimity among the Vedas on the origin of the four Varnas. None of the other Vedas agree with the Rigveda that the Brahmin was created from the mouth of the Prajapati, the Kshatriyas from his arms, the Vaishyas from his thighs and the Shudras from his feet. Ambedkar states:

> 'What a chaos? Why could the Brahmins not give a uniform and consistent explanation of the origin of the four Varnas?' [26]

On the issue of who created the four Varnas, there is no uniformity. This lack of uniformity has created a worst kind of confusion. Ambedkar writes:

> 'This chaos seems to be the result of concoction of the theory of Chaturvarna which the Brahmins quietly singled into the Rigveda contrary to established traditions? What was the purpose, what was the motive of the Brahmins who concocted this theory?'[27]

Concluding Remarks

Ambedkar has mentioned more than two dozens of riddles in Hinduism. A few of the riddles that have been mentioned above indicate, according to Ambedkar, that a chaos prevails in Hinduism for which the Brahmin or the superman is responsible. These riddles demonstrate that the true spirit of a religion is lacking in Hinduism; and its social order is fraught with formidable drawbacks. The four Varnas and its derivative caste system have led to the growth of graded inequality in the Hinduism – that its worst feature. The Superman under the mask of graded inequality has given an inhuman and degrading treatment to the untouchables or Shudras. That is why Ambedkar argues that the structure upon which the whole Hindu social order or its edifice has been built is moth-eaten and hollow. Since the Superman is unwilling to modify the basic feature of

Hinduism the salvation for the untouchables lies in conversion. A *Shudra* has no value in the Hindu social order and therefore it cannot provide a model for nation-building.

Ambedkar states that the Hindu social order or the established order is the law made by the Touchables. The Untouchables have nothing to do with it except to obey it and respect it. The Untouchables have no rights against the Touchable. For them, there is no equal right, no justice by which that which is due to the untouchables is allowed to them. Nothing is due to them except what the Touchables are prepared to grant. The Untouchables must not insist on rights. They should pray for mercy and favour and rest content with what is offered. Ambedkar, therefore, says:

> 'This Hindu social order (established order) is a hereditary order both in status as well as in function. Once a Touchable, always a Touchable. Once an Untouchable, always an Untouchable. …… In other words, the established order is based on an inexorable law of Karma or destiny which is fixed once for all and can never be changed. This destiny has no relation to the merits of the individuals living under it. An Untouchable however superior he may be mentally and morally is below a Touchable in rank, no matter how inferior he may be mentally or morally. A Touchable however poor he may be, must always take rank above an Untouchable however rich he may be.'[28]

Such is the picture of the Hindu Social order and under this established order, according to Ambedkar; nation-building is not possible. The Untouchability must be abolished and Ambedkar successfully abolished it under the new Constitution of India. Untouchability and nation-building cannot go together; the former must be abolished in practice too so that liberty, equality and fraternity may take roots and nation-building may proceed on healthy lines.

The basic essentials of a Nation, according to Ambedkar, are the social and psychological unity of the people, in the absence of which the dream of a nation is a mere chimera. In contrast to it, because of Varna and caste systems the Hindu social order is deeply fissured, giving rise to a fragmented society which is ruinous to the cause of nation-building. The infallibility of the Vedas and the structure of graded inequality have to be destroyed root and branch in order to unite the people in the social and psychological sense. That is the sure path towards nation-building.

References

1. *Dr Babasaheb Ambedkar Writings and Speeches*, Vol. 3, p. 72.
2. *Ibid.*, p. 77.
3. *Ibid.*, p. 78.
4. *Ibid.*, p. 92.
5. *Ibid.*, p. 100.
6. B. R. Ambedkar: *Annihilation of Caste* (Jalandhar, Bheem Patrika Publications, 1970), pp. 60-61.
7. *Ibid.*, p. 62.
8. *Ibid.*, p. 68.
9. *Ibid.*, p. 67.
10. Op. cit. Vol. 3, p. 100.
11. *Ibid.*, p. 105.
12. *Ibid.*, p. 106.
13. *Ibid.*, p. 115.
14. *Ibid.*, p. 123.
15. Op. cit. Radhakrishna, S: *The Hindu View of Life*, 1949, p. 93.
16. D. R. Jatav : *B. R. Ambedkar : A Vision of Man and Morals* (Jaipur, ABD Publishers, 1999), p. 90.
17. *Annihilation of Caste*, 1994, pp. 20, 37.
18. *Dr Babasaheb Ambedkar Writings and Speeches*, Vol. 4, p. 15.
19. *Ibid.*
20. *Ibid.*, p. 133.
21. *Ibid.*
22. *Ibid.*, p. 136.
23. *Ibid.*, p. 140.
24. *Ibid.*, pp. 8-9.
25. *Ibid.*, p. 52.
26. *Ibid.*, p. 203.
27. *Ibid.*, p. 204.
28. *Dr Babasaheb Writings and Speeches*, Vol. 5, p. 25.

CHAPTER–3

Emancipation of the Untouchables

Dr B.R. Ambedkar was one of the greatest builders of modern India. Apart from being the chief architect of India's Constitution, and the pioneer of Buddhist revival in the country, he was a dauntless champion of social change. His mission was to liberate and emancipate the untouchables of India from the yoke of Hindu social slavery. He certainly was not the first to have started the movement of social emancipation and political mobilisation of the untouchables, but he was perhaps more effective in highlighting the inhuman treatment to which they were subjected in the Hindu society. While earlier reformers had espoused the cause of social progress and welfare in general terms and had sought to improve the general conditions of society, their energy now required to be directed to the grievances of particular sections of the country. It is only on such a limited and defined canvas that the reformer's vision would gain precision and effectiveness. Ambedkar concentrated the force of his protestant and reformist spirit on the age-old abuses and disabilities of the untouchables in Hindu society.

Ambedkar's efforts to bring about the social change were qualitatively different from that of his predecessors. He at once stood for social change and liberation, economic emancipation and political advancement of the downtrodden millions – a task never undertaken by any high caste Hindu leader with so much vigour and force. His predecessors, not only in Maharashtra but all over the country, had raised their voice against the irrational customs which were responsible for the perpetuation of social backwardness. They raised issues like widow remarriage, child marriage, *Sati* system, dowry, death-feast, etc. which aimed at reforming the Hindu society. But none of them was for a fundamental and radical change in the social system as a whole. They did not boldly attack the ideological basis of the social institutions. Their concern was not the rejection but the reinterpretation of the scriptures in the light of contemporary exigencies. Ambedkar was remarkably free from these limitations.

Ambedkar symbolised the basic character of the non-Brahmin social reform movement in modern India. Although, it was a result as well as a part of a general national awakening and democratic consciousness, it succeeded in carrying the message of reform to classes which had so far remained untouched by it. Directed as it was to a particular section of the Indian society, it was yet capable of reforcing and quickening the wider stream of reform and hastening the forces of transformation of society. It has been correctly remarked that "Ambedkar combined in himself the role of a social reformer, a political leader and a spiritual guide of the untouchables. He, therefore, played a unique role in shaping the mind and the political outlook of his community."[1]

Ambedkar's thinking of social change was considerably influenced by Kabir and Phule. Kabir's teaching made him aware of the weaknesses of Hindu religion and of the need for reform in religious outlook and practice. Phule was considered by Ambedkar as "one of the greatest of our social reformers." He described Phule as "the greatest *Shudra* of modern India who made the lower classes of Hindus conscious of their slavery to the higher classes and who preached the gospel that for India social democracy was more vital than independence from foreign rule."[2] Under the influence of Phule, Ambedkar came closer to the liberal and reformist tradition in Maharashtra.

Moreover, Ambedkar overcame the limitations of the liberal reformist movement by consciously becoming a man of the masses, he not only believed in the driving force of principles and policies, but gave equal importance to the work of implementing them. In this sense, Ambedkar's main contribution was widening the base of the radical reformist theory and practice in India. That is why it is said:

> 'Ambedkar's approach towards the Hindu scriptures and their interpretation distinguished him from the early social reformers. He began to reconsider and reinterpret the sacred books with a forthright and a fearless critical spirit so that the Hindus may know that it is the doctrines contained in their sacred books which are responsible for the decline and fall of their country and their society. He also showed that what goes by the name of sacred books contain fabrications which are political in their motive, partisan in their composition and fraudulent in their purposes.'[3]

Besides, Ambedkar, after a careful study of the Hindu scriptures felt convinced that no reverence was due to it. According to him, the demand of the critical spirit was more imperative than the blind acceptance and reverence which such literature called for. He did not believe in fixed norms for any society. A norm must change with time and circumstances. No norms can be permanently fixed. There must always be room for revaluation of values of any norms. The possibility of revolving values remains open only when the scriptures are not invested with sacredness. The scriptures must be re-assessed on the basis of reason. Supremacy of reason was a cardinal principle in Ambedkar's social philosophy. His ideology of social change is based on the importance of Man and the supremacy of reason.

Ambedkar's ideology of social change is neither mysterious nor theological, nor a luxury for intellectual exercise. It is meant to eliminate all types of exploitation, thus, encouraging social cohesion. It is meant for the reconstruction of society, thus promoting liberty, equality and fraternity. These three words reflect his social philosophy. He did not borrow these words from the French revolution, but from the teachings of Buddha. His philosophy is meant to change the old world and to mitigate the existing misery from among the masses. It is keenly sensitive to the injustices and cruelties being done towards the untouchables. It is opposed to greed and exploitation, feudalism and fundamentalism, caste and untouchability. In fact, "his theory aims at mitigating human suffering and fighting against the social evils. It stands for social reconstruction and human creativity in all fields of life. It is meant to make life real and worthwhile."[4]

Ambedkar's ideology of social change is the outcome of a particular environment or his social background, which was full of hardships, trials and tribulations. He had witnessed and himself suffered atrocities at the hands of caste Hindus. He, therefore, squarely attacked the Hindu social order and vehemently criticised the inhuman treatment perpetrated by higher castes against the depressed classes. He repeatedly stressed the point that the Hindu society was infected with inequality, caste and untounchability. He was determined to exorcise the feelings of despair and inferiority from the minds of the untouchables; who had been forced to live the lives of sub-human beings.

Ambedkar's ideology and programmes of social change are quite comprehensive and broad. It is neither possible nor desirable to touch upon all the aspects relating to his ideology of social change. His concept and practice of social change is best reflected in his role regarding the removal of untouchability. In fact, he "emerged as a promising leader to break the centuries old shackles and liberate the untouchables from the age-old bondage of the Hindu society."[5]

Philosophy of Life

Ambedkar believed that every man should have a philosophy of life, for everyone must have a standard by which to measure his conduct. And philosophy is nothing but a standard by which to measure.

Ambedkar rejected the Hindu social philosophy propounded in the Bhagwat Geeta, because it is based on the *Triguna* of the Sankhya philosophy which is in his judgment a cruel perversion of the philosophy of Kapila, and which had made the caste system and the system of graded inequality the law of Hindu social life.

In his speech on October 3, 1954 (All-India broadcast),[6] Ambedkar said that positively speaking, his social philosophy may be said to be enshrined in three words: Liberty, Equality and Fraternity. He made it clear that he did not borrow his philosophy from the French Revolution. His philosophy had roots in religion and not in political science. He had derived them from the teachings of his Master, the Buddha. In his philosophy, liberty and equality had a place; but he added that unlimited liberty destroyed equality, and absolute equality left no room for liberty. Law had a place only as a safeguard against the breaches of liberty and equality; but he did not believe that law can be a guarantee for breaches of liberty or equality. He gave the highest place to fraternity as the only real safeguard against the denial of liberty or equality or fraternity, which was another name for brotherhood or humanity, which was again another name for religion.

He considered that law is secular, which anybody may break while fraternity or religion is sacred which everybody must respect. His philosophy had a mission. He had to do the work of conversion; for, he had to make the followers of *Triguna* theory to give it up and accept his. Indians today, he said, are governed by two different ideologies. Their political ideal set out in the Preamble to the Constitution affirms a life of liberty, equality and fraternity. Their social ideal embodied in their religion denies them.

Revolt against Four-Fold Varnas

Ambedkar was a bitter critic of untouchability, sanctioned by the Hindu scriptures. According to Rig Veda, there were four-fold Varnas in Hindu society – the Brahmin, Kshatriyas, Vaishyas and Shudras. It was stated that the Brahmins came from the mouth, Kshatriyas from the arms, Vaishyas from the thighs and Shudras from the feet of Brahma, the creator. The society thus was based on this mythical origin. It was known as *Chaturvarna*. It was regulated by the principle of graded inequality. The Brahmins were at the top, followed by Kshatriyas, Vaishyas and Shudras in descending order. This rule of graded inequality regulated their rights and privileges as well. Below these four Varnas came the untouchables or *Ati-Shudras*.

These unfortunate *Ati-Shudras* were damned as unseables, and untouchables whose mere 'touch' and even shadow would pollute the caste Hindus. They suffered from numerous social disabilities. Their children were not admitted into schools and the doors of the Hindu temples were closed to them. They were also denied the use of public tanks and other such places. Further, they could take up only the lower and degrading occupations. The more clean and paying jobs were not open to them on account of untouchability. In short, they were worst slaves and their children too were doomed for slavery as they had no choice but to serve the so-called high caste Hindus for no reward whatsoever. Thus, they were at the lowest rung of the social ladder and were denied all avenues of progress and self-elevation.

Ambedkar, who was born in this community of untouchables (Mahar) was opposed to the Varna system. He said:

> 'There cannot be a more degrading system of social organisation than the Chaturvarna. It is a system which deadens, paralyses and cripples the people from helpful activity.'[7]

In fact, Ambedkar rebelled against the Varna system. To him, it appeared utterly repellent and harmful. He wrote:

> 'The untouchables have no rights against the touchable. For them there is no equal right, no justice by which that which is due to the untouchables is allowed to them. Nothing is due to them except what the touchable are prepared to grant. The untouchables must not insist on rights. They should pray for mercy and favour and rest content with what is offered.'[8]

Untouchability, according to Ambedkar, had none of a just social order. The untouchable had no entry in the higher arts of civilisation and no way open to a life of culture. He must only sweep. He must do nothing else. Untouchability carried no security as to livelihood. The health of the untouchable was the care of nobody. Indeed, the death of an untouchable was regarded as a good riddance. There was a Hindu proverb which said, 'The untouchable is dead and the fear of pollution has vanished.'

The Varna system had established a hereditary order both in status as well as in function. Ambedkar said:

> 'Once a Touchable, always a Touchable. Once an Untouchable, always an Untouchable. Once a Brahmin, always a Brahmin. Once a sweeper, always a sweeper. Under it (Varna system), those who are born high, remain high; those who are born low, remain low. In other words, the established order is based on an inexorable law of Karma or destiny which is fixed once for all and can never be changed. This destiny has no relation to the merits of the individuals living under it.'[9]

The untouchable, while he is a free individual, had neither fair start, nor equal opportunity, nor square deal. From this point of view,

Ambedkar asserts that untouchability is not only worse than slavery but is positively cruel as compared to slavery. It is cruelty as compared to slavery because it throws upon the untouchables the responsibility for maintaining himself without opening to him fully all the ways of earning a living.[10] Thus, Rousseau's 'chained man', Marx's 'alienated man' and Ambedkar's 'broken man' are the human consequences of social exploitation as well as oppression.

Rejected the Dogma of Infallibility

Ambedkar held the views that the Vedas, *Manusmriti* and other Hindu scriptures are the bulwarks of Brahmanic theology. The Vedas are a lick knife whose blade is concealed in its handle and springs out at the touch of a button by a Brahmin. The Vedas have propounded a mischievous dogma – the dogma of the infallibility of the Vedas. He argued that this dogma must be destroyed root and branch, if India is to progress. This dogma has made the Hindu intellect ceased to grow, and has made the Hindu civilisation a stagnant and stinking pool. The Hindu scriptures are responsible for the four-fold classification of society.

Ambedkar pleaded that the sanctity of *Manusmriti* must go. It is responsible for graded inequality. In it, utterances and acts of Hindus are two poles apart. They have Rama on their tongues and knife under their armpit. They speak like saint but act like butchers. The laws of Manu ordained the lowest status to the untouchables. The humiliations, indignities and atrocities were heaped on them. They were the dumb victims of the Hindu social order and were made to suffer silently.

The Vedas say, "If a Shudra, hear the hymns then molten lead and glass be poured into his ears; if he utters the words of the Vedas his tongue must be slit; and if he remembers the Vedic mantras his body must be cut off by an axe or any other weapon." Ambedkar rejected outright such notions preached by the Vedas. He discarded the concepts of God, soul, infallibility of the Vedas, and worships, rites and rituals.

The Untouchables

Dr Ambedkar's work 'The Untouchables', published in 1948, is a sequel to his treatise called 'The Shudras'. He asserts that besides

Shudras, the Hindu society has produced three social classes whose existence has not received the attention it deserves. The first is the criminal tribes, the second the aboriginal tribes, and the third the untouchables. The first is taught to accept crime as an approved means of earning their livelihood; the second is left to live in full bloom of their primitive barbarism; and the third is treated as an entity beyond human intercourse and whose mere touch is enough to cause pollution.

The existence of these classes is an abomination; it arouses horror and disgust. The Hindu civilisation, gauged in the light of these social products, could hardly be called civilisation. It is a diabolical contrivance to suppress and enslave humanity. Its proper name would be infamy – a shameful disgrace. The existence of these classes has not occurred to the mind of the civilisation which is the most ancient and most unique. That the Hindu civilisation is the most ancient, one can understand and even allow. But how it is most unique, nobody could understand. If it means the existence of such classes, then it is a unique phenomenon. The inculcation of these beliefs in the sanity, superiority and sanctity of Hindu civilisation is due entirely to the peculiar social psychology of Hindu scholars.

The Hindu scholarship is confined to the Brahmins. No Brahmin scholar has produced a Voltaire. He is only a learned man; he is not an intellectual. The Brahmins have not been able to produce a Voltaire, because of their vested interest. Every Brahmins is interested in the maintenance of Brahmanical supremacy. A Voltaire among the Brahmins would be a positive danger to the maintenance of a civilisation which is contrived to maintain Brahmanic supremacy. The point is that the intellect of Brahmin scholar is severely limited by anxiety to preserve his interest. He himself would not play the part of an iconoclast even where it is necessary. And he would not allow such non-Brahmins as have the capacity to do so to play it.

Dr Ambedkar also presents his thesis on the origin of untouchability. He says, "The origin of untouchability lies buried in a dead past which nobody knows. To make it alive is an attempt to reclaim to history a city which has been dead since ages past and present it as it was in its original condition." He continues, "When the seed of untouchability could be said to have been sown? If it is not possible to fix an exact date, is it possible to fix an approximate date." The present day untouchables, the scheduled caste, were Buddhists in the distant past, and that they were dubbed as untouchables by the Brahmins when Buddhism declined. He considers the origin of untouchability as a result of hatred against Buddhists by the Brahmins. The roots of untouchability thus could be traced in the contempt and disgust which the Brahmins created against those who were Buddhists. 'The broken man' who embraced Buddhism hated the Brahmins because the Brahmins were the enemies of Buddhism. The Brahmins imposed untouchability against the 'broken man' because they would not leave Buddhism. The untouchability, he says, was born somewhere around 400 A.D. "It is born out of the struggle for supremacy between Buddhism and Brahmanism which has so completely moulded the history of India, the study of which is so woefully neglected by the students of Indian history." Untouchability is a corollary of the institution of caste, and not a separate institution. The untouchable formed the lowest stratum of Hindu society, they were in that position for centuries together. The touch or shadow or even voice of an untouchable was deemed by caste Hindus as polluting. They were born as untouchables; they lived and died as untouchables. As such, he described untouchability as 'a curse', 'an excrescence of Hinduism', 'a poison', 'a snake', 'a canker', ' a hydra headed monster', 'a great blot', 'a device of Satan', 'a hideous untruth; 'dyerism' and 'the most sinister'.

In addition, Dr Ambedkar's book on 'Riddles in Hinduism' published by the Government of Maharashtra in 1987, is useful for understanding the problem of untouchability. 'Riddles in Hinduism' is an exposition of the beliefs propounded by what might be called Brahminic theology. It is intended for the common mass of Hindus who need to be awakened to know in what quagmire the Brahmins have placed them and to lead them on to the road of rational thinking.

Struggle for Human Rights

Ambedkar was a man of action too. He made heroic efforts to accelerate social change and to achieve social equality. He rejected Pandit Motilal Nehru Committee Report (1928) in which the depressed classes were not recognised as a minority and no specific safeguards were contemplated for them. On the contrary, the Nehru Report opposed any safeguards for them.

The same year, Ambedkar submitted a Memorandum to the Simon Commission wherein he stressed the need for safeguards for the depressed classes. In his Dissent note to the Commission's Report, he forcefully pleaded for due representation of the depressed classes in the legislatures, executive and public services.

Further, at the first Round Table Conference (November, 1930), Ambedkar made a bold plea in favour of the depressed classes. Speaking about the position of the depressed classes in India, he said:

> 'It is one which is midway between that of the serf and the slave, and which may, for convenience, be called servile, with this difference, that the serf and the slave were permitted to have physical contact, from which the depressed classes are debarred. What is worse that this enforced servility and bar to human intercourse, due to their untouchability, involves, not merely the possibility of discrimination in public life, but actually works out as a positive denial of all equality of opportunity and the denial of those most elementary of civic rights on which all human existence depends.'

Impressed by the weighty arguments of Ambedkar, the British Government recognised the untouchables as a separate entity and granted them separate electorates along with other minorities in the Communal Award of August, 1932. Then Gandhi resorted to fast unto death (September, 1932) in order to have the Communal Award amended. The result was Gandhi-Ambedkar accord, or Poona Pact by which Gandhi conceded 'reservation of seats' for the depressed classes which he had refused to agree in London. By this Poona Pact the depressed classes were deprived of separate electorates and the double vote and in its place joint electorates and system of single vote was adopted. Ambedkar had reluctantly agreed to it because he was keen to save the life of Gandhiji.

Annihilation of Caste

Ambedkar believed in the annihilation of caste. In his presidential address prepared for the 1936 annual conference of the Jat-Pat-Todak Mandal of Lahore, he demolished the caste system totally. His address was not delivered as the conference was cancelled by the Reception Committee on the ground that the views contained in the address would be unbearable to the Conference. Ambedkar published his undelivered address in the form of a pamphlet, thus 'the posthumous child of the conference' has survived the passage of time as a great thesis on the annihilation of caste.

Ambedkar examined caste from two angles – the drawbacks of the system and what is the way out. Indicating the weakness of caste system, Ambedkar writes pungent, but true remarks. He asserts that caste is based on the dogma of predestination; it does not result in economic efficiency. It cannot and has not improved the race. It has disorganised and demoralised the Hindus. Its effect on the ethics of the Hindus is simply deplorable. It has killed public spirit; and destroyed the sense of public charity. It has restricted a Hindu's loyalty; it is confined only to his caste. Virtue has become caste-ridden and morality has become caste-bound. Neither there is sympathy to the deserving, nor is their appreciation of the meritorious. The four-tier classification of caste is most degrading; it is ridiculous and absurd. It forms 'the inner citadel of Hinduism'. It is riddled with puzzles. It is a serious threat to the unification of India.

Ambedkar, therefore, calls upon to annihilate the caste which is a great hindrance to social solidarity. The society, he says, must be based on reason and not on atrocious traditions of caste system.

Evil Effects of Caste System

Ambedkar in his broadcast on 'Voice of America' on 20th May, 1956, spoke on 'Prospects of Democracy in India.' He said that democracy in generally understood to be a political instrument. But this is primarily a mode of associated living. He said:

> 'The roots of democracy are to be searched in the social relationship, in the terms of associated life between the people who form a society.'[11]

To him, society connoted community of purpose and desire for welfare, loyalty to public ends and mutability of sympathy and co-operation. These ideals are not to be found in Indian society, because it consists of an innumerable collection of castes which are exclusive in their life and have no common experience to share and have no bond of sympathy. The existence of the caste system is a standing denial of the existence of those ideals of society and therefore of democracy.

Ambedkar argued that the Indian society is so imbedded in the caste system that everything is organised on the basis of caste. In the Indian society, caste exists in a glaring form. He stated:

> 'An Indian cannot eat or marry with an Indian simply because he or she does not belong to his or her caste. An Indian cannot touch an Indian because he or she does not belong to his or her caste. Go and enter politics and you can see caste reflected therein.'[12]

He held the view that in every field of Indian society caste system is a dominant factor. Go into the field of industry. What will you find? You will find that all the topmost men drawing the highest salary belong to the caste of the particular industrialist who owns the industry. The rest hang on for life on the lowest rungs of the ladder on a pittance. Go into the field of commerce and you will see the same picture. The whole commercial house is one camp of one caste, with no entry board on the door for others. Ambedkar frankly stated:

> 'Go into the field of charity. With one or two exceptions all charity in India is communal. If a Parsi dies, he leaves his money for Parsis. If a Jain dies, he leaves his money for Jains. If a Marwadi dies, he leaves his money for Marwadis. If a Brahmin dies, he leaves his money for Brahmins. Thus, there is no room for the downtrodden and the outcastes in politics, in industry, in commerce, and in education.'[13]

Ambedkar also pointed out other special features of the caste system which have their evil effects and which weaken the foundations of democracy. The first such special feature of the caste system lies in its being accompanied by what is called 'graded inequality.' Castes are not equal in their status. They are standing one above another. They are jealous of one another. It is an ascending scale of hatred and descending scale of contempt. This feature of the caste system has most pernicious consequences. It destroys willing and helpful co-operation.

The second evil effect in the caste system is that there is complete isolation in it. This manifests itself in the fact that the stimulus and response between two castes is only one-sided. The higher caste act in one recognised way and the lower caste must respond in one established way. It means that when there is no equitable opportunity to receive the stimulus from and to return the response from different caste, the result is that the influences which educate some into masters, educate others into slaves. The experience of each party loses its meaning when the free interchange of varying modes of life experience is arrested. It results into a separation of society, into a privileged and a subject class. Such a separation prevents social endosmosis.

There is a third characteristic of the caste system which depicts the evils thereof which cuts at the very roots of democracy. It is that one caste is bound to one occupation, and thereby it denies an individual to fulfil his pluralities of capacities and activities. A society to be democratic should open a way to use all the capacities of the individual. Stratification is stunting of the growth of the individual and deliberate stunting is a deliberate denial of democracy.

Thus, the caste system has many evils. The soul of the caste system is graded inequality, which is pernicious. The caste system has disabled the society. Neither there is unity in action nor one is able to know what is its common good. There is no knowledge of the end of existence. There is no criterion for rationality. As such, the mind of the Indians is distracted and misled by false valuations and false perspectives. It sets up number of different models and standards. It creates a disorganised and factional society. Under such conditions it is impossible for individual Indian to reach consistency of mind on the question of caste. The net result is that caste system is not to improve the prospect of democracy in India, but to put it in greater jeopardy.

Agenda for the Untouchables

Ambedkar had diagnosed the ills of the Hindu society and exposed the detestable condition of the untouchables in it. He also laid down an agenda or the prescription for the upliftment of the untouchables.

Ambedkar was prepared to go through any ordeal for the good of the untouchables. His mission was to wake them up to the causes of their misery and shame. He had resolved to lay down his life in enriching the noble ideals of self-respect and in bettering human life. Untouchables are not slaves. They are a warrior class. Nothing is more disgraceful for a brave man than to live a life devoid of self-respect and without love for the country. He made a solemn vow to die in the service and cause of those downtrodden people among whom he was born, he was brought up and he was living. He did not budge an inch from his righteous cause, or care for the violent and disparaging criticism by his detractors.

Ambedkar had laid down a long agenda for the upliftment of the untouchables. The main features of his agenda lie scattered in the speeches that he delivered from time to time. An effort is made here to put them in a condensed form.

Agitate and Organise

The first feature in his agenda was that his personal activities were not sufficient to bring about the redress of the grievances of the depressed classes. He said that they must agitate much more and organise themselves better. Agitation and organisation were essential for their liberation. Before leaving for London on 15 August, 1931, Ambedkar had addressed two separate meetings at Bombay (on 14th August). In those meetings he made very stirring speeches. He said:

> 'We must stand on our own feet and fight as best we can for our rights. So carry on your agitation and organise your forces. Power and prestige will come to you through struggle.'[14]

Untouchables not a Sub-Section

The second feature of Ambedkar's agenda was that the untouchables were not a sub-head or a sub-section of the Hindus, and that they were a separate and a distinct element in the national life of India. They were separate and distinct as the Muslims and like the Muslims of India the untouchables were entitled to separate political rights as against the Hindus. This was the fundamental basis of Ambedkar's politics.

Ambedkar upheld this view at the Round Table Conference. There was a contest between him and Gandhi on this point. Gandhi contested that the untouchables were a sub-section of the Hindus and consequently if any political power was to devolve from the hands of the British it should pass undivided into the hands of the Hindus who could be trusted to look after the interests of the untouchables. The stand taken by Ambedkar was totally different. He contended that the untouchables formed separate and distinct element in the life of the country. He stated that the Hindus, being their hereditary enemies, could not be trusted and far from using the political power for raising the untouchables the fear was that they would use it for perpetuating their subjection, and it was, therefore, absolutely necessary that there should be political partition between the untouchables and the Hindus so that the untouchables may get political power in their own hands to use it to promote their welfare, or to use it to save themselves against the tyranny and oppression of the Hindus. At the Round Table Conference the untouchables won and the Mahatma lost. The communal Award was the result of this contest. Its great virtue lay in the fact that the untouchables were recognised in the national life of India and entitled to claim separate political rights. That was the importance of the Communal Award.

Abandon Hero-Worship

The third feature was to abandon hero-worship. The ideas of hero-worship would bring ruin on the untouchables, as such, they must nip such ideas in the bud. By deifying an individual, they would be reposing faith for their safety and salvation in one single individual with the result that they would get into the habit of dependence and would grow indifferent to their duty. If they fall a victim to these ideas of hero-worship or superman, their fate would be no better than logs of wood in the national stream of life. Their struggle would come to naught. Ambedkar, therefore, said:

> 'You must abolish your slavery yourselves. Do not depend for its abolition upon God or Superman. Your salvation lies in political powers and not in making pilgrimages and observance of fasts. Devotion to scriptures would not free you from your bondage, want and poverty. Your forefathers have been doing it for generations, but there has been no respite nor even a slight difference in your miserable life in any way. Like your forefathers, you wear rags. Like them, you subsist on thrown out crumbs; like them, you perish in utter slums and hovels; and like them, you fall

easy victims to diseases with a death rate that rages among poultry. Your religious fasts, austerities and penances have not saved you from starvation.'[15]

Abandon Neutrality

The fourth feature was to abandon the attitude of neutrality. In the 1930's the main question before the untouchables was whether they should ally themselves either with the British Government or with the Indian National Congress. Ambedkar believed that the safety of the depressed classes lay in being independent of both, because of two reasons. Firstly, the British Government would never be able to solve their problem. And secondly, by joining the Congress the depressed classes would never be nearer to the solution of their problem. He stated that it was true that under the leadership of Gandhiji the Congress had no doubt passed a resolution condemning untouchability, but it has not done anything to give effect to it. The Congress had been providing moral support to eradicate untouchability, but very little was done to put it into practice. He saw no genuine effort on the part of the Congress to remove the stigma of untouchability. The Congress had been lukewarm and apathetic to the cause of the untouchables. Ambedkar, therefore, pleaded that the depressed classes should form an All-India organisation which would give voice to their opinions and provide them with the machinery for concerted action. Such an organisation should not be a bogus, or a make-believe organisation; it should be an effective one doing service to the depressed classes. An effective All-India organisation would encourage and energise the depressed classes and they would shed all their fears and begin to exercise their rights of humanity.

Attain Self-Elevation

The fifth feature was his appeal to the untouchables to attain self-elevation. At the Mahad Conference (1927), Ambedkar delivered his presidential address to the half-clad, embarrassed depressed classes. In an inspiring tone, he said:

> 'No lasting progress can be achieved unless we put ourselves through a three-fold process of purification. We must improve the general tone of our demeanour, re-tone our pronunciations and revitalise our thoughts.'[16]

He, therefore, asked the untouchables to take a vow from that moment to renounce eating carrion. It was high time that they must root out from their mind the ideas of highness and lowness among themselves. They must resolve not to eat the thrown-out crumbs. He said:

> 'We will attain self-elevation only if we learn self-help, regain our self-respect, and gain self-knowledge.'[17]

He further urged the assembled crowd to agitate for their rights. He tweaked their self-respect by telling them that it was utterly disgraceful to sell their human rights for a few crumbs of bread, and appealed to them fervently to do away with the humiliating, enslaving traditions. Self-elevation and self-respect was essential for the progress of the downtrodden.

Capture Political Power

The sixth feature was that the depressed must try to capture political power, in the absence of which their status would not improve. He exhorted the untouchables to capture political power, to be on their guard against any verbal and rosy promises, and urged them to believe only those leaders who had experience of their woes. At the meeting held near Bombay on 4th March, 1933, Ambedkar told the untouchables that the work of law-making and of its execution must be performed with their consent, help and will. He said:

> 'In short, law is the abode of all worldly happiness. You capture the power of law-making. It is, therefore, your duty to divert your attention from fast, worship and penance and apply it to capturing law-making power. That way lies your salvation. That way will end your starvation.'[18]

Thus, Ambedkar told the untouchables that they must be always watchful, strong, well-educated and self-respecting; and capture the power of law-making in order to attain and maintain success.

Again, while addressing the All-India Depressed Classes Congress at Kamptee in May 1932, Ambedkar said:

> 'It is very necessary that the political reins should come in the hands of the untouchables. For that, all of us should unite and

> secure a political status. Untouchability in India will not be eradicated so long as the untouchables do not control the political strings.'[19]

Further, the same feelings were expressed by Ambedkar in July 1942, at the All-India Depressed Classes Conference held at Nagpur, where he said:

> 'The only thing, therefore we can depend upon for our continued progress is the capture of political power. I have no doubt that is our only salvation, and that without it we will perish. It is on this question that we must concentrate all our attention. It is a question of life and death for us.'[20]

The untouchables, argued Ambedkar, must not be absorbed in the worthless mysteries of life, superstitions and mysticism; or sing songs of Rama, or hang *tulsi* leaves around their neck. These rituals would not eradicate their slavery. The most effective way would be to capture the instruments of political power. Once the untouchables capture law-making organs, they would be able to remove the foolish belief that their miseries were pre-ordained. In short, political power was the key to all social progress of the untouchables.

Change of Religion

The seventh related to Ambedkar's mission to bring about a social change by ending untouchability. In order to achieve this object, he fought relentlessly the unjust society on all the fronts – social, religious, economic and political. As a first step, he thought of reforming the Hindu religion. However, the two famous satyagrahas of Mahad (1927) and Nasik (1930-35) opened his eyes to the stark reality that it was futile to attempt to reform the decadent Hinduism. Therefore, at a Conference at Yeola (1935) he announced his intention to renounce Hinduism, which he ultimately did in 1956.

At Yeola, Ambedkar declared that the problem of untouchability is a matter of class struggle. It is a struggle between caste Hindus and the untouchables. It is not a matter of doing injustice against one man. It is a matter of injustice being done by one class against another. This class struggle has a relation with the social status. Those who are masters remain masters and those who are born in slavery remain slaves. The privileged remain privileged and the serfs remain serfs. This struggle indicates how one class should keep its relations with another class. This struggle starts as soon as the untouchables start claiming equal treatment with others. Ambedkar said:

> 'In a class structure, there is on the one hand, tyranny, vanity, pride, arrogance, greed, selfishness, and on the other insecurity, poverty, degradation, loss of liberty, self-reliance, independence, dignity and self-respect.'[21]

Ambedkar continued that the Untouchability is not a short or temporary feature, it is a permanent one. It is eternal, because the religion which has placed the untouchables at the lowest level of the society is itself eternal, according to the belief of the Hindu caste people. No change, according to time and circumstances, is possible. Ambedkar stated:

> 'You (untouchables) are at the lowest rung of the ladder today. You shall remain lowest forever. This means, the struggle between Hindus and untouchables shall continue forever. How will you survive through this struggle is the main question? And unless you think over it, there is no way out. Those who desire to live in obedience to the dictates of the Hindus, those who wish to remain their slaves; they do not need to think over the problem. But those who wish to live a life of self-respect and equality, will have to think over this. How should we survive through this struggle? For me, it is not difficult to answer this question. Those who have assembled here will have to agree that in any struggle one who holds strength becomes the victor. One, who has no strength, need not expect success. This has been proved by experience, and do not need to cite illustrations to prove it.'[22]

Ambedkar argued that the untouchables are not only low in the eyes of the Hindus, but they are the lowest in the whole of India, because of the treatment given to them by the Hindus. At Yeola, he said:

> 'If you have to get rid of this shameful condition, if you have to cleanse this filth and make use of this precious life, there is only one way and that is to throw off the shackles of Hindu religion and the Hindu society, in which you are bound. The taste of a thing

can be changed. But the poison cannot be made *Amrit*. In short, so long as we remain in a religion which teaches a man to treat another man as leper, the sense of discrimination on account of caste which is deeply rooted in our minds cannot go. For annihilating castes and untouchability, change of religion is the only antidote.'[23]

In fact, the Hindu religion did not appeal to Ambedkar's conscience. Neither did it appeal to his self-respect nor to his dignity. He believed that religion is for Man and not Man for religion. He, therefore, argued that to get human treatment, the depressed should convert themselves. He said:

'Convert for getting organised. Convert for becoming strong. Convert for securing equality. Convert for getting liberty. Convert so that your domestic life may be happy.'[24]

Conversion is Essential

The last feature was conversion. Ambedkar viewed the matter of conversion through two aspects – social as well as religious; material as well as spiritual. He held that the downtrodden had no enough power to survive in a struggle against the caste-Hindus. They lacked three types of strength known to man, that is, man-power, wealth and mental strength. So far as man-power was concerned, they were in a minority. Financial strength was also very weak. They had no trades, no business, no service, and no land. As regards their mental strength, the condition is still worst. Their confidence, vigour and ambition had completely vanished on account of exploitation through centuries. They had become helpless, unenergetic and pale. Everywhere, there was an atmosphere of defeatism and pessimism. Even the slightest idea that they could do something did not arise in anybody's mind. The Hindus were practicing injustice and tyranny against them only because they were helpless. They could not face tyranny without strength; or could not possess enough strength to face the tyranny. As such, Ambedkar asserted that the strength required to face this tyranny needed to be secured from outside.

In addition, the social and religious environment was against the upliftment of the untouchables. The casteism and religious fanaticism that prevailed in the country, had a very peculiar effect on the minds and morality of the people. The higher castes were not pained by the poverty and sufferings of the untouchables. Looking at the social milieu which was in favour of the higher castes, Ambedkar pleaded that the strength needs to be brought from outside. He said:

> 'You (downtrodden) must realise one thing, that is, unless you establish close relations with some other society, unless you join some other religion, you cannot get the strength from outside. It clearly means, you must leave your present religion and assimilate yourselves with some other society. Without that, you cannot gain the strength of that society. So long as you do not have strength, you and your future generations will have to lead your lives in the same pitiable condition.'[25]

Ambedkar held the view that the conversion was necessary both for material gains and spiritual well-being. He criticised the Hindu religion because it was not a true religion. There was no place for an individual in Hindu religion, because it was constituted on a class-concept. A religion which did not recognise the individual was not acceptable to Ambedkar. He did not accept a religion in which one class had a right to gain knowledge, another had only a right to use arms, the third one to trade and the fourth only to serve. Such a religion based on *Chaturvarna* was not beneficial to the untouchables. The downtrodden could not develop himself at all in the Hinduism. Three factors were required for the uplift of an untouchable – sympathy, equality and liberty. These factors did not exist in Hinduism.

The Hindus did not look with sympathy towards the downtrodden. They had no sense of brotherhood towards them. Inequality too was widespread in Hinduism. No where in the world such a system existed where a man was treated so low as not to touch another man. Ambedkar boldly stated:

> 'Can anybody believe that there exists an animal called man (untouchable) by whose touch man becomes impure, water is polluted, and God becomes unworthy for worship? Is there any difference between the treatment meted out to an untouchable and a leper? Though people feel nauseated thinking of a leper, they at least have sympathy for him. But people have nausea as well as hatred against you. Your condition is worse than the leper.'[26]

The majority of the Hindus, wrote Ambedkar, believed that the untouchables were a stigma, because they were impure. The Hindus regarded them as unequals. The untouchables had been thrust into this condition because they had continued to be Hindus. Making a scathing attack on the meanness found among the Hindus, Ambedkar wrote:

> 'The Hindus can be ranked among those cruel people whose utterances and acts are two poles apart. They have this Ram on their tongue and a knife under their armpits. They speak like saints and act as butchers. Do not keep company with those who believe that the God is omnipresent, but treat men worse than animals, they are hypocrites. Do no keep contact with those who feed ants with sugar but kill men by prohibiting them from drinking water, they are hypocrites.'[27]

Thus, the untouchables were not low in the eyes of the Hindus alone, but they were the lowest in the whole of India, because of the treatment given to them by the Hindus. To get rid of this shameful condition, to cleanse this stigma and make this precious life graceful for the untouchables, Ambedkar pleaded, that there was only one way and that was to discard the Hindu religion and the Hindu society.

Ambedkar gave some more weighty reasons for the change of religion by the untouchables. He said that the Hindu social order denied social liberty to the untouchables. Neither they had physical freedom nor freedom of the mind. In fact, they had no freedom; they were worse than slaves. In his opinion, in Hinduism, conscience, reason, thoughts had neither any importance nor any scope. Hence, so long as the untouchables were a part of the Hindu religion, they could not expect to have freedom of thought. The whole of the Hindu religion was the creation of the high caste Hindus for the welfare and prosperity of the high-castes. To which the Hindus called a religion, had assigned a role of the slaves to the untouchables. Thus, the Hinduism had marred their progress, sacked their mental freedom and made them slaves. As such, they must change their religion.

There was one more potent factor for the change of religion by the untouchables. This was the caste system imbedded in Hinduism. Ambedkar was of the opinion that castes could not be abolished by inter-caste dinners or stray instances of inter-caste marriages. He wrote:

> 'The caste is a state of mind. It is a disease of the mind. The teachings of the Hindu religion are the root cause of this disease. We practice the casteism, we observe the untouchability, because we are asked to do so by the Hindu religion in which we live. A bitter thing can be made sweet. The taste of salty and stringent things can be changed. But the poison cannot be made nectar (Amrit). To talk of annihilating castes while living in the Hinduism is like talking of changing the poison into nectar.'[28]

In short, Ambedkar argued, so long as the untouchable remained in the religion which taught a man to other man as filthy, the sense of discrimination on account of caste which was deeply rooted in the Hindu religion, could not be abolished. For annihilation the castes and the untouchability from among the untouchables, change of religion was the only antidote. The principal argument of Ambedkar in favour of conversion was that through it the untouchables would secure social freedom, spiritual as well as material gains. The conversion was the only right path of freedom which would ultimately lead to equality. The conversion was not the path of escapism. It was not the path of cowardice; it was the path of wisdom. Stating specifically, that 'man is not for religion, religion is for man,' Ambedkar appealed to the untouchables in the following words:

> 'To become human, convert yourselves. To get organised, convert yourselves. To achieve strength, convert yourselves. To secure equality, convert yourselves. To get liberty, convert yourselves. To make your domestic life happy, convert yourselves.'[29]

For the emancipation and advancement of the untouchables, the change of religion appeared necessity to Ambedkar. He characterised Hindu religion as 'a diabolical creed', which had forced the untouchables to lead a life of degradation, and heaped all sorts of indignities on them, kept them poor and ignorant. There was no rationale in continuing to accept a degraded and lowly position. To change this degraded and disgraceful existence into a golden life, conversion was absolutely necessary.

Taking refuge in the words of the Buddha, Ambedkar told the untouchables:

> 'Be your own guide. Take refuge in your own reason. Do not listen to the advice of others. Do not succumb to others. Be truthful. Take refuge in truth. Never surrender to anything. If you keep in mind this message of Lord Buddha at this juncture, I am sure, your decision will not be wrong.'[30]

Memorandum to the Cabinet Mission

Ambedkar's memorandum to the Cabinet Mission was a significant one. On 5th April, 1946, Dr Ambedkar on behalf of All-India Scheduled Castes Federation submitted a Memorandum to the Cabinet Mission. In that memorandum, he pleaded for adequate representation of the depressed classes in the legislature, executive and services.

That memorandum also stated the condition of the untouchables in the village system of India. It stated that the existing village system had the effect of making the scheduled castes in the villages slaves of the Caste Hindus. It had the effect of making untouchability permanent. Under the village system, the Memorandum, said:

> 'The Scheduled Castes are not allowed to live inside the village. They have to live on the outskirts. They are not allowed to take water from the village well. They are not allowed to send their children to the village schools. No barber in the village will shave them… they have no independent means of livelihood. They own no land…they form a mass of landless labour, utterly destitute, a class of hereditary paupers …. They have to do forced labour… they have to live a life of degradation, dishonour and ignominy from generation to generation. It is a state of eternal perdition. They cannot wear clean clothes, they cannot wear ornaments, they cannot eat rich food, they cannot sit on a chair in the presence of a Hindu and they must do all the dirty jobs.'[31]

Such was the condition of the Untouchables around the independence of the country. A radical change was brought about subsequently by Ambedkar in the new Constitution of India.

The Abolition of Untouchability

From his early childhood, Ambedkar had dedicated himself to the upliftment of the untouchables among whom he was born. It was not that there were no temptations in his way. If he had considered his own interests, he could have been anything he wanted to be, and if had joined the Congress he would have reached to the highest place in that organisation. But as he said:

> 'I had dedicated myself to the upliftment of the untouchables and I have followed the adage which says that it is better to be narrow-minded if you wish to be enthusiastic about a cause which you wish to accomplish.'[32]

Ever since Ambedkar began to understand the meaning of life, he had always followed one principle in life and that was to serve his untouchable brethren. He had never given so much attention to any other problem than the betterment of untouchables. He boldly stood for guarding the interests of the untouchables. That was the principal aim of his life. He was the voice of the untouchables. There was no other voice of the untouchables, except him. In the concluding session of the Con-Assembly, he said:

> 'I came into the Constituent Assembly with no great aspiration than to safeguard the interests of the Scheduled Castes or the Untouchables.'[33]

Ambedkar had not the remotest idea that he would be called upon to undertake more responsible functions. He was therefore greatly surprised when the Con-Assembly elected him to the Drafting Committee. He was more than surprised when the Drafting Committee elected him to be its Chairman. He said:

> 'There were in the Drafting Committee men bigger, better and more competent than myself such as my friend Sir Alladi Krishna Swami Ayyar. I am grateful to the Constituent Assembly and the Drafting Committee for reposing in me so much trust and confidence and to have chosen me as their instrument and given me this opportunity of serving the country.'[34]

On behalf of the Drafting Committee, Ambedkar submitted the Draft of the new Constitution of India as settled by the Committee to the Constituent Assembly on 21st February, 1948. In that Draft Constitution, Article 11 was regarding the abolition of untouchability. In the Constitution of India which was enacted by the Assembly, this article is numbered 17. Article 17 says:

> 'Untouchability is abolished and its practice in any form is forbidden. The enforcement of any disability arising out of 'untouchability' shall be an offence punishable in accordance with Law.'[35]

Besides, the abolition of untouchability, special provisions have been incorporated in the Constitution of India, regarding reservation of seats for Scheduled Castes and Scheduled Tribes in the parliament, legislatures, public services and educational institutions.

Concluding Remarks

Dr Ambedkar had done a yeoman's service to the cause of the untouchables or the depressed classes. His independent thinking and action had brought about a phenomenal change in the status of the untouchables. He had not only infused confidence in untouchables but he had also awakened the caste Hindus.

By his struggle, sacrifice and scholarship, Ambedkar was able to abolish untouchability, thus strengthened the Hindu social structure. His entire life was a life of service and sacrifice. His mission was to free the millions of untouchables from the shackles of slavery and serfdom. He succeeded in his mission in full measure.

But for the constant struggle and ceaseless efforts of Ambedkar, the observance of untouchability in Hindu society in India would never have been removed and banned. He stood for social liberation, economic emancipation and political advancement of the untouchables – a task which he successfully completed with vigour and force. He brought about a great social change by the abolition of untouchability. As a social reformer, a political leader and a spiritual guide of the untouchables, he played a unique role in shaping the mind and the political outlook of the depressed classes. In fact, he brought about a social revolution of major significance in India. He filled the dead cells of the untouchables with "new energy, new blood and new inspiration. That energy, vision and consciousness would hold on inspite of difficulties and danger."[36]

References

1. K. Majumdar and Bhanwar Singh (eds): *Ambedkar and Social Justice* (New Delhi, Radha Publications, 1997), p. 2.
2. Ibid.
3. *Ibid.,* pp. 2-3.
4. D. R. Jatava: *B. R. Ambedkar : A Vision of Man and Morals* (Jaipur, ABD Publishers, 1999), p.vi.
5. *Dr Babasaheb Ambedkar Writings and Speeches*, Vol. 17, Part One (Education Department, Government of Maharashtra, 2003), p. xvi.
6. *Dr Babasaheb Ambedkar Writings and Speeches*, Vol. 17, Part Three, p. 503.
7. Op. cit. D. C. Ahir: *The Legacy of Dr Ambedkar* (Delhi, B. R. Publishing Corporation, 1990), p. 287.
8. *Dr Babasaheb Ambedkar Writings and Speeches,* Vol. 5, 1989, p. 25.
9. *Ibid.*
10. A. K. Majumdar and Bhanwar Singh, p. 60.
11. *Dr Babasaheb Ambedkar Writings and Speeches*, Vol. 17, Part Three, p. 519.
12. *Ibid.,* p. 520.
13. *Ibid.*
14. *Ibid.,* p. 65.
15. *Ibid.,* p. 89.
16. *Ibid.,* Vol. 17, Part One, p. 4.
17. *Ibid.*
18. *Ibid.,* Vol. 17, Part Three, p. 89.
19. *Ibid.,* p. 79.
20. *Ibid.,* pp. 251-52.
21. Op. cit. D. C. Ahir: *The Legacy of Dr Ambedkar* (Delhi, B. R. Publishing Corporation, 1990), p. 287.
22. Op. cit., *Ibid,* p. 21.
23. *Ibid.,* p. 22.
24. *Ibid.,* p. 23.
25. *Dr Babasaheb Ambedkar Writings and Speeches*, Vol. 17, Part Three, p. 121.
26. *Ibid.,* p. 124.
27. *Ibid.,* p. 126.
28. *Ibid.,* pp. 130-131.
29. *Ibid.,* p. 145.

30. *Ibid.*, p. 147.
31. *Ibid.*, Vol. 17, Part Two, pp. 176-177.
32. *Ibid.*, p. 1321.
33. *Ibid.*, Vol. 13, p. 1208.
34. *Ibid.*
35. The Constitution of India, p. 12.
36. *Dr Babasaheb Ambedkar Writings and Speeches*, Vol. 17, Part Three, p. 68.

CHAPTER–4

Uproot Caste

Dr Ambedkar, a constructive social reformer and legal philosopher, has shown abundant originality and profundity of his convictions and conceptions in his small treatise 'Annihilation of Caste'. His treatise can be compared with the writings of the best minds of the East and the West. It is the outcome of his vast erudition. Apart from dismantling the caste system, Ambedkar also depicts the ideal society in 'Annihilation of Caste.'

He observes that caste is a derivative of the Chaturvarna and, as such, it is an important feature of the Hindu social order. Caste is anti-social and anti-nationhood, because of its negative effects which weaken social cohesion and social solidarity. The task of healthy nation-building is wellnigh impossible unless caste is completely destroyed. Caste has destroyed the hopes of happiness of the millions of depressed and neglected classes. It has made them less and less confident and happy; it has made the society sick and hence not wanted.

Ambedkar's small treatise 'Annihilation of Caste' is a frontal attack on caste. It excels all his other treatises and is regarded as a valuable heritage. He observes that the reformers among the high-caste Hindus were enlightened intellectuals, who confined their activities to abolish the enforced widowhood, child-marriage, etc., but they did not feel the necessity for agitating for the abolition of castes nor did they have courage to agitate against it. According to him, the political revolutions in India were preceded by the social and religious reforms led by saints. But during the British rule, issue of political independence got precedence over the social reform and therefore social reform continued to remain neglected. Pointing to the socialists, he remarked that the socialists will have to fight against the monster of caste either before or after revolution. He asserts that caste is not based on division of labour. It is a division of labourers. As an economic organisation also, caste is a harmful institution. He calls upon the Hindus to annihilate the caste which is a great hindranace to social solidarity and to set up a new social order based on the ideals of liberty, equality and fraternity in consonance with the principles of democracy. He advocates inter-caste marriage as one of the solutions to the problem. But he stresses that the belief in the 'Shastras' is the root cause of maintaining castes. He therefore suggests, 'Make every man and woman free from the thraldom of the *Shastras*, cleanse their minds of the pernicious notions founded on the *Shastras* and he or she will interdine and intermarry.' According to him, the society must be based on reason and not on atrocious traditions of caste system.[1]

The main argument that he develops in this treatise is that, 'it is not possible to break caste without annihilating the religious notions on which the caste system is founded.' He writes:

> 'The real method of breaking up the caste system was not to bring about inter-caste dinners and inter-caste marriages but to destroy the religious notions on which caste was founded.'[2]

Ambedkar was deeply interested in nation-bulding and he regarded caste as the greatest impediment towards nation-building. He was not satisfied with the half-hearted approach of the reformers of Hindu society because they refused to analyse the whole issue on the basis of logic. He was sure that the best method of abolishing caste is the destruction of notions of Hindu religion on which the super-structure of caste thrived. He was aware of the fact that he had arrived at as to the best method of destroying caste, and that method might be startling and painful, but that alone is a necessary step towards nation-building.

While advocating the destruction of the caste system, Ambedkar gives a number of cogent arguments. His whole analysis is rational and logical. It is necessary to highlight the main points of his attack on caste, so that one may have a clear picture of the hindrances that block the path of social oneness and nation-building.

Precedence of Social or Political Reform

Ambedkar's views on the precedence of social or political reform appear to be overlapping. At one stage he gave precedence to social reform; whereas on other occasions he spoke about the precedence of political reform.

The first point relates to the cause of social reform. The path of social reform, argues Ambedkar, like the path to heaven at any rate in India, is strewn with many difficulties. Social reform in India has few friends and many critics. The critics fall into two distinct classes. One class consists of political reformers and the other of socialists.

It was at one time recognised that withut social reforms or efficiency no permanent progress in the other fields of activity was possible, that owing to mischief wrought by the evil customs, Hindu society was not in a state of efficiency and that ceaseless effort must be made to eradicate these evils. Ambedkar states that it was due to the recognition of this fact that the birth of the Indian National Congress (1885) was accompanied by the foundation of the Social Conference. While the Congress was concerned with defining the weak points in the political organisation of the country, the Social Conference was engaged in removing the weak points in the social organisation of the Hindu society. For some time the Congress and the Conference worked as two wings of one common activity and they held their annual sessions in the same pandal. But soon the two wings developed into two parties – a Political Reform Party and a Social Reform Party, between whom there raged a fierce controversy. The Political Reform Party supported the National Congress and Social Reform Party supported the Social Conference. The two bodies thus became two hostile camps. Ambedkar writes:

'The point at issue was whether social reform should precede political reform. For a decade the forces were evenly balanced and the battle was fought without victory to either side. It was however evident that the fortunes of the Social Conference were ebbing fast. The gentlemen who presided over the sessions of the Social Conference lamented that the majority of the educated Hindus were for political advancement and indifferent to social reform... the number of those who attended the Social Conference was very much smaller...Thus, in course of time the party in favour of political reform won and the Social Conference vanished and was forgotten.'[3]

Ambedkar states that the speech delivered by W. C. Bannerji in 1892 at Allahabad as president of the eighth session of the Congress, gave a death-blow to the Social Conference. Bannerji said:

> 'I, for one have no patience with those who say we shall not be fit for political reform until we reform our social system. I fail to see any connection between the two.'[4]

Thus, the Congress gave precedence to political reform and neglected social reform. The Congress proved conclusively that social reform had no bearing on political reform. Ambedkar did not agree with this view-point of the Congress, because he gave precedence to social reform. He drew upon the treatment of the untouchables for proving his thesis. Ambedkar states:

> 'Under the rule of the Peshwas in the Maratha country the untouchable was not allowed to use the public streets, if a Hindu was coming along lest he should pollute the Hindu by his shadow. The untouchable was required to have a black thread either on his wrist or in his neck as a sign or mark to prevent the Hindus from getting themselves polluted by his touch through mistake...'[5]

Ambedkar, having stated a number of such facts, defended the case for social reform. He believed that the political reform could not with impunity take precedence over social reform in the sense of reconstruction of society. He stated that history bears out the preposition that political revolutions have always been preceded by social and religious revolutions. Hence, the emancipation of the mind and the soul of the untouchables is a necessary preliminary for the political expansion of the people. He firmly adhered to the maxim that no political progress is possible without first introducing social emancipation or reform.

Then, turning to the Socialists, Ambedkar stated that: 'Can the Socialists ignore the problem arising out of the social order?

The Socialists of India apply the economic interpretation of history to the facts of India. They propound that man is an economic creature, that his activities and aspirations are bound by economic facts, that property is the only source of power. They, therefore, preach that political and social reforms are but gigantic illusion and that economic reform by equalisation of property must have precedence over other kind of reform. Ambedkar argues that the above view of the socialists is a narrow one, and that economic motive is not the only motive by which man is actuated. That economic power is the only kind of power no student of human society can accept. There are other sources of power, such as, religion, social status, etc. which the socialists have disregarded. Defending the case of precedence of social reform, Ambedkar asks the socialists:

> 'Can you have economic reform without first bringing about a reform of the social order?...If socialism is a practical programme and is not merely an ideal, distant and far off, the question for a socialist is not whether he believes in equality. The question for him is whether he minds one class ill-treating and suppressing another class as a matter of system, as a matter of principle and thus allow tyranny and oppression to continue to divide one class from another.'[6]

Thus, Ambedkar could not see how a socialist state in India could function for a second without having to grapple with the problems created by the prejudices which made Indian people observe the distinctions of high and low, clean and unclean. He, therefore, states that the problem of social reform is fundamental and that for the socialists or others there is no escape from it. No political reform is possible, no economic reform is possible, and no nation-building is possible, unless the monster of high and low caste is abolished, and that the social reform must be given precedence over political reform and economic reform.

On other occasions, namely Ambedkar's address at Belgaum on 24 May, 1932, he said that political reform must precede social reform and without political power to the depressed classes their status would not improve.[7] By gaining control over the political power, the depressed classes could influence the enactment of social legislation, aiming towards the removal of social evils. Again, addressing the Scheduled Castes Federation on 24 April, 1948, he stated that 'political power is the key to all social progress'[8] and as such its precedence must be realised so that the depressed classes may achieve their salvation if they capture this power. Further, on 27 October, 1951, he in his speech at Jullunder, said that the depressed classes must have one power and that is the political power, and it must be won. He told the depressed classes that 'without political power we cannot exist in this world.'[9] These statements reveal Ambedkar's precedence for political power.

Defenders of Caste

Ambedkar observes that it is a pity that caste has its defenders. It is defended on the grounds of division of labour, purity of race and economic efficiency. Ambedkar refutes these defences.

Firstly, Ambedkar argues that caste system is not merely division of labour; it is also a division of labourers. Civilised society undoubtedly needs division of labour, but in no civilised society is division of labour, accompanied by this unnatural division of labourers into water-tight, compartments. Caste system is not merely a division of labourers which is quite different from division of labour – it is a hierarchy in which the divisions of labourers are graded one above the other. In no other country is the division of labour accompanied by this gradation of labourers. Further, Ambedkar says that this division of labour is not spontaneous; it is not based on natural aptitudes. The stratification of occupation which is the result of the caste system is positively pernicious. The division of labour brought about by the caste is not a division based on choice. Individual sentiment, individual preference has no place in it. Moreover, it is based on the dogma of predestination. Ambedkar, therefore, states that caste is a harmful institution, because it involves the subordination of man's natural powers and inclinations to the exigencies of social rules.

Secondly, Ambedkar rejects the biological argument given by its supporters to defend the caste system. The defenders of caste say that its object is to preserve purity of race and purity of blood. This is an erroneous argument. Ambedkar asserts that ethnologists are of opinion that men of pure race exist nowhere and that there has been a mixture of all races in all parts of the world. Especially this is the case with the people of India. There is hardly a class, or caste in India which has not a foreign strain in it. There is an admixture of alien blood not only among the warrior classes – the Rajputs and the Marathas – but also among the Brahmins who are under the happy delusion that they are free from all foreign elements. As such, Ambedkar is of the opinion that the caste system cannot be said to have grown as a means of preventing the admixture of races or as a means of maintaining purity of blood. It came into being long after the different races of India had commingled in blood and culture. To defend caste on biological ground, or heredity and eugenics, therefore, is a gross perversion of facts. Ambedkar writes:

> 'The caste is a social system which embodies the arrogance and selfishness of a perverse section of the Hindus who were superior enough in social status to set it in fashion and who had authority to force it on their inferiors.'[10]

And lastly, Ambedkar states that caste does not result in economic efficiency. Caste cannot and has not improved the race. Caste has however done one thing. It has completely disorganised and demoralised the Hindus. The Hindu society, according to Ambedkar, is a myth; it does not exist; it is only a collection of castes. Each caste is conscious of its existence. Its survival is the be all and end all of its existence. Castes do not even form a federation. A caste has no feeling that it is affiliated to other castes except when there is a Hindu-Muslim riot. On all other occasions each caste endeavours to segregate itself and to distinguish itself from other castes. Each caste neither dines nor marries among itself, but each caste prescribes its own distinctive dress. There is no Hindu 'consciousness of kind'. In every Hindu the consciousness that exists is the consciousness of his caste. That is the reason why the Hindu cannot be said to form a society or a nation. Ambedkar emphatically states that Indians are not a nation, that they are only an amorphous mess of people. There is no fundamental unity among them. The essentials which make a nation are lacking in Hindus. The ideal Hindu is 'like a rat living in his own hole refusing to have any contact with others.' Men constitute a nation when they have things which they possess in common. To have similar thing is totally different from possessing things in common. In short, Ambedkar writes:

> 'The caste system prevents common activity; it has prevented the Hindus from becoming a society or nation with a unified life and a consciousness of its own being.'[11]

Exposing the weaknesses of the arguments given by the defenders of the caste system, Ambedkar characterises the caste as 'a stigma' upon the Hindu society. Caste generates 'anti-social spirit' which is highly dangerous for the growth of nation-building.

Caste Cultivates Anti-Social Spirit

According to Ambedkar, the worst feature of the caste system is that it cultivates or generates anti-social spirit among the Hindus. What is surprising is that one caste enjoys singing a hymn of hate against another caste! The literature of the Hindu is full of caste genealogies in which an attempt is made to give a noble origin to one caste and an ignoble origin to other castes. This anti-social spirit is not confined to caste alone. It has gone deeper and has poisoned the mutual relations of the sub-castes as well.

Citing an instance from his own province (Maharastra), Ambedkar writes:

> 'In my province the Gulak Brahmins, Deorakha Brahmins, Karada Brahmins, Palshe Brahmins and Chitpavan Brahmins, all claim to be sub-divisions of the Brahmin caste. But the anti-social spirit that prevails between them is quite as marked and quite as virulent as the anti-social spirit that prevails between them and other non-Brahmin castes.'[12]

This anti-social spirit is the outcome of the interests of its own group or sub-caste, which shut full interaction among groups. This anti-social spirit, this spirit of protecting its own interests is a marked feature of the different castes, living in isolation from one another. The Brahmin's primary concern is to protect 'his interest' against those of the non-Brahmins and the non-Brahmin's primary concern is to protect their interests against those of the Brahmins. Ambedkar, therefore, argues that the Hindus, are not merely an assortment of caste but they are so many warring groups each living for itself and for its selfish ideal. This is a feature of the caste system which is deplorable.

Position of the Aboriginal Tribes

Ambedkar states that the Hindu caste system has excluded the aboriginal tribes from its fold, which constituted a significant number about 13 millions in 1936. These aborigines, states Ambedkar, have remained in their primitive uncivilised state in a land which boasts of a civilisation thousands of years old. They remained uncivilised and some of them follow pursuits which have led to their being classified as criminals. Living in the midst of civilisation, the tribes are still in a savage state and are leading the life of hereditary criminals! But the Hindus, says Ambedkar, have never felt ashamed of it. Ambedkar writes:

> 'Civilising the aborigines means adopting them as your own, living in their midst, and cultivating fellow-feeling, in short, loving them. How is it possible for a Hindu to do this? His whole life is one anxious effort to preserve his caste. Caste is his precious possession which he must save at any cost.'[13]

The whole argument of Ambedkar is that caste is, therefore, the real explanation as to why the Hindu has let the savage remain a savage in the midst of his civilisation without blushing or without feeling any sense of remorse or repentance. Not only has the Hindu made no effort towards the humanitarian cause of civilising the savages but the higher-caste Hindus have deliberately prevented the lower castes who are within the pale of Hinduism from rising to the cultural level of the higher castes. The Hindu is more interested in safeguarding his caste interests; he has never undertaken a mission of civilising the aboriginal tribes.

Hindu Religion is not a Missionary Religion

The basic drawback in Hindu religion, according to Ambedkar, is that it is not a missionary religion. Had it been a missionary religion it could have spread over the face of India? The Hindu religion could not become a missionary religion because of the caste system that grew up among the Hindu. And caste is inconsistent with conversion.

The convert has no place in the social life of the Hindus. The problem is where to place the convert, in what caste?

Ambedkar, therefore, says:

> 'Unlike the club the membership of a caste is not open to all and the sundry. The law of caste confines its membership to persons born in the caste. Castes are autonomous and there is no authority anywhere to compel a caste to admit a new-comer to its social life. Hindu society being a collection of castes and each caste being a close corporation there is no place for a convert.'[14]

Thus, Ambedkar argues that it is the caste which has prevented the Hindus from expanding and from absorbing other religious communities. So long as castes remain, Hindu religion cannot be a made a missionary religion and *Shudhi* will be both a folly and a futility.

Sanghatan is Impossible

On account of castes it is impossible for the Hindus to make *Sanghatan*. *Sanghatan* here means strength, unity, fellow-feeling and oneness. Ambedkar observes that such a *Sanghatan* is visible among the Sikhs or Mohammedans. A Sikh or Mohammedan derives his strength from *Sanghatan* which makes him brave and fearless. All Sikhs will come to the rescue of a Sikh when he is in danger and that all Mohammedans will rush to save a Muslim if he is attacked. The Hindu can derive no such strength. He cannot feel assured that his fellows will come to his help. Being one and fated to be alone he remains powerless.

Ambedkar continues to state that among the Sikhs and Mohammedans there is the spirit of fellow-feeling which is produced on account of their associated mode of life. There is no mode of associated life among the Hindus. Among the Sikhs and Muslims there is social cement which makes them *Bhais* (brothers), but there is no such social cement among the Hindus, and one Hindu does not regard another Hindu as his *Bhai.* This difference is undoubtedly a difference due to caste. The lack of associated mode of life or social cement among the Hindus is on account of their caste system.

Ambedkar states that the Hindus suffer from a worst kind of disease, that is, 'indifferentism'. This indifferentism is the result of caste system which has made *Sanghatan* and co-operation even for a good cause impossible. So long as caste remains, there will be no *Sanghatan* and so long as there is no *Sanghatan* the Hindu will remain weak and meak.

Effect of Caste on the Ethics

The caste has exercised a negative effect on the zeal of the reformers and the ethics of the Hindus.

Ambedkar observes that a caste is capable of organising itself into a conspiracy to make the life of a reformer a hell. Caste in the hands of the orthodox has been a powerful weapon for prosecuting the reformers and suppressing their zeal.

Further, Ambedkar says that the effect of caste on the ethics of Hindus is simply deplorable. He states:

> 'Caste has killed public spirit. Caste has destroyed the sense of public charity. Caste has made public opinion impossible. A Hindu's public is his caste. His responsibility is only to his caste. His loyalty is restricted only to his caste. Virtue has become caste ridden and morality has become caste-bound. There is no sympathy to the deserving. There is no appreciation of the meritorious. There is no charity to the needy. Suffering as such calls for no response. There is charity but it begins with the caste and ends with the caste.'[15]

Broadly speaking, Ambedkar argues that a Hindu is unwilling to acknowledge and follow the leadership of a great and good man, except the case of Mahatma Gandhi. A Hindu is willing to follow a leader if he is a man of his caste. A Brahmin will follow a leader only if he is a Brahmin, a Kayastha if he is a Kayastha and so on. The capacity to appreciate merits in a man apart from his caste does not exist in a Hindu. There is appreciation for virtue but only when the man is a fellow caste-man. The whole morality is as bad as tribal morality. A Hindu has committed treason against his country in the interest of his caste. This caste ethics or morality of the Hindus is a formidable obstacle towards the creation of society or nation.

Caste has greatly retricted or narrowed the minds of the Hindus that the idea of nation is beyond their comprehension.

Social Order and Nation-Building

There is a close relationship between the Hindu social order and nation-building. Ambedkar had no doubt that unless the Hindus change their social order they can achieve little by way of progress. They cannot mobilise the community either for defence or for offence. They cannot build anything on the foundations of caste. They cannot build up a nation, they cannot build up morality. Anything that they will build on the foundation of caste will crack and will never be a whole.

Caste generates forces that separate groups and classes. It creates clevages in society and hampers the forces that unite. It undermines the social significance of group life. The strength of society or nation depends upon the presence of points of contact, possibilities of interaction between different groups which exist in it. These are called 'organic filament'. Ambedkar calls them 'the elastic threads' which help to bring the disintegrating elements together and to reunite them. He asserts that there is no integrating elements together and to reunite them. He asserts that there is no integrating force among the Hindus to counteract the disintegration caused by caste. While among the non-Hindus there are plenty of these 'organic filaments' which bind them together. If a Hindu breaks his caste, writes Ambedkar, he is sure to be outcasted. But this is not so among the non-Hindus (Sikhs, Muslims and Christians). This shows the difference in the social significance of caste to Hindus and non-Hindus. Further, he says that among the non-Hindus, caste is only a practice, not a sacred institution. They do not regard caste as a religious dogma; with them it is only a survival; whereas religion compels the Hindus to treat isolation and segregation of castes as virtue.

Ambedkar writes:

> 'Religion does not compel the non-Hindus to take the same attitude towards caste. If Hindus wish to break caste, their religion will come in their way. But it will not be so in the case of non-Hindus. It is, therefore, a dangerous delusion to take comfort in the mere existence of caste among non-Hindus, without caring to

> know what place caste occupies in their life and whether there are other 'organic filments', which subordinate the feeling of caste to the feeling of community. The sooner the Hindus are cured of this delusion the better.'[16]

Ambedkar considered the question regarding the reform of the Hindu social order, and such a reform is impossible without abolishing caste. To him, the basic question was: How to abolish caste? He observes that the steps like abolition of sub-castes and inter-caste dinners are inadequate. He is convinced that the real remedy is inter-marriage. Fusion of blood, he stresses, can alone create the feeling of being kith and kin and unless this feeling of kinship, of being kindred, becomes paramount the separatist feeling – the feeling of being aliens – created by caste will not vanish. He writes :

> 'The real remedy for breaking caste is inter-marriage. Nothing else will serve as the solvent of caste.'[17]

Though Ambedkar recognises that inter-marriage is a prescription for the disease, it is not popular among the Hindus. He observes that inter-marriage is not popular among the Hindus, because the idea of inter-marriage is repugnant to the beliefs and dogmas which the Hindu regard as sacred. He argues that caste is not a physical object like a wall of bricks or a line of barbed wire which prevents the Hindus from commingling and which has, therefore, to be pulled down. He says that caste is a notion, it is a state of mind. The destruction of caste does not therefore mean the destruction of a physical barrier. He asserts that it means a notional change. He recognises that the Hindus observe caste not because they are inhuman or wrong headed; they observe caste because they are deeply religious. Hence, he writes:

> 'Hindus are not wrong in observing caste. In my view, what is wrong is their religion, which has inculcated this notion of caste. If this is correct, then obviously the enemy, you must grapple with, is not the people who observe caste, but the Shastras which teach them this religion of caste. ...The real remedy is to destroy the belief in the sanctity of the Shastras.'[18]

As such, Ambedkar argues that the methods like inter-dining or inter-marrying or celebrating inter-caste marriages are futile methods of achieving the desired end, or they are 'like forced feeding brought about by, artificial means.' He stresses that the real remedy is to destroy the belief in the sanctity of the *Shastras*, or free every man and woman from the thraldom of the *Shastras*. The Hindu social order cannot be reformed unless the caste is broken, and caste cannot be broken, unless the minds of every man and woman are cleansed of the pernicious notions contained in *Shastras*, or the belief of the sanctity of the *Shastras* is broken. The sanctity of the *Shastras* can be broken, says Ambedkar, if the people take the stand that Buddha took; if they take the stand which Guru Nanak took. They must not only discard the *Shastras*, they must deny their authority, as did Buddha and Nanak. What Ambedkar emphasises is that the notion of the sacredness of caste must disappear? Once that is done the Hindu social order would be rejuvenated and a genuine nation-building would be possible!

One must not forget that the social order is the structure and nation-building is a super-structure. Caste is a disease; it saps the foundations of social order or weakens the structure. Any attempt to create a society or nation on a weak structure is bound to fail; it would not survive for long. Ambedkar, therefore, pleads that the caste must be annihilated and the sanctity of the sacredness of the *Shastras* must be done away with in order to develop durable foundations for nation-building.

No nation-building is possible without social amalgamation. Ambedkar did not agree with Gandhi and the Congress when they said that India is a nation. Neither did he agree with the Muslim League when they said that Hindus and Muslims could not be welded together into a nation. He said:

> 'My belief is that we are not a nation. But my confident hope is that we can be a nation provided proper processes of social amalgamation are set forth.'[19]

Hence an important step would be the annihilation of caste, which if put in motion can accelerate the processes of social amalgamation. So long as caste survives; the social amalgamation is not possible.

Religion of Principles: Necessity of

Ambedkar observes that the Hindu religion is not a true religion because it is based on rules and not principles. He draws a distinction between principles and rules because he regards that this distinction is real and important. He states that rules are practical; they are habitual ways of doing things according to prescription; but principles are intellectual, they are useful methods of judging things. Rules seek to tell an agent just what course of action to pursue; principles do not prescribe a specific course of action. He therefore asserts that this difference between rules and principles makes the acts done in pursuit of them different in quality and in content. He argues that doing what is said to be good by virtue of a rule and doing good in the light of a principle are two different things. The principle may be wrong but the act is conscious and responsible. The rule may be right but the act is mechanical. He writes:

> 'Religion must mainly be a matter of principles only. It cannot be a matter of rules. The moment it generates into rules it ceases to be religion, as it kills responsibility which is the essence of a truly religion act.'[20]

So said, Ambedkar observes that Hindu religion is not a true religion; it is only a code of rules. He states that the Hindu religion as contained in the *Vedas* and the *Smritis*, is nothing but a mass of sacrificial, social, political and sanitary rules and regulations, all mixed up; it is nothing but a multitude of commands and prohibitions, or a code of ordinances. He stresses that since Hindu religion is a code of rules, it tends to deprive moral life of freedom and spontaneity and to reduce it to a more or less servile confirmity to externally imposed rules. He says that under Hindu religion there is no loyalty to ideals or principles, there is only conformity to commands. Its rules are not the same for one class as for another. This iniquity is made perpetual in that they are prescribed to be the same for all generations. He states that the objectional part is that this code has been invested with the character of finality and fixity. He, therefore, pleads that this code of eternal rules must be dismantled, because it is a crippling disease. He states:

> 'I have, therefore, no hesitation in saying that such a religion must be destroyed and I say, there is nothing irreligious in working for the destruction of such a religion.'[21]

While Ambedkar condemns a religion of rules, he must not be understood to hold the opinion that there is no necessity for a religion. He believes in a true religion which is the foundation of society or nation. He urges that these ancient rules of life must be annulled. It means a religion of rules must be destroyed, and its place be taken by a religion of principles, which alone can lay claim to being a true religion. He is convinced of the necessity of religion, but it must be a true religion based on principles. A true religion must have a doctrinal basis – a basis that is in consonance with liberty, equality and fraternity, in short, with democracy. It means a complete change from the religion of rules to that of religion of principles. It means a complete change in the fundamental notion of life or in the value of life. It means a complete change in outlook and in attitude towards men and things. It means discarding the authority of the *Shatras* and destroying the religion of the *Shastras*. It means new life.

Ambedkar's concept of a true religion is meant to destroy caste and to eradicate untouchability. Caste is a feature of Hindu religion which is a religion of rules or a code of rules. Caste is a by-product of code of rules incarnate. The code of rules is the poison which has spoiled Hinduism. Caste would be killed and a new society or nation would be born in its true sense if Hinduism moves ahead from the religion of rules to the religion of principles.

Caste survives in a religion of rules, because such a religion is inimical to progress and is a hindrance to a strong and a viable society or nation. A religion of rules is fixed, eternal and stagnant; whereas in a religion of principles there is nothing *sanatan*, in it everything is changing and that change is the law of life for individuals as well as for society. In a changing society, there is always a constant revolution, discarding a religion of rules and setting new standards for a religion of principles. A religion of rules looks upon the present as empty and upon the future as remote; whereas a religion of principles is ever living and growing, making an attempt to find out suitable morality, beliefs, habits and outlook.

A religion of principles based on an ideal of justice, if universally practiced would be able to create a strong nation; whereas a religion of rules encrusted with caste would weaken a nation and in the long run it might be unfit for survival.

Caste is Contrary to Reason

Ambedkar makes an emphatic rejection of caste on the ground that it is contrary to reason. A Hindu must follow either Veda, Smriti or Manusmriti. These scriptures he regards infallible. Ambedkar condemns this approach absolutely because rationalism as a canon of interpreting the Vedas and Smritis is neglected. Thus, where a matter is covered by the Vedas or the Smriti, a Hindu cannot resort to rational thinking. He writes:

> 'Even when there is a conflict between Vedas and Smritis on matters on which they have given a positive injection, the solution is not left to reason. When there is a conflict between two Smritis, both are to be regarded as of equal authority, but no attempt is to be made to find out which of the two accords with reason. When there is a conflict between Shruti and Smriti, the Shruti must prevail, but here too, no attempt must be made to find out which of the two accords with reasonging. Again, when there is a conflict between two Smritis, the Manusmriti must prevail, but no attempt is to be made to find out which of the two accords with reason. It is, therefore, clear that in any matter on which the Shrutis and Smritis have given a positive direction, a Hindu is not free to use his reasoning faculty.'[22]

The point that Ambedkar emphasises is that a Hindu must abide by the directions of *Vedas*, *Smriti* and *Shrutis*. He is not permitted to apply reason for their interpretation. As such, caste and *Varna* are matters, which are dealt with by the *Vedas* and the *Smritis* and consequently, appeal to reason can have no effect on a Hindu. So far as caste and *Varna* are concerned, the scriptures and *Shastras* do not permit the Hindu to use his reason in the decision of the question, but they have taken care to see that no occasion is left to examine in a rational way the foundations of his belief in caste and *Varna*.

Ambedkar observes that the *Vedas* and *Smritis* are beyond reflective thought, that is, active application of reason towards their interpretation is forbidden for a Hindu. They simply direct him to maintain caste. The Hindu scriptures have given caste a perpetual lease of life and have smothered reflective thought which would have otherwise led to the destruction of the notion of caste.

Ambedkar states that the *Vedas* and *Smritis* have commanded the Hindu in unmistakable terms to preserve caste. The Hindu, therefore, is deprived of reason and morality, which are regarded as the two most powerful weapons in the armoury of a reformer. To deprive the Hindu of the use of these weapons is to disable him for action. Ambedkar frankly states:

> 'How are you going to break-up caste, if people are not free to consider whether it accords with reason? How are you going to break-up caste if people are not free to consider whether it accords with morality? The wall built around caste is impregnable and the material, of which it is built, contain none of the combustible stuff of reason and morality.'[23]

Ambedkar believes that because of the absence of two powerful weapons – reason and morality – the Hindu is incapable of breaking-up the caste. He thinks that breaking-up of caste amongst the Hindus is 'wellnigh impossible', and at any rate, it would take ages before a breach is made. He believes that the only way to bring about a breach in the caste system is to apply the dynamite to the Vedas and the *Shastras*, which deny any part to reason or morality. He asserts that unless the religion of *Shrutis* and the *Smritis* is not destroyed, nothing substantial would be gained. His considered view is that caste is contrary to reason, and unless Vedas, *Smritis* and *Shrutis* are not interpreted through the application of reason and morality, it would not be possible either to make a breach or to break-up the caste system.

Social Vitals of Nation-Building

There are a number of factors – social, economic, cultural and political – that shape the making of a nation. Ambedkar lays more emphasis on social factors and points out the social ills that have hampered the growth for society or nation. He pleads for their removal.

Ambedkar gives the following catalogue for nation-building:[24]

(i) The caste has ruined the Hindus; 'it has played its ignoble and destructive role in the history of India'; it must be annihilated;

(ii) That the reorganisation of the Hindu society on the basis of *Chaturvarna* is impossible because the *Varna Vyavastha* is like a leaky pot. It is incapable of sustaining itself by its own virtue and has an inherent tendency to degenerate into a caste system unless there is a legal sanction behind it which can be enforced against everyone transgressing his *Varna*;

(iii) That the reorganisation of the Hindu society on the basis of *Chaturvarna* is harmful because the effect of the *Varna Vyavastha* is to degrade the masses by denying them opportunity to acquire knowledge and to emasaculate them by denying them the right to be armed;

(iv) That the Hindu society must be reorganised on the religious basis which would recognise the principles of liberty, equality and fraternity;

(v) That in order to achieve this object the sense of religious sanctity behind caste and *Varna* must be destroyed; and

(vi) That the sanctity of caste and *Varna* can be destroyed only by discarding the divine authority of the *Shastras*.

Broadly speaking, Ambedkar's assertion towards building a strong, vibrant and cohesive society or nation lies in destroying the infallibility or divine sanction attached with the *Vedas*, *Smritis* and *Shrutis*. Once that is destroyed the path of annihilation of caste and *Varna Vyavastha* would be gradually cleared, and a new society or nation based on the grand principles of a true religion would emerge – which can safely be characterised as the genuine social vitals of nation-building.

While interpreting the ideology of Ambedkar, it can be said that so long as social ills of untouchability and caste prevail in a society, the nation-building is hardly possible, because they create deep fissures and clevages among the people, thereby prevent harmonious social relations. The worst sufferers of *Varna Vyavastha* have been the untouchables, that is why Mahatma Gandhi once wrote: 'Untouchability is a snake with a thousand mouths through each of which it shows its poisonous fangs.'[25] That is why Ambedkar upehelds that the destruction of the divinity of *Vedas* and *Shastras* is essential, because the social evils of untouchability, Varna and caste originate from them. The infallibility of the *Vedas*, or the belief in their divinity is once broken, the task of nation-building would be an easy one.

Remove Basis of Smriti Religion

Ambedkar wished to cultivate the sense of a common nationality among the Indians, and for the attainment of this ideal nothing should be done which would harden local patriotism, group consciousness and inequality. He says:

> 'I am of the opinion that the most vital need of the day is, to create amongst the people the sense of a common nationality, a feeling not that they are Indian first and Hindus, Mohammedans or Sindhis and Canaree afterwards, but they are Indians first and Indians last.'[26]

Being a creative iconoclast, Ambedkar believes that such a sense of common nationality would not evolve in the presence of caste system, and that it is impossible to annihilate the caste, unless the basis of caste is destroyed, which is the religion of Vedas, *Smritis*, *Shrutis* and *Shastras*. His slogan, therefore, has been 'Remove basis of Smriti religion'.

Ambedkar states that whatever may be the metaphysical basis of a religion, those religious principles upon which depends the ethical system and the social practices of a people must be considered to be the principal element of that religion. He argues that though Hinduism is based on the conception of *Absolute Brahma* the practices of the Hindu community as a whole are founded on the doctrines of inequality as pronounced in *Manusmriti*. Refuting the argument propounded by some people that religion is not essential, he emphatically writes: 'I consider the foundation of religion to be essential to the life and practices of society,' and continues:

> 'At the root of the Hindu social system lies *Dharma* as prescribed in Manusmrti. Such being the case I do not think it possible to abolish inequality in the Hindu society unless the existing foundation of the *Smriti* religion is removed and a better one laid in its place. I, however, despair of the Hindu society being able to reconstruct on such a better foundation.'[27]

Ambedkar emphasises that the cause of nation-building would not advance with the help of legislatures, but it would advance with the removal of caste and untouchability, that is, the abolition of inequality in the Hindu society. It means removing the basis of inequality which in reality is *Smriti* religion. Destroy Smriti religion, he asserts, and with its destruction the traditionl social set-up held under the tentacles of caste-ridden graded inequality for centuries together would gradually crumble. That would organise the society on modern lines breaking down its age-long framework rooted in *Smritis*. That would bring a complete change in social, economic and political life of the Indian society, giving birth to a virile nation.

Divine Law is a Hindrance

The basic hindrance to the task of nation-building has been the divine law of Manu or Yajnavalkya, which gave birth to *Chaturvarna* and caste, thereby prevented the Hindu society from repairing itself. The decay of the society lay in its failure to take upon itself the task of removing the defects in its structure. Instead of removing the defects the society submitted to be governed by the law laid down by the law-makers like Manu. The true function of law consists in repairing the faults in society which, Ambedkar feels, had been sadly neglected.

Ambedkar points out that the difference between ancient Hindu society and modern society lies in the fact that in the former law-making was not the function of the people. Law was made by God or by the law-giver. The function of society was merely to obey law that was made either by the divine power or the law-maker. This was the fundamental reason for Hindu society not having any continuous civilisation.

Ambedkar states that the true function of law consists in repairing the faults of the society. Unfortunately the Hindu society never dared to assume the function of repairing its own defects; consequently it decayed. He writes:

> 'One of the reasons for the decay of Hindu society is that it was governed by law which had either been made by Manu or Yajnavalkya. Law that has been laid down by these law-makers is divine law. The result was that Hindu society was never able to repair itself.'[28]

Ambedkar draws attention to the fact that India has been in a conflict between ecclesiastical law and secular law long before the

Europeans sought to challenge the authority of the Pope (Kautilya's *Arthshastra* lays down foundations of secular law); but unfortunately in India ecclesiastical law triumphed over secular law. He regards it as one of the greatest disasters in this country. 'The unprogressive character of Hindu society,' he argues, 'was due to the notion that law cannot be changed.'

Interpreting Ambedkar, it may be said that the triumph of ecclesiastical law over secular law, or the total acceptance of the divine law of Manu or Yajnavalkya, the Hindu society was never able to repair itself. Because of the blind belief in the divine law, the institutions of *Chaturvarna* and caste survived ceaselessly in Hindu society, retarding the growth of nation-building.

Caste Creates Social Clevages

Caste creates social cleavages. It hampers the successful working of democracy. It creates glaring inequalities in the society. Its outcome is the emergence of an oppressed class or a suppressed class. It gives birth to a class which has all the privileges and another class which has to carry all the burdens of society. Such a society or nation based on high and low castes has within itself the germs of a bloody revolution and perhaps it would be impossible for the democracy to cure them.

Caste divides the house and a house divided against itself cannot create a nation. Deep clevages between caste and caste, or class and class, are one of the greatest hindrances in the success of democracy. Caste creates a privileged few who are not willing to surrender their privileges. It creates a wide gulf between the higher and lower castes which is likely to destroy democracy and bring into existence something quite different. There was no doubt in Ambedkar's mind that if one examines the history of democracy in various parts of the world; he will find that one of the causes for the breakdown of democracy is the existence of these social cleavages.

Therefore, Ambedkar pleads the destruction of caste or its ally class, in order to create a social order, leading to social cohesion and social solidarity. Having examined the institution of caste from varied angles, Ambedkar argues in favour of its annihilation so that a viable society or a nation can be build.

Final Observations

Ambedkar pleads in favour of annihilation or uproot of caste, because it is like a canker or an evil, having a dangerous influence that spreads and affects the health of the society or nation. Like the termites, caste does a lot of damage by eating the vitality of nation.

Ambedkar makes a rational analysis of caste and points out its various weaknesses and debilities. It does not lead to division of labour; instead it is division of labourers, that is, an hierarchy in which the labourers are graded one above the other. It is a harmful institution, because it is based on the dogma of predestination. Neither it preserves the purity of race nor purity of blood. It nurtures a social system, embodying the arrogance and selfishness of caste Hindus. It does not promote economic efficiency. It generates anti-social spirit, promotes disunity and disrupts harmonious social relations. It gives birth to many warring groups in society, each living for itself and for its selfish ends. It has prevented the lower castes from rising to the cultural level of the higher castes. It has made no effort towards the humanitarian cause of civilising the tribes.

Caste has prevented Hinduism from becoming a missionary religion. It has blocked the Hindus from expanding and from absorbing other religious communities. It has undermined the strength, unity and oneness of the Hindu society. Indifferentism among the Hindus is the result of caste system.

Further, Ambedkar says that the effect of caste on the ethics of Hindus has been deplorable. It has prevented the Hindus from developing the idea of nation. It lacks organic filaments that unite society; on the contrary, it encourages disintegrating element that saps the foundations of Hindu social order. It is the very antithesis of social amalgamation. It is a phenomenon of Hindu religion which is not a true religion because it is a religion of rules and not a religion of principles. It is contrary to reason and morality. It creates social cleavages which are harmful in a democracy.

Hence, Ambedkar argues that for building a strong nation: (i) the caste must be uprooted or annihilated; (ii) the *Varna Vyavastha* has ruined the Hindu society, it must be destroyed; (iii) the society must be based on the religion of principles; and (iv) that the divine authority or the religion of Vedas, *Smritis*, *Shuritis* and *Shastras* must be removed. Along with the destruction of religious notions upon which caste is founded, inter-dinning, inter-marriage, social conscience and social legislation must be encouraged or adopted, so that a virile society or nation, having strength and energy may emerge. However, Ambedkar was well aware that the annihilation of caste or tearing apart the religious notions of *Smritis* are extremely difficult, even impossible, unless there is a leader like Kemal Pasha in India.

References

1. *Dr Babasaheb Ambedkar Writings and Speeches*, Vol. 1 (New Delhi, Ministry of Social Justice and Empowerment, 2014), pp. xiv-xv.
2. B. R. Ambedkar: *Annihilation of Caste* (Jalandhar, Bheem Patrika Publications, 1995), p. 15.
3. *Ibid.,* pp. 25-26.
4. *Ibid.,* p. 26.
5. *Ibid.,* p. 27.
6. *Ibid.,* p. 38.
7. *Dr Babasaheb Ambedkar Writings and Speeches*, Vol. 17, Part Three (New Delhi, Ministry of Social Justices and Empowerment, 2014) p. 82.
8. *Ibid.,* p. 388.
9. *Ibid.,* pp. 417, 419.
10. *Annililation of Caste,* p. 45.
11. *Ibid.,* p. 47.
12. *Ibid.,* p. 48.
13. *Ibid.,* p. 50.
14. *Ibid.,* p. 53.
15. *Ibid.,* p. 56.
16. *Dr Babasaheb Ambedkar Writings and Speeches*, Vol. 1, pp. 65-66.
17. *Ibid.,* p. 67.
18. *Ibid.,* p. 68.
19. *Dr Babasaheb Ambedkar Writings and Speeches*, Vol. 17, Part Two (New Delhi, Ministry of Social Justice and Empowerment, 2014), p. 318.
20. *Dr Babasaheb Ambedkar Writings and Speeches*, Vol. 1, p. 75.
21. *Ibid.,* p. 76.
22. *Annihilation of Caste*, p. 84.
23. *Ibid.,* p. 87.
24. *Dr Babasaheb Ambedkar Writings and Speeches*, Vol. 1, pp. 86-87.

25. Op. cit. Mohan Dass Namishray: *Caste and Race: Comparative Study of B. R. Ambedkar and Martin Luthar King* (Jaipur, Rawat Publications, 2003), p. 42.
26. *Dr Babasaheb Ambedkar Writings and Speeches*, Vol. 17, Part One (New Delhi, Ministry of Social Justice and Empowerment, 2014), p. 66.
27. *Ibid.*, p. 236.
28. *Dr Babasaheb Ambedkar Writings and Speeches*, Vol. 17, Part Three, p. 386.

Chapter–5

Indian Constitution and Social Change

The Constitution of India is a very effective instrument or a tool towards promoting the cause of social change in the country. It aims to secure an egalitarian society, based on the principles of secularism, liberty, equality and a just social order. The chapters on preamble, the directive principles of state policy, and the fundamental rights, are meant to usher in a social revolution in a traditional society, which for centuries had been dominated by narrow religious and caste loyalties and feudalistic outlook. Based on the ideology of liberal democracy, the Constitution aims to promote peaceful social transformation. All in all, the Constitution is a marvellous document saturated with the ideals of social justice and social change or transformation.

The Indian Constitution mirrors basic values about who shall govern and in what direction. In addition to, structuring, allocating and limiting power, it performs 'aspirational goals'. Through its institutional arrangements and commandments, it reflects a particular vision of a good and achievable social order. The Constitution thus reflects vision of Ambedkar's social ideology and constitutionalism in a remarkably way.

Ambedkar's social ideology was moulded by his personal experiences of untouchability in his early life, and by his Western education. The social ideology that he developed ultimately led him to emerge as the champion of the oppressed. Because of his early sufferings due to the practice of untouchability, he relentlessly fought against the social evils. It was because of his incessant struggles that the untouchability was at last abolished through the Constitution of India in whose drafting he played a significant role. Great persons like Buddha, Phule, Ranade, John Dewey and J. S. Mill influenced Ambedkar's social ideology. The stamp of Ambedkar's ideology is clearly visible over the pages of the Indian Constitution.

Ambedkar himself explicitly says, "If you ask me, my ideal would be a society based on Liberty, Equality and Fraternity"[1].He also defended these ideals by meeting the objections raised against them in Constituent Assembly particularly. On fraternity, he argues that an ideal society involves maximum facilities for communications between individuals and groups, and this is best achieved by fraternity. But what is fraternity? His answer is that "it is only another name for democracy." Democracy is necessary to generate what he calls "social-endosmosis" by which he means a social system that provides for "varied and free points of contact with other modes of association". And he states, 'it is an attitude of respect and reverence towards fellowmen'.

Pre-Constitution social order in India was based upon certain inhuman as well as cruel religious practices. At the height of it, certain social lawless laws were ordained by Hindu lawgivers like Manu and others who sanctified such inhuman customs and practices. Custom of untouchability was one of them. The system was a gold mine to caste Hindus because they were getting millions of untouchables to serve as their retinues to enable the Hindus to maintain pomp and show and to cultivate a feeling of pride and dignity befitting a master class which cannot be fostered and sustained unless there is beneath it a servile class to look down upon. Ambedkar's viewpoint was that, the system of untouchability was not merely a religious system but more than that. It was also an economic system which was worse than slavery. In slavery the master at any rate had the responsibility to feed, clothe, and house the slave and keep him in good condition lest the market value of the slave should decrease. But in the system of untouchability the Hindu took no responsibility for the maintenance of the untouchable. As an economic system it permitted exploitation without obligation. Untouchability was not only a system of unmitigated economic exploitation, but it was also a system of uncontrolled economic exploitation.

In India, the castes were not merely non-social but often they were anti-social. This was particularly true of the Hindus towards the untouchables. A few facts will suffice to show how anti-social the Hindus were towards the untouchables. For instance, the Hindus did not allow the untouchables to take water from a well. They did not allow their entry in schools. They did not allow them to travel in the same railway compartment. They did not allow them to wear clean clothes or jewellery. They did not allow untouchable to own land. They did not allow them to sit when the Hindu was standing. They were not isolated acts of a few bad men among the Hindus. They were the emanations of the permanent anti-social attitude of the Hindu community against the untouchables.[2]

Some protagonists of Hinduism believed that untouchability is a vanishing thing and therefore there is no use recognising the untouchables as a separate element in the national life of India. Ambedkar argued that those who raise this point did not seem to make a distinction between untouchability as a touch-me-not-ism and untouchability as a mental attitude manifesting itself in social discrimination. The two are quite different. Ambedkar said:

> 'It may be that untouchability as a touch-me-not-ism may gradually vanish in towns, although I am doubtful if this is happening in any appreciable degree. But I am quite certain Untouchability as a propensity on the part of the Hindus to discriminate against the Untouchables will not vanish either in towns or in villages within an imaginable distance of time...You cannot untwist a two-thousand-year-twist of the human mind and turn it in the opposite direction.'[3]

Since untouchability was a problem of an attitude of the Hindu, Ambedkar was of the firm view that, unless Hindus change their attitude, untouchability will not vanish.

These were the distinguishing features of the Indian social order based on caste system which justified why the Indian Constitution took account of it and provided constitutional safeguards for the betterment of the untouchables.

Thus, the Indian Constitution ushers in an egalitarian social order guaranteeing social justice to every citizen and to protect the liberties of people from onslaughts of autocratic and arbitrary use of executive authority. The inception of the Indian Constitution in 1950 was a significant event, not only in the political history of India but also in the history of 'social justice' and 'human rights'. At the same time, it has opened up new avenues of human welfare and development in the Indian sub-continent by providing equal rights and privileges to the citizens at large. The Constitution of independent India is more than a mere legal manuscript – it is meant to structure the norms of governance, define the functions of various key institutions as well as political actors – for the society as a whole and particularly for the underprivileged sections who were exploited in multiple ways over the centuries especially due to the prevailing dominant social order of Hindu society. The process of Constitution making during the 1940s was thus laden with various sets of expectations and requirements. In fact, it was assumed that the new constitution would be effective enough to terminate the unending patterns of exploitation based on gender, caste and religion and bring increasingly sought changes in the deeply hierarchical and unequal social structure, so one could live with dignity and possess equal civil rights. It was indeed the first moment in the lives of millions of people, particularly the depressed communities when they received an equal treatment and entitlement after the adoption of new Constitution.

Ambedkar articulately advocated the cause of the empowerment of broken men (marginal sections) in the society, waged an ideological war with Congress Party and Gandhi. Thus, he was looked upon as the saviour of scheduled castes and tribes in the country, and a political opponent of Gandhi and Congress politics.

Ambedkar's unique idea of social justice, his dynamic political thought, his liberal views on constitutionalism, his progressive concepts of rights of the people, his vision of an ideal society, and above all, his concern for the welfare and development of the poor, depressed class, the dumb millions, or the *dalits*, not only echoed during the debates and deliberations in the Constituent Assembly, but also reflected each and every part of the Constitution of India.

Dr Ambedkar, as a Chairman of the Drafting Committee, played a leading role in mandating the State to create a new social order in independent India through the incorporation of several provisions in the form of Fundamental Rights, Directive Principles of State Policy and affirmative state action. The Preamble itself, which specifies the objectives containing the unalterable basic structure of our Constitution, promises to secure Justice, Liberty, Equality and Fraternity to all its citizens.

Drafting of the Indian Constitution was a mammoth task. With about 444 articles and 12 schedules, Indian Constitution qualifies as the longest Constitution of the world. Eminent historian Ramchandra Guha describes the process of drafting of Indian Constitution as follows:

> 'The proceedings of the Constituent Assembly of India were printed in eleven bulky volumes. These volumes some of which exceed 1,000 pages are testimony to the loquaciousness of Indians, but also to their insight, intelligence, passion and sense of humour. These volumes are little known treasure-trove, invaluable to the historians but also a potential source of enlightenment to the interested citizen. In them we find many competing ideas of the nations, of what language it should speak, what political economic system it should follow, what moral values it should uphold or disavow.'[4]

Hence, in the history of social change in modern India, Ambedkar because of his struggles and role in the Con-Assembly has secured a solitary or pre-eminent place for himself.

Constitutional lawyers for a long time believed that the scope and function of Constitutional Law was to prescribe the shape and form of the political structure of society leaving the social and economic structure unchanged. Dr Ambedkar, the chief architect of the Constitution of India, however, had a strong conviction that, if democracy is to live up to its principle of one man, one value, the time has come to take a bold step and define both the socio-economic structure as well as the political structure of the society by the law of the Constitution. As a consequence, the Constitution of India is not just a pedantic legal text, but it is a living document of social change.

During the process of Constitution making, tall claims were made by many members of the Constituent Assembly. Dr S. Radhakrishnan, member of Constituent Assembly, believed that India must have a 'socio-economic revolution' designed not only to bring about the real satisfaction of the fundamental needs of the common man; but to go much deeper and bring about 'a fundamental change in the structure of Indian society'. Dr Rajendra Prasad, assured the nation that the Assembly and the government's aim was "to end poverty and squalor and its companions, hunger and disease; to abolish distinction and exploitation and to ensure decent conditions of living."[5] K. Santhanam, member of the Constituent Assembly, described the situation in terms of three revolutions. "The political revolution would end with independence. The social revolution meant to get (India) out of the medievalism based on birth, religion, custom and community and reconstruct her social structure on modern foundation of law, individual merit, and secular education. The third revolution was economic one, the transition from primitive rural economy to scientific and planned agriculture and industry."[6] At midnight of 14th August, 1947, Pandit Nehru in one of his famous speeches declared that, "Long years ago we made a tryst with destiny, and now the time comes when we shall redeem our pledge, not wholly or in full measure, but very substantially."[7] Such views were held by many members of the Constituent Assembly.

Dr Ambedkar made all efforts to embody his ideology and above all declared goals or objectives of the Constitution. The text prepared by Ambedkar offered a wide range of constitutional safeguards and guarantees to all citizens, for instance, socio-economic rights, civil liberties, freedom of religion, the abolition of untouchability and prohibitions of all forms of discrimination among others. He argued for extensive economic and social rights of depressed classes. In addition to constitutional rights, he eventually won the Assembly's support for introducing a system of reservations of jobs in civil services, schools and colleges particularly for members of scheduled castes and scheduled tribes. These measures are popularly known as the '*Policy of Inclusion*' that makes endeavours to include the deprived and overlooked classes in the society. In this way, Ambedkar was a valiant fighter for the cause of social justice and social equality, and thus known as the leader, liberator, emancipator, representative of the voices of the socially neglected classes. He fought his entire life for the upliftment of the depressed classes.[8] On 17th December, 1946, Ambedkar stated in the Constituent Assembly:

> 'I know today we are divided politically, socially, and economically. We are a group of warring camps, and I may go even to the extent of confessing that I am probably one of the leaders of such a camp.'[9]

In this way, he explicitly mentioned his commitment for the depressed sections of society.

Ambedkar on Constitutionalism

Constitutionalism denotes a kind of political order with certain political objective like protection of individuals' rights and limitation on powers of governments, while constitution is a necessary means for achieving such objectives. However, the fundamental difference between them lies in the fact that while constitutionalism is based on ideology; the basis of legitimacy of a constitution is law. Yet, the two are closely related since the constitution is the means and constitutionalism the end.

Ambedkar, like other great leaders of his generation, was influenced by the western liberal ideas. During his stay in America (1913-16), England (1920-21) and Germany (1922-23) for higher studies in Political Science, Economics and Law, he was exposed to the Western liberal thought on constitution and constitutionalism. His advocacy for parliamentary democracy, federal constitution, supremacy of the constitution as a fundamental document, fundamental rights with necessary restrictions, safeguards for minorities and provisions relating to amendment of the Constitution, emanating from his exposures to the western liberal ideas as well as his own ideas as a distinguished social and political thinker and a jurist, had been manifested in the framing of India's Constitution.

Dr Ambedkar justified the merits of the parliamentary system *vis-à-vis* a non-parliamentary system, while moving the Draft Constitution in the Constituent Assembly on November 4, 1948, he argued: [10]

> '...The Parliamentary system differs from a non-Parliamentary system inasmuch as the former is more responsible than the latter

> but they also differs as to the time and agency for assessment of their responsibility. Under the non-Parliamentary system, such as the one exists in the U.S.A., the assessment of the responsibility of the Executive is periodic. It takes place once in the four years. It is done by the electorate. In England, where the Parliamentary system prevails, the assessment of the responsibility of the Executive is both daily and periodic. The daily assessment is done by members of Parliament, through questions, resolutions, no-confidence motions, adjournment motions and debates on addresses. Periodic assessment is done by the electorates at the time of the election which may take place every five years or earlier. The daily assessment of responsibility which is not available under the American system is, it is felt, far more effective than the periodic assessment and far more necessary in a country like India. The Draft Constitution in recommending the Parliamentary system of Executive has preferred more responsibility to more stability.'[11]

As regards the forms of the Constitution, the Draft Constitution proposed a federal constitution inasmuch as it sought to establish a dual polity consisting of the Union at the Centre and the States at the periphery, each endowed with sovereign powers to be exercised in the field assigned to them respectively by the Constitution. Ambedkar observed:

> '...There are two weaknesses from which federation is alleged to suffer. One is rigidity and other is legalism. That these faults are inherent in federations; there can be no dispute. A federal constitution cannot be but be a written constitution and a written constitution must necessarily be a rigid constitution. A federal constitution means division of sovereignty by no less a sanction than that of the law of the constitution between the Federal Government and the States, with two necessary consequences (i) that any invasion by the Federal Government in the field assigned to the States and vice-versa is a breach of the Constitution; and (ii) such breach is a justiciable matter to be determined by the judiciary only. This being the nature of federalism, a federal constitution cannot escape the change of legalism. These faults of federal constitution have been found in a pronounced form in the Constitution of the United States of America.'[12]

Dr Ambedkar and the Constituent Assembly's solution to these twin problems were to ensure that Parliament would have overwhelming superiority over the State legislature. Therefore, Article 249 grants parliament the power to legislate with respect to a matter in the State List in the national interest. Article 250 enables Parliament to legislate in any matter in the State List if a proclamation of emergency is in operation. And Article 252 enables Parliament to legislate for two or more states by consent and adoption of such legislation by any other State. And the other major method adopted to enable flexibility as explained by Ambedkar was "the second means adopted to avoid rigidity and legalism is the provision for facility with which the Constitution could be amended."[13]

Finally, Ambedkar spoke of another way in which the drafters created a unique way to ensure that while the country would have federation, and also have an abiding uniformity in essential mechanisms of governance. Therefore, Ambedkar said that, "the Draft Constitution has sought to forge means and methods whereby India will have federation and at the same time will have uniformity in all basic matters which are essential to maintain unity of the country. The means adopted by the draft constitution were three (i) A single judiciary, (ii) Uniformity in fundamental laws – civil and criminal, and (iii) a common all-India civil services to man important posts.[14]

"In assuaging the rigour of rigidity and legalism", observed Ambedkar, "the Draft Constitution follows the Australian plan on a far more extensive scale than has been done in Australia. Like the Australian Constitution, it has a long list of subjects for concurrent powers of legislation." Yet, as he noted further:

> 'The biggest advance made by the Draft Constitution over the Australian Constitution is in the matter of exclusive powers of legislation vested in Parliament. While the exclusive authority of the Australian Parliament to legislate extends only to about three matters, the authority of the Indian parliament as proposed in the Draft Constitution will extend to 91 matters. In this way Draft Constitution has secured the greatest possible elasticity in its federalism which is supposed to be rigid by nature.'[15]

Responding to the objection of some critics to the description of India in Article 1 of the Draft Constitution as a *Union of States* instead of *Federation of States*, Ambedkar made the following enlightening observations –

> 'It is true that South Africa which is a Unitary State is described as a Union. But Canada which is federation is also called a Union. Thus the description of India as a Union, though its Constitution is federal, does no violence to usage. But what is important is that the use of the word "Union" is deliberate. I do not know why the word 'Union' was used in the Canadian Constitution. But I can tell you why the Drafting Committee has used it. The Drafting Committee wanted to make it clear that though India was to be a Federation, the Federation was not the result of an agreement by the States to join in a Federation and the Federation not being the result of an agreement, no State has the right to secede from it. The Federation is a Union because it is indestructible. Though the country and the people may be divided into different States for convenience of administration the country is one integral whole, its people a single people living under a single imperium derived from a single source. The Americans had to wage a civil war to establish that the States have no right of secession and that their Federation was indestructible. The Drafting Committee thought that it was better to make it clear at the outset rather than to leave it to speculation or to dispute.'[16]

The provision relating to amendment of the Constitution also came in for a 'virulent attack' from the critics of the Draft Constitution on the ground that the provisions contained in the Draft made amendment difficult. Ambedkar, while responding to this criticism, used his expertise in constitutional jurisprudence to argue vigorously –

> 'I must repudiate the charge because it is without foundation. To know how simple are the provisions of the Draft Constitution in respect of amending the Constitution one has only to study the provisions for amendment contained in the American and Australian Constitutions. Compared to them those contained in the Draft Constitution will be found to be simplest. The Draft Constitution has eliminated the elaborate and difficult procedures such as a decision by a convention or a referendum. The powers of amendment are left with the Legislature, Central and Provincial.

It is only for amendments of specific matters and they are only a few that the ratification of State Legislature is required. All others articles of the Constitution are left to be amended by 2/3 majority of each House members present and voting… It is difficult to conceive simpler method of amending the Constitution.'[17]

Dr Ambedkar being a great visionary clarified the position of the Constituent Assembly and the future Parliament very lucidly in the following words:

'The Constituent Assembly, in making a Constitution has no partisan motive. Beyond securing a good and workable Constitution it has no axe to grind. In considering the articles of the Constitution it has no eye on getting through a particular measure. If the future Parliament met as a Constituent Assembly, its members will be acting as partisans seeking to carry out amendments to the Constitution to facilitate the passing of party measures which they have failed to get through Parliament by reason of some article of the Constitution which has acted as an obstacle in their way. Parliament will have an axe to grind while the Constituent Assembly has none. That is the difference, between the Constituent Assembly and the future Parliament. That explains why the Constituent Assembly though elected on limited franchise can be trusted to pass the Constitution by simple majority and why the Parliament though elected on adult suffrage cannot be trusted with the same power to amend it.'[18]

Concluding his historic speech while moving his Draft Constitution in the Constituent Assembly, Ambedkar made the following observations:

'No Constitution is perfect and the Drafting Committee suggesting certain amendments to improve the Draft Constitution. But the debates in the Provincial Assemblies give me courage to say that the Constitution as settled by the Drafting Committee is good enough to make in this country a start with. I feel that it is workable, it is flexible and it is strong enough to hold the country together both in peace time and in war time. Indeed, if I may say so, if things go wrong under the new Constitution, the reasons will not be that we had a bad Constitution. What we will have to say is, that Man was vile.' [19]

Ambedkar's contribution in the framing of India's Constitution was unparalleled. Even his stern critics in the Constituent Assembly were ultimately convinced with his unique idea of social justice, his liberal views on constitutionalism, his progressive concept of rights of people, his vision of an ideal society and his enlightening deliberations on the Constitution. Ambedkar ultimately provided the path of social change through the Constitution.

Ambedkar as a Social Engineer

The Constitution of India is a remedial answer to the system of age old social injustice in the form of caste system.[20] Prof. A. M. Rajasekhariah has rightly stated,

> 'He (Ambedkar) strove his utmost to incorporate into the Constitution of India such provisions as would help establish a new social order based on lofty principle of political, economic and social justice for one and all. He tried to bring in about all the necessary changes in the Hindu society in order to make it more democratic one.'[21]

The various important contributions of Ambedkar in the Constitution, which had impact on social justice and social change, are described below.

Fundamental Rights

Part III of the Constitution, which provides for Fundamental rights is the greatest gift of the Constitution-makers, especially of Ambedkar. In his book, 'Ranada, Gandhi and Jinnah', Ambedkar has expressed that the idea of making a gift of fundamental rights to every individual is no doubt very laudable. But the essential question which has to be answered is how to make them effective? According to him rights would be recognised and enforced only if there is a 'social conscience' to do the same. The judiciary, parliament and law all together would come to rescue the Fundamental Rights if there is an opposition from the community.

Eradicating Untouchability and Reservation Policy

Ambedkar himself had to face the evil of untouchability. The abolition of untouchability was one of the important goals of his life.

Article 17 of the Indian Constitution abolishes untouchability. The contribution of Ambedkar in removing untouchability was aptly lauded by Dr Mono Mohan Das, member of Constituent Assembly, in the following words:

> 'I cannot resist the temptation of saying a few words about our great and eminent Law Minister and Chairman of the Drafting Committee Dr Ambedkar. It is an irony of fate that the man who was driven from one school to another, who was forced to take his lesson outside the class room, has been entrusted with this great job of framing the Constitution of free and independent India and it is he who has finally dealt the death blow to this custom of untouchability, of which he himself was the victim in his young days'.

Ambedkar had realised very early that declaration of rights and equality of opportunity would in practice be rendered ineffective if adequate safeguards for the protection and promotion of weaker sections were not provided in the Constitution. The reservations would be, and has also proved to be the most effective such measure.

He was clear that a reservation in jobs is not a concession or a privilege extended to depressed classes. It is their legitimate right. It is in recognition of their fundamental right of equality– Article 16 (1). He said, "We have to safeguards two things, namely principle of equality of opportunity and at the same time satisfy the demand of communities which have not had so far representation in the State."[22] Ambedkar also held that reservation should always be for minority of seats, otherwise it would nullify the principle of equality of opportunity. His stand has been vindicated by various judgments of the Supreme Court. In Thomas[23] and ABSK[24] cases Supreme Court held that Article 16 (4) is a facet, an illustration or a method of application of Article 16 (1), because opportunity can never be equal among human beings who have unequal capacities to grasp it. Since reservation in jobs is not a permissible exception but a necessary ingredient of the right to equality of opportunity, Supreme Court has held it to be a fundamental right of the scheduled castes and scheduled tribes. Ambedkar's another contention that reservation should be for a minority of seats has been proved right by Supreme Court Judgement in *Indira Sawhney vs Union of India Case*, 1992, wherein the Supreme Court has put a ceiling of 50 per cent for reservation in jobs.[25]

On the issue of reservation in politics Ambedkar had stated that "a representative government is better than an efficient government."[26] 'Objective Resolution' of the Draft Constitution itself guaranteed equality and freedom of expression together with adequate safeguards for minorities, backwards and tribal areas and depressed and other backward classes.

Initially, he wanted separate electorates for the depressed classes for at least first ten years, thereafter to be substituted by the joint electorates. He, however, gave up this demand at the insistence of Gandhi and with some concessions contended for joint electorates.

These principles acted as guidelines for the draftsmen throughout the constitution-making process and provide a strong foundation for inclusion of reservations for the underprivileged which was essentially aimed at removing inequality.

Uniform Civil Code and Hindu Code Bill

Ambedkar had a view that the Indian personal laws are not valid on the basis of established legal principles and are in some way very traditional and discriminatory against women. To bring a reformation in personal laws he proposed a Uniform Civil Code, which would replace all the personal laws (which were religiously guided) and will be applicable to all the people irrespective of their religion, caste or creed. Article 44 of the Indian Constitution provides for a Uniform Civil Code. In the Constituent Assembly while presenting his view on Civil Code, he stated:

> 'I personally do not understand why religion should be given this vast, expansive jurisdiction, so as to cover the whole of life and to prevent the legislature from encroaching upon that field. After all, what are we having this liberty for? We are having this liberty in order to reform our social system, which is so full of inequities, discriminations and other things, which conflict with our fundamental rights.'[27]

Ambedkar had achieved only partial success in reforming the personal laws. It was in the form of Article 44, which read: "The state shall endeavour to secure for the citizens a uniform civil code throughout the territory of India."

Bringing to the fore, a Hindu Code Bill to bring about a reformation in Hindu personal laws was a fight Ambedkar had to fight single handedly with only superfluous support from Nehru. The Hindu Code Bill aroused profound opposition not only from traditionalists like Hindu Mahasabha but also from big Congress figures like Rajendra Prasad and Sardar Patel. Prasad in a letter to Patel criticised the Bill as one whose "new concepts and new ideas are not only foreign to the Hindu law but are susceptible of dividing every family."

Finally, successive amendments made to the Bill, killed it. Ambedkar who had lived up his life as a true social reformer could not absorb the shock that his proposal was a vindictively negated. He chose to leave Nehru government on this issue. For him it was more important to uphold constitutional values, rule of law and equality than the position in the government. A uniform civil code is still a dream. But the primary purpose of the Hindu Code Bill, which was removing discrimination against women in personal laws, is achieved as now Hindu Succession Act provides 'equal' inheritance rights to women also. Thus, Dr Ambedkar might have lost his fight then but with the amendment of personal laws, upholding the principles of equality, he has succeeded today.[28]

Economic Vision and Human Rights

As parliamentary democracy, in Ambedkar view, was unmindful of the adverse consequences of liberty for the poor, the downtrodden and the disinherited, he was highly critical of the doctrine of *laissez faire*, which is an important aspect of western liberal democracy. According to him, liberty from the control of the State is another name for the dictatorship of the private employer. To him the oppression and exploitation of the most human beings by a few was the result of lack of social ownership of the means of production. Therefore, if the new social order based on equality, liberty and fraternity was to be established, parliamentary democracy must be accompanied by State socialism. His constitutional vision of State socialism included state ownership of land and basic industries.

A necessary corollary to his vision of State socialism was the absence of a fundamental right to property, because he was of the view that this would not only generate economic inequality but further widen the gap between rich and poor, instead of reducing it. He said, "No landlord means no tenants, and no landless labourer".

However, there was an extreme form of difference of opinion in the Constituent Assembly over right to property. The extent of difference can be judged from the fact that the Drafting Committee had to leave a blank space in the Draft Constitution. This was done with an idea that this could be finalised by the Congress Party. Later on, in the Congress Party, except Nehru all gave support for making property as a fundamental right.

Ambedkar in his model Constitution had provided a separate clause on "Protection Against Economic Exploitation". He emphasised the idea of including specific economic rights like right to work, right to adequate living wage and better standard of living in the list of fundamental rights. He doubted the value of fundamental rights for unemployed and rightly observed that a man without job was prone to relinquish his fundamental rights in order to gain his living. He could not, however, incorporate his total vision of economic structure in the Constitution. He had to be satisfied by incorporating them as Directive Principles which though are fundamental in the governance of the country but are not judicially enforceable. Circumstances permitted him this much, but even this by no means is insignificant. He brought radical reforms in the wages, working conditions and social security by introducing and pushing through the new labour legislation and modification of old one, when he became the Labour Minister.

Dhananjay Keer appropriately calls him as the first legislator in India to introduce a Bill for the abolition of the serfdom of the agricultural tenants. Thus, Ambedkar's struggle to secure human rights to weaker sections in particular and to all the citizens in general was endless.

Indian Constitution is a document vibrant with a social and economic ideology geared to the goal of socio-economic justice. To lay down the foundation of this document of social restructuring in 1947, there was no one better prepared for the job of constitution-crafting than Ambedkar. With his vast funds of knowledge of constitutional law and grassroots experience of country's complex socio-economic and political issues, he set out his thinking about the nation's constitutional needs. As a consequence, the doctrine of Rule of Law, Part III and IV of the Constitution, that is Fundamental Rights and Directive Principles of State Policy, an independent judiciary as an arm of social revolution, the charter of equality, liberty and justice: social, economic and political to all, along with some constitutional safeguards to the downtrodden groups (SCs, STs, OBCs, minorities and women) form the core of social revolution.

These constitutional convictions are as follows:

1. The Preamble has authorised the state and its three principal organs –legislature, executive and judiciary – to take all necessary measures to create a sustainable social order in which every citizen could be assured of all inclusive justice without any discrimination on grounds of religion, race, caste, sex, decent, place of birth and residence.
2. Articles 14, 15, 16 ensures equal protection of law, non-discrimination by the State on ground of religion, caste, sex or place of birth particularly in matters relating to employment, absence of any disability or restriction among citizens in the matter of access to public places or use of public places of public resort. Articles 15 and 16 commands the State to make special provision through reservation or otherwise in favour of Scheduled Castes, Tribes, Women, Children as well as other backward classes of citizens.
3. Article 17 abolishes untouchability and made criminal prohibition of its practice in any form.
4. Articles 23 and 24 prescribe prohibition against exploitation and traffic in human beings and forced labour.
5. Articles 25, 29 and 30 provides for equal entitlements of every person to freedom of conscience and the right to freely profess, practice and propagate ones religion, protection of interests of minorities and their right to establish and administer educational institutions.
6. Article 38 directs the State to secure a social order for the promotion of welfare of the people by elimination of

inequalities in status, facilities and opportunities including social order founded on justice: social, economic and political.

7. Article 39 lays down the State policy towards securing adequate means of livelihood for every citizen, equal pay for equal work to men and women and preventing concentration of wealth to the common detriment.
8. Article 39A assures equal justice under law and towards that end providing free legal aid to the poor.
9. Article 45 directs the State to provide free and compulsory education to all children within 10 years of the commencement of the Constitution.
10. Articles 46 directs the State to promote educational and economic interests of Scheduled Castes, Scheduled Tribes and other weaker sections and also commands the State to protect them from social injustice and all forms of exploitation. Article 335 directs the State to maintain the claims of SCs and STs to services and posts.
11. Along with the policy of reservation of job quota and in educational institutions for the SCs, STs, Articles 330, 332 and 334 provide reservation of seats for SCs and STs in the House of People and in the Legislative Assemblies of the State.
12. Article 338 makes the provision for National Commission for the SCs and STs to advise on the socio-economic development of the SCs and STs and to evaluate their progress under the Union and States.
13. Article 340 provides for the Commission to investigate the conditions of backward classes and to make recommendationed as to the steps that should be taken by the state.

Reservation for depressed classes as envisaged by Ambedkar in the Constitution was of three kinds, namely:

(i) Reservation to the Lok Sabha and State Assemblies (Articles 330 and 332).

(ii) Job reservations (Articles 16 (1), 16 (4) and 335) and

(iii) Reservation in the admissions to educations institutions (Articles 15 (4) and 46).

Thus, along with the general constitutional guarantees, there are specific safeguards for the downtrodden groups. These provisions speak for the State's commitment and conviction to create a just, humanitarian social order, an egalitarian society premised on the constitutional spirit of liberty, equality, fraternity and justice.

In the mid-twentieth century liberal constitutional States were held with the responsibility of the social and economic changes in the society. Accordingly, Ambedkar emphasised for such changes through Law of Constitution. Obviously, Ambedkar regarded Part IV of the Constitution as of great value and that would serve as the guiding principle for all State actions and if the rulers dare to disobey this constitutional-national agenda will have to pay the heavy price.[29] While justifying the constitutional place of Directive Principles, he said:

> 'The Draft Constitution as framed only provides a machinery for the government of the country. It is not a contrivance to install any particular party in power as has been done in some countries. Who should be in power is left to be determined by the people as it must be, if the system is to satisfy the tests of democracy. But whoever captures will not be free to do what be likes with it. In the existence of it, he will have to respect these instruments of instructions which are called Directive Principles. He cannot ignore them. He may not have to answer for breach in a Court of Law. But he will certainly have to answer for them before the electorate at election time. What great value these directive principles possess will be realised better when the forces of right contrive to capture power.'[30]

Ambedkar's firm desire was to make all Directive Principles of State Policy justicible and sought for a comprehensive programme for the social and economic revolution. But the powerful lobby in the Assembly favouring the supremacy to civil and political rights over social and economic rights emerged as victorious and accorded unenforceable status to the Directive principles – a pool of half-hearted compromises. The most unfortunate part is that even the

Supreme Court of India in its early decisions echoed the voice of *status quoists*. K. T. Shah supported Ambedkar by saying that, there must be a specified time limit within which all the Directive Principles must be made justiciable, otherwise they would be mere 'pious wishes' and much window dressing for the social revolution.

The record of the Constituent Assembly reveals that Ambedkar tried a lot for socio-economic planning and warned that if socio-economic rights were not taken seriously future governments may fall down. He emphasised on the construction of a virtual bridge between the classes of the society. According to him, it would be difficult to maintain the unity of the country if the difference among the classes were not met.

Speaking on the Third Report of SC, ST Commission in the Rajya Sabha on 6th September 1954, Ambedkar said:

> 'What is untouchability? Let us understand it very carefully. Untouchability, so far as I understand it, is a kind of mental disease of Hindu…It is a mental twist; every Hindu believes that to observe untouchability is the right thing… I cannot see how you blame the Hindu. For thousands of years, by the teaching of this dirty law they have got inculcated in their mind the doctrine that untouchability is most sacred thing. He must not touch this, he must not touch that; he must not eat this, he must not eat that, etc. That is the position and all that we can do is seeing that untouchability which, as I said, is a mental twist of the Hindus does not protrude so much into public life as to involve the civil liberties of the people.'

Ambedkar had unhesitatingly rejected the Hindu social philosophy, because it did not satisfy the requirements of his ethical standard. His ethical norm teaches and adheres to the ideals of liberty and equality; whereas the Hindu social order denies them not only in theory but also in practice. The Hindu social philosophy also falls in contradiction with the Constitution of India which affirms a life of justice, liberty, equality and fraternity. The caste system is virtually a denial of all social and political ideals as contained and visualised in the Constitution of India. To say it differently, Ambedkar always stood for a harmonious relation between political ideals and social practices; otherwise a life of self-contradictions would be perpetuating in our land. Sooner the life of self-contradiction is removed and replaced by a new social system; the better is for Indian people.

In Ambedkar's social and political scheme of things, though liberty and equality have prominent place, yet to him, it is not unlimited liberty, because it destroys the true sense of equality and similarly, it is not absolute equality, because it leaves no room for liberty. Only the proper relation between liberty and equality can help both the individual and society. In Ambedkar's idea of social life, law also plays a very significant role, but only as a safeguard against the branches of liberty and equality. He gave the highest place to fraternity as the only real safeguard against the denial of liberty and equality. Fraternity is another name for brotherhood among men which is another name for religion, because religion has nothing to do with metaphysical speculations. Law is secular, he told us, which anybody may break, while fraternity or religion is sacred which everybody regards sacred. Since people give more importance to fraternity (religion) than law, fraternity provides good ground for the protection of liberty, equality and social justice.

In Ambedkar's vision of social relations, morality, precisely called as 'Human brotherhood' has been given a prominent place in order to bring men together. Law is important, but it has been given a secondary place. The social and ethical philosophy of Ambedkar encourages the people to organise themselves on the basis of liberty, equality and fraternity.

It is an open fact that Ambedkar suffered a lot in life due to the denial of human rights to him being an untouchable. The untouchables were in those times less than human beings and worse than beasts. It has been rightly observed, the untouchables, who were segregated, had no civic, religious and political rights. It was then Ambedkar's aim to create those rights, to prepare his people's heads, hearts and hands to secure Man rights, and to make them real men, real countrymen, out of sixty millions virtual slaves.

Indian Constitution and Ambedkar's Deweyan Experiment

If we investigate the Indian Constitution in the light of B. R. Ambedkar as student of John Dewey, we will find evidence that

Ambedkar's ideas on democracy were Deweyan in their emphasis upon experimentation. Ambedkar studied with Dewey at Columbia University between 1913 and 1916 and often credited the latter for having a lasting impression on his thinking.

If we look at Dewey's *Democracy and Education* exclusively since most of Ambedkar's, explicit and implicit, Dewey quotes come from this work. The provisions in the Indian Constitution dealing with remedial treatment for disadvantaged citizens, variously called 'positive discrimination and compensatory discrimination' are the Ambedkar's significant efforts to exercise democratic experimentalism. The second important example is the attempted passage of the Hindu Code Bill in 1951. This Bill proposed comprehensive reform to clarify, standardise and streamline Hindu personal law. Both these examples, when viewed in light of Dewey-Ambedkar perspective of democracy where democracy is not just a matter of routine elections, but is the nature of sociality itself, in which social harmony and fraternity ought to be more important.

Democracy, as Dewey scholars point out has been at the core of the nerve centre of Dewey's thinking in all fields. In that sense the theme of democracy is the very expression of Dewey's pragmatism. Democracy was never a mere form of government where the majority rules for Dewey.

According to Dewey, true democracy is 'radical' as its end "requires great change in existing social institutions, economic, legal and cultural. The radicalism of true democracy is not only in its end but also in its means, and its process that need to include everyone. Dewey emphasises the necessity of an inclusive plan for a democratic society." Ambedkar's community was excluded from all forms of social participation. So like Dewey he wanted their involvement in all field through Constitution.

What sets Ambedkar apart from other leaders of Mahar among other untouchable communities who worked towards the goal of ending social oppression for their untouchability is the fact that he was the first one to clearly envision that change has to be sought through political means and not religious means. Zelliot proposes that it could be because of his 'Western education', 'I think it is not simply for his Western education because that would apply to Gandhi as well since the latter too benefited from a Western education, but envisioned a solution that drew deeply from his Hindu ethos. Instead, Ambedkar's commitment followed from a more specific aspect of his Western education, namely, his conviction that Deweyan democratic ideals and their associated means and goals are the only viable means of social change. This results in Ambedkar's 'intensely secular humanist mission' with its secure confidence that only 'a pragmatic and flexible democratic system' can raise status of untouchables and effect improvements.'[31] This confidence fueled Ambedkar's life-long and indomitable commitment to the fashioning of various instruments of Indian democratic system until his death in 1956. This involvement included; his 1919 presentation before the very important Southborough Committee on Franchise Commissioned by the British Government to review and revise voting rights of Indian especially the minorities; his participation in the Round Table Conference of early 1930s, especially the Second one in 1931 where Ambedkar was able to convince the British Government for separate electorate for the Untouchables though subsequently he had to relinquish this demand due to Gandhi, who feared that this measure was going to threaten Hindu Unity;[32] his role as the Chairman of the Drafting Committee of the Indian Constitution; his role as the first Law Minister in the Cabinet of Prime Minister Nehru; and also the numerous political parties he founded to use as a platform to enable the full participation of the marginalised and backward communities within the Indian democratic landscape.

How influential was Ambedkar in the process of producing the Indian Constitution as the Chairman of its Drafting Committee? This has been a contentious issue especially with Ambedkar's detractors like Arun Shourie[33] arguing that since the Drafting Committee didn't compose the primary texts of the articles, but the various specialised subcommittee did and further the final version had to be discussed and passed in the plenary sessions of the Constituent Assembly, Ambedkar's role in the shaping of the Indian Constitution was merely peripheral. Ambedkar, with his iconoclastic critique of the Indian ruling class and its heroes, remains a sticking nail, an uncomfortable guest at nationalist celebrations of India's might. In fact, it is this unease that prompted fundamentalist caste Hindu authors like

Arun Shourie to portray Ambedkar as a traitor to Indian nationalism and supporter of the British colonialism.

On the other side of the debate, as Jaffrelot documents, are a number of scholars who argue that Ambedkar played a central role in the shaping of the Constitution and that "it was only by virtue of his competence that Ambedkar was appointed head of the Drafting Committee."

In fact, Ambedkar was a member of multiple of the subcommittees and also the fact that as a Chairman of the Drafting Committee he 'guided and channelled' all discussion on the various draft first within the Drafting Committee and later the final version on the floor of the Constituent Assembly, it seems reasonably to surmise that at least some parts of the Indian Constitution reflected his vision.

It is Ambedkar's intellectual and political contributions that lie at the heart of the development of the reservation policy that prevail in India to this day. It is undeniable the "reservations in education, in legislature and in government employment have brought about into universities and political process many individuals who otherwise would have entered neither and they attest to the paradoxical erosion of the caste system as caste allegiance facilitates upward mobility."[34]

Dewey considered democracy to be radical since it 'requires great change in existing social institutions' and, in a similar spirit, Ambedkar came to the conviction that a truly communal life where every Indian participates was not possible without a thorough overhaul of the age old Hindu social order and caste system and this focused his involvement with the Hindu Code Bill. "While Constitution outlined favourable framework for social reform, particularly by abolishing untouchability and by prohibiting all discrimination based on caste, race and sex," "Ambedkar was determined to attack the ills of Indian society in a more concrete fashion."Ambedkar saw the project of Indian democracy and annihilation of the existing Hindu caste system as integrally intertwined.

In his address on 'Prospect of Democracy in India', a talk for Voice of America, on 20th May 1956, Ambedkar comments that the caste System 'militates against democracy,' because it is characterised by 'graded Inequality,' where the system becomes "an ascending scale of hatred and descending scale of contempt."[35] The Hindu Code Bill was an 'omnibus measure' that aimed for a through revision and modernisation of various Hindu personal law codes. Various aspects of this Bill included marriage, and divorce, property ownership and inheritance, women's rights, adoption, and most controversially the role of caste in a Hindu identity. This Bill was not only a 'cornerstone of the modernisation of India', but it also served as the basis of the secularisation of its political space. This Bill became one of Ambedkar's defining projects as the Law Minister in the Nehru Cabinet.

The Hindu Code Bill also provided a concrete location for Ambedkar's idea of Indian democratic experimentalism. But it brought him into direct confrontation with most of his colleagues as they did not share his conviction. One of the forceful opponents was Rajendra Prasad, the President of the Constituent Assembly, who argued that this Bill was discriminatory since it only aimed to 'secularize' Hindu personal law while leaving the personal laws of minority communities untouched. More importantly, as Austin puts it, his fear was that "this Bill would force 'revolutionary changes' in Hindu life; and he also found the measure unnecessary as for him "Hindu law was evolving in ways making legislative changes unnecessary."[36] Unfortunately, the opponents' voices proved too strong and under tremendous pressure from his Congress colleagues Nehru decided to postpone bringing the Bill to the Parliament after the general election 1952. This became one of the main reasons for resigning from the Nehru Cabinet in 1951, and in declaring his resignation, Ambedkar wrote,

> 'To leave inequality between class and class, between sex and sex, which is the soul of Hindu society untouched and to go on passing legislation relating to economic problems is to make a farce of our Constitution and to build a palace on a dung heap. This is the significance I attached to the Hindu Code.'[37]

However, in spite of Ambedkar's disappointment, this Bill was split in four parts and brought to the Parliament where significant aspects of the Hindu Code Bill were passed in subsequent years. So even in this regard Ambedkar's democratic experimentalism seemed to get the Indian democracy started on the right track.

N.A. Palkhivala has rightly observed:

> 'Dr Ambedkar was too big a man to harbour thought of vengeance and vendetta, ill-wills or revenge towards those who had been exploiting casteism from times immemorial. He gave Indian Constitution, which guarantees equality to all as its basic feature, and ensures truly egalitarian society, where no class would be unprivileged, underprivileged on the ground of religion, race, caste, sex and decent place of birth or residence'.

The Constitution and its architects have tried a lot to bring a socio-economic revolution through peaceful democratic and constitutional means. Some constitutional safeguards although not to the level of Ambedkar's expectations have been provided in the Constitution as the affirmative action to uplift the backward classes, especially children, women, SCs and STs. But the fate of this social and economic revolution has been sealed by ruling class and the successive governments in the country. Due to neglect of social revolution aspect of the Constitution the goal of creating a 'just' society has remained merely on the paper. Taking the cognizance of this kind of pathetic situation, the former President of India, K.R. Narayanan in one of his addresses to the nation, said:

> 'We have to ponder over the condition of not only women in our society, but of the Dalits, the tribals and other weaker sections. Untouchability has been abolished by law but shades of it remain in the ingrained attitudes nurtured by the caste system. Though the constitutional provisions of reservation in educational institutions and public services flow from our Constitution; these provisions remain unfulfilled through bureaucratic and administrative deformation or by narrow interpretations of these special provisions. It seems, in the social realm, some kind of a counter-revolution is taking place in India. It is forgotten that these benefits have been provided not in the way of charity, but as human rights and as social justice to a section of society who constitutes a big chunk of our population, and who actually contribute to our agriculture, industry and services as landless labourers, factory and municipal workers. These are signs that our privileged classes are getting tired of the affirmative action provided by constitutional provisions.'

The prevailing stark realities in the country had compelled President K.R. Narayanan to observe that : (i) Fifty years into our life in the Republic we find that justice – social, economic and political – remains an unrealised dream for millions our fellow citizens. (ii) Tragically, the growth in our economy has not been uniform. It has been accompanied by great regional and social inequalities. (iii) There is our greatest national drawback; the status of women and our greatest national shame, the condition of the dalits, the erstwhile untouchables.

Dr Ambedkar had articulated the agenda of the social and economic revolutions through his struggles and the Indian Constitution. The Constitution could be considered as the foremost legacy of the struggles of Ambedkar. But as Granville Austin very well said:

> '...a Constitution, however 'living', is inert. It does not 'work', it is worked –worked by human beings whose conduct may shape, whose energies it may canalise, but whose character it cannot improve, and whose tasks it cannot perform...The politics of working the Constitution confronted Indians with two apparent incompatibilities: the first was between aspects of their culture and the pursuit of a democratic and reformed society; the second was among constitutional provisions carrying the strands of the seamless web. These difficulties had to be surmounted, circumvented, or accommodated in the conditions prevailing in the country.'

To what extent the constitutional agenda of social change has worked out is a matter of great debate. In fact, Ambedkar visualised the futility of the constitutional safeguards in the hands of majority in the country that he thought of being communal in character, and as such as essentially undemocratic. He held the firm views that:

> 'In India the majority is not a political majority. In India, the majority is born, it is not made. That is the difference between a communal majority and a political majority. A political majority is not a fixed or a permanent majority. It is a majority which is always made, unmade and remade. A communal majority is a permanent majority fixed in its attitude. One can destroy it but one cannot transform it.'[38]

Ambedkar's above analysis of India's political as well as communal majority, and its evil effects on the constitutional institutions and functionaries, perhaps reveals the reasons that obstruct the path of social and economic change in India. The basic hindrance towards social change is the lack of social democracy in our country. Ambedkar had visualised this and he had stated in the Constituent Assembly that the Constitution had created political democracy, whose success would depend upon establishing social and economic democracy. For accelerating the wheels of social change, what is required is an effective and healthy social and economic democracy. Let us not forget that social change, social democracy and economic democracy –all are co-related.

Thus, the framers of the Constitution of India adopted a holistic view of social change, which is enshrined in the preamble, fundamental rights and the directive principles of state policy of the Constitution. The possibility of ensuring social change in contemporary era is linked not only with a vibrant and dynamic economic equality but to social order too. The social and economic democracy suggests removal of social inequalities that impede the effective exercise of freedom for securing well-being. Also, it implies the fulfillment of the needs of various groups of diverse background. Social change has significance in the context of Indian society which is divided into castes, depressed and backward classes and they create walls and barriers of exclusiveness on the basis of superiority and inferiority. Such inequalities pose serious threat to Indian democracy. The concept of social change has taken within its sweep the objective of removing inequalities and affording equal opportunities to all citizens in social, economic and political affairs. The country, while passing through the process of social change, is in the quest for finding out ways for a better and just socio-economic order. The search for a new model of social change and socio-economic order is the need of the hour. Recent trends in globalisation, urbanisation, mobilisation of the poor and depressed classes in search of better life conditions and social justice and social transformation movements compel us to think afresh.

References

1. *Dr Babasaheb Ambedkar Writings and Speeches*, Vol. 1 (New Delhi, Ministry of Social Justice and Empowerment, 1979), p. 57.

2. *Dr Babasaheb Ambedkar Writings and Speeches*, Vol. 9 (New Delhi, Ministry of Social Justice and Empowerment, 2014), p. 194.
3. *Ibid,* p. 195.
4. Ramchandra Guha: *India after Gandhi: The History of the World's Largest Democracy*, (London, Macmillian, 2007), pp.103-104.
5. *Constituent Assembly Debate*, Vol. V, (New Delhi, Official Report, Reprinted by Lok Sabha Secretariat, Second reprint, 1989), p. 2.
6. Granville Austin: *The Indian Constitution Cornerstone of Nation*, (New Delhi, Oxford University Press, 2000), p. 26.
7. *Constituent Assembly Debate*, Vol. V, p. 4.
8. Kamal Kumar*: Indian Constitution: The Vision of B. R. Ambedkar,* (IOSR e-Journal of Humanities and Social Sciences, Vol. 19, Issue 3), p. 30.
9. *Thus Spoke Ambedkar*, Vol. 1, (Jalandhar, Buddhist Publishing House, 1963), p. 133.
10. For full text of Ambedkar speech, see Constituent Assembly Debate, Vol. VII. pp. 31-34.
11. *Constituent Assembly Debate*, Vol. VII, pp. 32-33.
12. *Constituent Assembly Debate,* Vol. VII, (4th Nov. 1948).
13. *Ibid.*
14. *Ibid.*
15. *Dr Babasaheb Ambedkar Writings and Speeches*, Vol. 13, (New Delhi, Ministry of Social Justice and Empowerment, 2014), p. 56.
16. *Constituent Assembly Debate*, Vol. VII, pp. 42-43.
17. *Ibid.,* Vol. VII, pp. 43-44.
18. *Ibid.,* Vol. VII, (4th Nov. 1948).
19. *Dr Babasaheb Ambedkar Writings and Speeches*, Vol. 13, (New Delhi, Ministry of Social Justice and Empowerment, 2014), p. 1210.
20. *Indian Constitution*, Article 15, clause 3.
21. Bhupender Kumar Ahluwalia and Shashi Ahluwalia : *Dr Ambedkar and Hindu Rights*, Vivek Publishing Company, 1981, p. 72.
22. *Constituent Assembly Debates,* Vol. 1. p. 59.
23. A.I.R. 1976, S.C. p. 490.
24. A.I.R. 1981 S.C. p. 298.
25. M. K. Kishore: *Dr B. R. Ambedkar* (ed.) Mohammad Shabbir: *Ambedkar on Law, Constitution and Social Justice,* (Jaipur, Rawat Publication, 2011), p. 242.
26. Kalyani Shankar: *Gods of Power: Personality Cult and Indian Democracy*, (London, Macmillian, 2005), p. 281.
27. Christophe Jaffrelot: *Ambedkar and the Uniform Civil Code, Outlook,* http/ /www. Outlook, India. com (March 7, 2013).

28. Section 6, Hindu Succession (Amendment) Act, 2005, *Hindu Women entitled to Equal Property Rights*; The Indian Express, March 7, 2013.
29. Mohammed Shabbir (ed.): *Ambedkar on Law, Constitution and Social Justice,* (Jaipur, Rawat Publications, 2011), p. 252.
30. *Constituent Assembly Debate*, Vol. VII, 4th Nov. 1948, p. 41.
31. E. Zelliot : *From Untouchability to Dalit*: *Essays on Ambedkar Movement* (Delhi, Manohar, 2001), p. 11.
32. C. Jaffrelot : *Dr Ambedkar and Untouchability: Fighting the Indian Caste System* (New York, Columbia University Press, 2005), p. 4.
33. Arun Shourie : *Worshipping False Gods : Ambedkar and the Facts which have been Erased,* (New Delhi, ASA Publishing, 1997).
34. Suresh Mane *: Constitution and Dr Ambedkar's Vision for Social Change*, Mohammad Shabbier (ed.): *Ambedkar on Law, Constitution and Social Justice* (Jaipur, Rawat Publications, 2005), p. 266.
35. *Ibid.*, p. 266.
36. G. Austin : *Working A Democratic Constitution: A History of the Indian Experience*, (New Delhi, Oxford University Press, 1999), p. 22.
37. *Dr Babasaheb Ambedkar Writings and Speeches*, Vol. 14, Part II, (New Delhi, Ministry of Social Justice and Empowerment, 1995), p. 1326.
38. *Dr Babasaheb Ambedkar Writings and Speeches*, Vol. 1, Education Department, Government of Maharashtra, 1979.

CHAPTER–6

The Policy of Reservations

The policy of reservations for the Scheduled Castes and Scheduled Tribes has been clearly introduced under the Constitution of India, 1950. The reservations commenced from 1952 for a period of ten years, but extendable after the expiry of the said period. From 1952 till date it is in existence. In addition to the reservations for SC's and ST's, there came into existence reservations for 'Other Backward Classes' (OBC) in 1990's on the basis of the recommendations of the Mandal Commission Report.

The key feature of this policy is the reservations of seats in legislatures, government jobs, panchayat raj and educational institutions for the persons belonging to each of the above categories. The percentage of reservations is calculated on the basis of population (according to 1931 census) of each category or group. As per census of 1931, the percentage of population of Scheduled Castes was 15.05, Scheduled Tribes 7.51 and OBCs 52.10 in the country. The percentage of population of each category varies from state to state. As such, broadly speaking, the state-wise reservation percentage is given in the following Table:[1]

S.N.	State	SC	ST	OBC	Total
1.	West Bengal	22	6	7	35
2.	Kerala	10	-	40	50
3.	Uttar Pradesh	21	2	27	50

(Contd...)

4.	Bihar	15	1	34	50
5.	Assam	7	15	15	37
6.	Jharkhand	11	27	12	50
7.	Karnataka	15	3	32	50
8.	Uttaranchal	19	4	14	37
9.	Delhi	15	7.5	27	49.5
10.	Maharashtra	13	7	32	52
11.	Andhra Pradesh	15	6	25	46
12.	Gujarat	7	15	27	49
13.	Rajasthan	15	7.5	27	49.5
14.	Madhya Pradesh	16	20	14	50
15.	Haryana	15	7.5	27	49.5
16.	Tamil Nadu	18	1	50	69
17.	Orissa	15	7.5	27	49.5
18.	Himachal Pradesh	15	7.5	5	27.5
19.	Chhattisgarh	15	18	14	47
20.	Punjab	20	5	22	47
	All India	**15**	**7.5**	**27**	**49.5**

Hidden Form of Reservations

From the above description, it would seem to many that reservations are a new thing in India, but if one dares to peep into the past history of the country, he would come to realise that its roots are embedded in the social system of Hinduism that operated from the Vedic times to framing of the Constitution of India, 1950. The whole thing revolves around the meaning of reservations. One writer while defining reservations says:

> 'India has been a nation of reservations and, by reservation, I mean the system of fixed identities, immovable social positions and reserved privileges and obligations. India's history, culture, economy and polity are not only the monuments of above said system of reservations; they also continue to be determined by it.'[2]

Reservations, one should not forget, are the bedrock of Hindu social system based on the Vedic scriptures, especially *Rig Veda* and *Manusmriti*. The Hindu social system rooted in *Chaturvarna* is, in fact, the real founder of reservations. The four Varnas of this system are Brahmins, Kshatriyas, Vaishyas and Shudras, who had their 'birth-based fixed social status and duties.' In the Hindu Varna or hierarchical system, the Brahmins occupied the highest positions, and they had the monopoly over the functions related to wisdom, education and spiritual leadership. The *Kshatriyas* held the second position and their duty was warriorship. The third place was held by *Vaishyas*; they were the appetite class and their duty was production, trade and commerce. The lowest position was held by *Shudras* who were considered untouchables and unseeables. They were prohibited from spiritual leadership, education, warriorship, production and commerce. Their only duty was to serve the top three *Varnas*. They had no privileges and for centuries were exploited and oppressed by the three higher *Varnas*. They could not move up to higher Varnas; they were thus totally an alienated class, that lived in bondage and servitude to the caste Hindus. This naturally resulted in 'complete social, spiritual, educational and economic deprivation of *Shudras* or untouchables, leaving them unable to recognise or fight for their own humanity.' This *Varna* system in a hidden way or covertly sanctioned or recognised Reservations of privileges and positions for the three higher castes and continued for centuries till the end of the British rule in India. It was against this *Varna* system that Dr B. R. Ambedkar, the foremost exponent of the abolition of untouchability in the twentieth century, had revolted and finally succeeded in the eradication of untouchability through the mechanism of Constitution.

This chapter is mainly concerned with the reservations provided to SCs/STs in the Constitution of India.

Evolution of Reservations

The present reservation system embedded in the Constitution of India has a long history. It would be desirable to mention a few landmarks in the evolution of reservation system.

Prior to independence of the country, reservations in favour of Backward Classes (BCs) were introduced in some Presidency areas and princely states. In 1882, Hunter Commission was appointed. Mahatma Jyotirao Phule made a demand of free and compulsory education for depressed classes along with proportionate representation in government jobs. In 1891, there was an agitation for reservation of government jobs in the princely State of Travancore against the recruitment of *non-natives* into public service overlooking qualified *native* people. In 1901-02, reservations were introduced in the Princely State of Kolhapur by Shahu Maharaj Chatrapati Sahuji Maharaj, Maharaja of Kolhapur; it was in favour of non-Brahmin and backward classes. He provided free education to everyone and opened several hostels in Kolhapur to make it easier for everyone to receive the education. He also made sure everyone got suitable employment no matter what social class they belonged. He also appealed for a class-free India and the abolition of untouchability. The notification of 1902 created 50 per cent reservation in services for backward classes/ communities in the State of Kolhapur. This is the first official instance (Government Order) providing for reservation for depressed classes in India.

It was in the nineteenth century that a social reformer from Maharashtra, namel, Jyotiba Phule carried on a forceful crusade against the practice of untouchability. He called attention to the plight of victims of caste discrimination in Maharashthra. He is rightly regarded as a pioneer of untouchability eradication in India in general and Maharastra in particular. The movement for eradication of untouchability started by Mahatma Phule was further carried on by Chatrapati Shahu with full strength, vigour and earnestness. Hence, Shahu Maharaj earned the position of an apostle of the rising movement of the untouchables after him.[3] When Shahu Maharaj took the administration of the state of Kolhapur in his hands in 1894, majority of the state officials were Brahmins. Other backward classes remained aloof from education and consequently from state services. Thus, from the beginning Shahu realised the necessity of setting on the right track the whole social machine which for ages had strayed along lines harmful to national growth. To do this he had to embark on a strenuous campaign against the evils of the traditional hierarchy of castes. He set about his work systematically, his first step, to this effect was the reservation of 50 per cent of posts for backward classes including untouchables. In the year 1902, Shahu Maharaj was invited to England to attend the coronation of his majesty king Edward VII. During this sojourn in England, he issued the order from England, to the effect that 50 per cent posts for the Kolhapur state services should be reserved for the backward class candidates. This was indeed a landmark in his carrier as social reformer. Shahu Maharaj was keen on extending all facilities for education of the lower classes. By the order of 1911, he exempted them completely from the school fees. He granted in 1919 Scholarships to students for school education.

Dr Ghurey evaluates the work initiated by Jyotiba Phule and Chatrapati Shahu Maharaj in following words:

> 'Phuley's was a revolt against Caste in so far as Caste denied ordinary human rights to all the members of Hindu society and not merely a non-Brahmin movement to cast off the diminution of Brahmins. The movement did not receive any support from the Brahmins in general. Even among the non-Brahmins the progresses of Phule's ideas were slow. It was Shahu Maharaj who infused new life into the agitation so much so that Montagu and Chelmsford, in their Indian political reforms had to grant the demands.'[4]

To end the discriminative treatment to the untouchables in the state departments, the Maharaja issued prompt orders to all the authorities directing them to follow his instructions in this respect rigorously. His order of 15th January 1919 was thus:

> 'All officers in the state, revenue, judicial or general department must treat the untouchables who have entered the state services with kindness and equality. If any state officers have any objection to treat the untouchable according to the above order, he will have to give notice of resignation within six weeks from the receipt of this order and resign his post. He will be entitled to no pension. His Highness expects every subject of his should be treated like a human being and not like a beast.'[5]

Forward-thinking Maharajas in 'native' states like Baroda, Kolhapur, and Travancore, took progressive initiatives.[6] Ambedkar, from the Mahar caste of Maharashtra, was one beneficiary. The Mahars had a long association with the British-organised Indian Army, in which Ambedkar's father and grandfather had served. The Maharaja of Baroda, sponsored Ambedkar's study abroad, first at Columbia University in New York, where Ambedkar obtained a Ph.D. in Economics, and later at London University, where he earned a D.Sc. and entrance to the Bar from Grey's Inn.

The Princely State of Mysore, influenced by the social reform movement in the former Madras Presidency, particularly the social revolt sponsored by the Justice Party, had developed its own rudimentary policy of reservation as far back as 1874. During the period between 1874 and 1895, the Government of Mysore reserved 20 per cent of middle and lower level jobs in police department for Brahmins and 80 per cent for Muslims, Hindus and Indian Christians, again from 1914, the Government of Mysore introduced a system of nomination of qualified backward class candidates to the post of Assistant commissioners. Even so it was realised that the backward classes including SCs and STs could not break the monopoly of the Brahmins in the State Government service.

The social reform movement and the resultant communal order in the Madras province and the monopoly of the Brahmins in Mysore Government jobs created a lot of discontent among the backward classes. No government could ignore the demands of a vast majority of the people for a share in the government service. As a positive response to this demand, the first Backward Classes Committee under the Chairmanship of the Chief Judge of Mysore High Court, Leslie. C. Miller, was appointed and this Committee which submitted its report within a record time of about 11 months. It laid the basic foundation for the future formulation of the reservation policy for the backward classes in the State of Karnataka, created in 1956. In fact, the report which runs over 31 pages brizzles with original ideas about the criteria to be adopted for identifying backward classes, measures needed for promoting their education and the reasons for compromising merit with equality of representation in Government Service.[7]

In what is now Kerala, the Maharaja of erstwhile State of Travancore announced the "Temple Entry Proclamation" in 1936, in what has been called a "pioneer effort in the field of reforms relating to the eradication of untouchability before independence." Stating that "none of our Hindu subjects should, by reason of birth or caste or community, be denied the consolations and solace of the Hindu faith," the Maharaja declared the removal of all bars on those denied entry to temples controlled by Travancore government.[8]

Thus, it could be said that the progressive rulers of the princely states of Baroda, Kolhapur, Mysore and Travancore had taken steps towards reservations of the backward and depressed classes, even before the dawn of Indian independence.

In a nutshell, the evolution of reservations have been described by Mulchand S. Rana in the following words:

> 'The thought of reservation has its roots way back in the year 1902, when Chhatrapati Shahuji Maharaj, a small ruler in the then Kolhapur state in Maharashtra in pre-independence days introduced reservation in the jobs, of his small kingdom for the 'Antayas', i.e., the Shudras or the backwards. This was followed by another little larger state of Mysore in South India introducing reservation in the state in the year 1921, on the basis of report of Millar Committee… The Millar Committee appointed in 1918, was the first Committee appointed in India for suggesting upliftment measures for the socially deprived people. Immediately, thereafter in 1921 itself, the sprawling Madras Presidency introduced reservation for the backward classes including scheduled castes. The large Bombay Presidency also initiated the process in 1931 following the report of the State Committee for the depressed classes and backward castes.'[9]

British Period

The reservations during the British rule in India took a different turn. It started with the introduction of Morley-Minto reforms in1909. Its key feature was communal electorates and reservation of seats for the Muslims in the Legislative Councils. This type of reservations based on the demand of the Muslim League which was established in 1906 gave birth to communal politics in India.

The communal representation that commenced in 1909 was retained in Montagu-Chelmsford Reforms and the Government of India Act of 1919. It was at this stage that Dr B. R. Ambedkar had started his struggle for the liberation of the depressed classes or the dalits. He pleaded for the representation of depressed classes in the councils on the ground of separate interests which required protection.[10] He stated that the untouchable classes must have their own men in the Councils to fight for the redress of their grievances.

The question of depressed classes also gained the attention of the Simon Commission, appointed in 1927. Dr Ambedkar on

29 May 1928, submitted a memorandum to the Simon Commission, demanding protection of the interests of depressed classes through adequate representation. He made it clear that the depressed classes and untouchables were synonymous and they must be treated as distinct minority separated from the Hindu Community.[11] The Simon Commission rejected separate electorates for the depressed classes; but it recommended the continuation of separate electorates for the Muslims, Sikhs and the Europeans. However, the Commission recommended that in all the eight provinces of the British, there should be some reservation of seats for the depressed classes on a scale which would secure a substantial increase in the number of members of Legislative Councils drawn from the depressed classes.

The next important event was the first Round Table Conference held in London in November 1930. Dr Ambedkar and Rai Bahadur R. Srinivasan represented the depressed classes. The Indian National Congress did not participate in the first Round Table Conference. In this Conference, Ambedkar pleaded for separate electorates for the depressed classes. Separate electorate meant a territorial constituency comprising exclusively of untouchables only in which they alone would vote for their handpicked candidates.[12]

The second Round Table Conference was held in 1931. Ambedkar and Srinivasan represented the depressed classes. The Indian National Congress participated in the second conference and its representative was Mahatma Gandhi. Ambedkar in this Conference again pleaded separate electorate for the depressed classes, which Gandhi opposed tooth and nail. After the end of the second R.T.C., Ramsay MacDonald announced his famous 'Communal Award' on 17 August, 1932. An essential feature of this Award was the acceptance by the British Government of separate electorates for the depressed classes. As per this Award, the untouchables were given two votes, one in general constituency and another in a special constituency of untouchables to be carved out in areas where they were most numerous.[13]

Gandhi was greatly perturbed by the decision (Communal Award) of the Prime Minister. His main objection was that the Award would take untouchables away from Hindus and Hinduism and that the interest of Hinduism would suffer. He believed that separate electorates for the untouchables would surely vivisect and disrupt Hinduism. In a letter to Samuel Hoare, then Secretary of State for India, Gandhi wrote:

> 'I do not mind the untouchables being converted to Islam or Christianity. I should tolerate that, but I cannot possibly tolerate what is in store for Hinduism if there are these two decisions set up in every village… Therefore, I want to say with emphasis that I will resist it with my life.'[14]

The Prime Minister Ramsay MacDonald tried to assure Gandhi and through him the Hindus that this Award would not take away the untouchables from Hindus and Hinduism. He stated that such a step was necessary to safeguard the rights and interests of the untouchables; and that 'we are convinced that such an Award is necessary under present conditions.'

Since Mahatma Gandhi was totally opposed to the 'Communal Award', he went on 'Fast unto death' in Poona Yarwada Jail and the Hindu press came out with wide propaganda that Ambedkar was bent upon killing the father of the Nation. Gandhi's 'fast unto death' created a great stir throughout country. Even Ambedkar's life was threatened. The fanatics among the Hindus openly said, 'If Gandhi were to die, they would burn the houses of all the untouchables in the whole of India.' Under these alarming circumstances, Ambedkar reluctantly agreed to amend the Award in accordance with the wishes of Gandhi.[15] This led to the concluding of Poona Pact between Gandhi and Ambedkar on September 24, 1932. Though Ambedkar was quite unhappy with the pact because it deprived the depressed classes of their genuine rights, but in order to save Gandhi's life, he had signed the pact. After signing the pact, a dissatisfied Ambedkar expressed his feelings to the press in the following words:

> 'People call Mr. Gandhi as Mahatma, but I can't call him 'Mahatma', I can't even call him a human being. I brought a fruit from London for my people. I was thinking to hand it over to my people, and hoping to see that they would enjoy it. But meanwhile Mr. Gandhi snatched the fruit from my hand, he squeezed the fruit and gave the juice to his people and threw the rind on the face of my people. Today, I am facing as a person on whose face rind of the fruit has been thrown.'

The Poona Pact had occurred as a compromise between the depressed classes and the Hindu Community. It declared the scheme of reservation of seats for the depressed classes out of general electorates in the provincial as well as in Central legislature through election by joint electorates. It also declared about the representation of these classes in the public services. The numbers of seats reserved for the depressed classes were increased to equal their proportion of population with representatives being chosen in general from both communities.[17]

Then came the Government of India Act, 1935. It was the first statute during the British rule, which incorporated the provisions for reservation to the depressed classes (scheduled castes and scheduled tribes and many other backward castes).

However, the objective of the British behind the reservation provisions and the one by the framers of the Indian Constitution was quite different. Explaining the objective of the British Government, Mulchand S. Rana writes;

> 'The Britishers were interested merely in maintaining the balance of power in society to facilitate their rule… They simply used to device of reservation as a tool to manage the then mounting social tensions along with penetrating fight for freedom… Thus, the reservation policy of the British was half-hearted, short-sighted and ill-motivated…'[18]

The framers of the Indian Constitution not only regularised these provisions through its various articles, but also 'cast a duty bound obligation on the state to look after their overall development through numerous welfare measures for these categories who have lagged behind for centuries together due to peculiar social inequalities deeply rooted in the country.[19] Thus, under the Constitution of India reservation is 'not a number gave of apportioning a percentage of vacancies for the eligible community candidates; but it is a mission of abscission of deeply, rooted abject social animosity.' Reservation, it must be understood, is a revolutionary step embedded in our Constitution; it is meant to remove social backwardness and to establish social harmony. It provides constitutional support to those who are deprived of adequate opportunities and equal treatment from the vast majority of the society for centuries. It is a campaign to spread the message of social justice and fraternity.

Reservations Under the Constitution of India, 1950

During extended debates in the Constituent Assembly, strong moral and intellectual arguments were put forward by Ambedkar and some others, which highlighted the conditions and needs of Dalits. As a result, the Constitution of free India, which had its preamble based on principles of justice, liberty, equality and fraternity, was made to include definitive and specific provisions to help preferentially those who have been systematically oppressed throughout the history of India.

Ambedkar had realised very early that declaration of rights and equality of opportunity would in practice be rendered ineffective if adequate safeguards for the protection and promotion of weaker sections were not provided in the Constitution. Reservations would be, and has also proved to be the most effective such measure.

The two important features of the constitutional provisions for the uplift of the weaker section are: the principle of 'Non-discrimination and equal opportunity' and the provisions enshrined in the Constitution empowering the state to take steps to ensure equal opportunity.

Article 16 provides for "equality of opportunity for all citizens in the matters relating to employment or appointment to any office under the State". It bans discrimination, particularly in any employment or appointment to any office under the state on grounds of religion, race, caste, sex, descent, place of birth, residence, or any of them. In fact, Article 17 abolished the tradition of untouchability which sanctified discrimination and exclusion of the erstwhile untouchables. The Article states: "Untouchability is abolished and its practice in any form is forbidden". Accordingly, the Constitution empowered the state with the responsibility to ensure non-discrimination and equal opportunity in practice.

Article 46, a 'Directive Principle of State Policy' states: The State shall promote with special care the educational and economic interests of the weaker sections of the people, and, in particular, of the Scheduled Castes and the Scheduled Tribes, and shall protect them from social injustice and all forms of exploitation. Such provisions in the constitution relates to government services, education, political representation and others.

Reservations for depressed classes as envisaged by Ambedkar in the Constitution are of three kinds, namely:

1. ***Government Services***: The Constitution provides safeguard for both appointment and promotion in the government services for weaker sections. **Article 16 (4)** empowers the State to make "any provision for the reservation in appointments, or posts in favour of any backward class of citizens". **Article 16 (4 A)** enables the State to make provision for reservation in matters of promotion to any group or groups of posts in the services under the State in favour of the SCs and STs. **Article 335** states: 'The claims of the members of the Scheduled Castes and Scheduled Tribes shall be taken into consideration, consistently with the maintenance of efficiency of administration, in the making of appointments of services and posts in connection with the affairs of the Union or of a State'.
2. ***Education***: In the case of education, the provision relates to non-discrimination in educational institutions, equal representations, and measures for educational promotions. Article 15 (4) states that "Nothing in this article shall prevent the State from making any special provision for the advancement of any socially and educationally backward classes of citizens or for the Scheduled Castes and the Scheduled Tribes". Article 29(2) provides protection for admission and against discrimination in any educational institution maintained by the State or receiving aid out of State funds on grounds only of religion, race, caste, language or any of them.
3. ***Political Safeguards:*** The Constitution empowers the State to take steps to provide due representation to the SC/STs. Various articles contains provisions for the reservation of seats for the SC/STs in the nation's legislative bodies in proportion to their population:
   I. Central Legislative Assembly (Article 330),

II. Legislative Assembly of the States (Article 332),
III. In Municipalities (Article 243 T),
IV. In various Panchayat (local self government) level bodies, namely, village, taluk (block) and district (Article 243 D).

Reservation as a Policy – Employment, Education and Legislature[20]

The Indian Government's approach towards the SC/ST population has primarily been shaped by the provisions in its Constitution which basically guarantees equality before the law, and empowers the State to make special provisions to promote the educational and economic interest of the SC/ST and to provide legal and other safeguards against discrimination in multiple spheres.

The government has applied a two-fold strategy which includes:

(a) Legal safeguards against discrimination,
(b) Pro-active measures in the form of 'reservation policy' for state sector and state supported sectors, and
(c) Policy in the form of informal affirmative action for private sector (namely, agriculture and private industry, in which more than 90 per cent of the SC/ST workers are engaged) as part of a general developmental or empowering measure.

Anti-discriminatory measures include enactment of Anti-untouchability Act of 1955 (renamed as protection of Civil Rights Act in 1979) and Schedule Caste/Tribe Prevention of Atrocities Act, 1989. Under the first Act, practice of untouchability and discrimination in public places and services is treated as offence. The second Act provides legal protection to SC/STs against violence and atrocities by the high castes.

Reservation for both SC/ST in government services, educational institutions and political bodies like legislature also falls under anti-discriminatory, but pro-active measures. These pro-active measures have been used to ensure proportional participation of the SC/ST in various public domains.

The reservation policy is confined to a tiny state-run and state-supported sector, whereas the vast private sector where more than

90 per cent of the SC/ST population workers are engaged are excluded. They therefore remain unprotected from exclusion and discrimination. In the absence of reservation policy in the private sector, the state has used 'general programmes' for economic, educational and social empowerment of the SC/ST. The focus has been to improve the private ownership of fixed capital assets (land and non-land), education, and improved access to social needs like housing, health, drinking water, electricity and others. The strategy for improving or building the private ownership of capital assets, education and social needs, which has been generally taken as a part of the anti-poverty programme, is also used as a method of earmarking quotas in an informal manner for the SC/ST population of the country.

Reservation in Government Sector

It is important to note that the Indian affirmative action policy is confined to government and government-aided sector of services and educational institutions; the private jobs and educational institutions are completely excluded from the purview of the policy. Accordingly, the reservation policy is operative mainly in three spheres: government jobs, admission to public educational institutions and seats in central, state and local legislatures and bodies. Over a period of time, as the government sphere expanded, so did the scope of reservations to include newer spheres like: government housing, government spaces for shops and commercial activities and a number of other small spheres.

The most important is the reservation in government services. Article 16(A) permits reservation in favour of backward castes and in pursuance of this provision, the government has made reservation for SC/ST in proportion to their share of population. There is also reservation in promotion of employed persons. The government services generally include government civil service, public sector undertakings, statutory and semi-government bodies, voluntary agencies, etc. which are under the control of the government or receiving grant-in-aid. However, there are also certain services at the central level that do not come within the purview of reservation policy: these prominently include the defense and the judiciary.

Reservation policy is accompanied by an array of other special provisions designed to facilitate and enhance the probability of the reserved groups to compete for government jobs. These include: relaxation of minimum age for entry into the service, relaxation in minimum standard of suitability within reasonable limits (subject to required minimum qualification), relaxation in fee, and provision for pre-examination training, separate interview for SC/ST persons, provision of expert from SC/ST background on selection committee and others.

Reservation in Education Sector

Second important sphere of reservation is in the education sector. **Article 15** provides the prohibitions of discrimination on grounds of religion, race, caste, sex or place of birth. Article 15(4) empowers the State to make special provisions for the advancement of the SC/STs. Under this provision, the State has reserved seats for SC/ST students in educational institutions: in colleges and universities, including technical, engineering and medical colleges run by the central and state governments and government aided educational institutions. These provisions are supported by a number of financial schemes which include scholarships, special hostels for SC/ST students, concession in fees, grants for books, remedial coaching, etc. **Article 29 (2)** provides full protection of interests of minorities and prohibits discrimination in admissions in educational institutions based on religion, race, caste and languages or any of them. **Article 46** provides specific directives to the state to preferentially promote educational and economic interests of scheduled castes, scheduled tribes and other weaker sections.

Reservation in Legislative Bodies

Third most important sphere of reservation is representation in the central and state legislatures. A legislative reservation is one of the specific and mandatory constitutional provisions dedicated to SC/STs. Under Articles 330, 332 and 334 of the Constitution, seats are reserved for SC/STs in the central and state legislatures in direct proportion to their population size. Similarly, reservation is provided in local level bodies at the district, taluk and village levels. The constitutional provision for reservation in legislative bodies for the SC/STs is complemented by statutory provisions which enhance political participation from the SC/ST population. For instance, they are required to make smaller election deposits.

Implementation and Monitoring

The Central Government has developed administrative mechanisms for regulating, monitoring and implementing the reservation policy and other affiliated programmes. These institutions can be divided into:

(a) ones that are directly involved in regulation (i.e. preparing rules relating to reservation from time to time) and monitoring the fulfillment of the required quotas in the central government services,
(b) those acting as investigative agencies in the event of violation of reservation rules, and
(c) those that are concerned with policy-making and overseeing the overall development of the SC/STs.

Department of Personnel and Training

The Department of Personal and Training (DOPT) is the division located in the Ministry of Personnel, Public Grievance and Pension. It regulates and monitors the reservation policy in government services. Its main function is to enforce or modify the rules, as well as, monitor the fulfillment of quotas as per given rules in central government services. Each ministry and government supported organisation has an administrative unit known as the 'SC/ST Cell' with liaison officers responsible for ensuring that instructions with regard to the implementation of reservation policy are strictly complied with. The DOPT through the administrative heads of the ministries and organisations, monitor and regulate reservations at the central level.

National Commission for Scheduled Castes and Scheduled Tribes

The other important independent organisation is the National Commission for SC and ST. It functions as the investigating agency on specific complaints from SC/ST employees regarding service and promotion matters. The matters may be related to incidences of discrimination, violation of reservation policy, etc. The Commission has the power of functioning as a Civil Court and has the authority to summon an employer for enquiry and action. The Commission also oversees the development of SC/STs, prepares report about their progress annually, which is accordingly, discussed in the Parliament.

Committee of Parliament on Welfare of Scheduled Castes and Scheduled Tribes

Committee of Parliament on Welfare of SCs /STs is another body (comprising of SC/ST Members of Parliament) entrusted with the task of examining the progress regarding the representation of SC/STs. It attempts to make suitable recommendations for effective implementation of policies and programmes.

Ministry of Social Justice and Empowerment and Ministry of Tribal Affairs

At the policy framing level are the Ministry of Social Justice and Empowerment, Ministry of Tribal Affair and Committee of Parliament on Welfare of SCs/STs. The Ministries are the nodal bodies which oversee the task for the development of the SC/STs. The ministries are responsible for the overall development of the SC/ST population. They carry out various schemes related to education, and economic development.

Financial Mechanisms

Funds for the operation of reservation policy and for general development programmes of SC/STs come through the annual budget of the government.

Constitutional Provisions of Special Significance

Article 17 is very noteworthy in emancipation of the depressed class. It provides for the abolition of untouchability and also makes the practice of untouchability an offence punishable in accordance with the law. Some of the following articles in the Indian constitution have become of special significance in the ongoing debate over reservations.

Article 334 provides that reservation of seats and special representation for scheduled castes and scheduled tribes would cease after fifty years.

Article 335 is of special importance because it provides for the consideration into claims of schedules castes and scheduled tribes to be consistent with maintenance of efficiency of administration.

This article, as will be pointed out later, has given significant discretionary and discriminatory powers to the people in positions of authority to the detriment of Dalits.

Impact of Reservation Policy

India is one of the few countries of the world that offers job and educational reservations to the depressed and backward communities of the country, so as to uplift them. This technique has received worldwide praise and generally positive views. The policy of Reservation is special preferential treatment, it is very much necessary to bring equality among unequal. However, this system has its own merits and demerits to offer.

Due to our lack of knowledge and even most of the books depicted Dr Ambedkar as a 'villain' to higher caste people and hero to SC/ST's. But the truth is that he was fighting for equality not only in terms of social aspect, but also in terms of economical aspects and political aspects.

To reduce the gap between rich and poor, low caste and high caste, one religion and other religion, policy of reservation was necessity during the times of independence. India needed an overall growth, wherein every individual no matter what caste he belonged to, no matter what religion he belonged to, no matter how rich or poor he was, giving opportunity everyone, was the only solution.

Nobel Laureate Amartya Sen, in their study (2002), brought out the emerging evidences of the efficient reservation policy as very important factor in Tamil Nadu.

"One observation of major interest, for instance, is that the 'social distance' between medical officer/doctors and patient are almost nil in Tamil Nadu. This is helped by the fact that, large proportion of doctors is SC/ST's and OBC's and Women (about 45-50 per cent of medical officers are women) in Tamil Nadu. In addition, social reform movements, the policies of affirmative action (69 per cent of reservation) have substantially eroded the privileged access of upper castes to medical profession."

Impact of Reservation in Employment Sector[21]

There has been a striking increase in the numbers of SC/ST government employees. In 1960, there were 2,18,000 SC employees which increased to 6,41,000 in 1991, and 5,40,000 in 2003. The corresponding increase in the percentage of SC employees to total government employees increased from 12 per cent in 1956 to about 16 per cent in 2003- fairly proportionate to their percentage share in population. In the case of ST, the numbers increased from about 3,80,000 in 1960 to 2,03,000 in 1991 and further up to 2,11,000 in 2003; a corresponding increase in percentage from 2 per cent in 1960 to 6 per cent in 2003.

If we take the total number of employees in three services – government, public sector undertaking and public sector banks – we will notice that the number of employees in these three services has increased from 7,88,000 to 9,10,000 for SCs and from 2,45,000 to 3,69,000 for STs during the period, 1978-2004. The percentage of total employees also improved between 1978 and 2004; from 15 per cent to 17 per cent in the case of SCs and from 4.7 per cent to 6.9 per cent in the case of STs.

Thus, the share of SC/ST in the government services has improved quite significantly but there are, however, variations between different types of jobs. Generally, reservations are fairly proportionate to the required percentage in group C and D jobs, but unsatisfactory in the case of A and B category jobs, and also in several categories of technical and university jobs, the fulfillment of quotes fell short.

Impact of Reservation in Education

The limited evidence indicates that the student enrollment has increased under reservation. According to the report of *Indian Institute of Dalit Studies 2007*, the proportion of graduate students was around 3.3 per cent for SCs and 0.8 per cent for STs in 1981– which is highly disproportionate to the actual population share of SC/STs. By the late 1990's, the proportion of SC students to the total number of students enrolled rose to 7.8 per cent and for the STs, it rose to 2.7 per cent. This is nevertheless low if look at the actual share of the SC/ST population to the total population – 16 per cent and 8 per cent respectively. Hence, it is difficult to estimate how many SC/ST students have benefited by the reservation policy. One estimate indicates that in 1996/97, roughly 5,10,000 SC students and 1,80,000 ST students were enrolled. Of these, roughly about 2,00,000 students from both the categories may have been enrolled in desirable programmes in higher education where reservation matters.

Therefore, there is a substantial amount of catching up to do in order to reach the required level of 16 per cent and 8 per cent reservation for SC/STs.

Impact of Reservation on Legislature

The constitutional provisions for reservation in public sector employment and educational institutions are mere authorisations empowering the State to make special provisions in favour of discriminated groups. But, the legislative reservations are specifically provided in the Constitution itself.

Legislative seats in each state are reserved in proportion to the population of SC/STs in the state. Thus, in 2004, 75 seats (13.81 per cent) of 543 seats in Lok Sabha were reserved for SCs and 41 seats (7.55 per cent) for STs. Of the total number of seats reserved in all the states' legislative assemblies (Vidhan Sabhas), more than 2000 seats were reserved for SC and STs. In the case of political reservation, two problems continue to receive attention. Firstly, the government has been delaying the updating of the percentage share of seats for SC/STs in the central and state legislatures as per the recent changes in population figures. The present allocation of seats for SC/ST is based on the population census of 1981, whereby the population share of SCs is about 14 per cent and STs about 7.55 per cent. Whereas, according to the latest population census of 2001, their population is about 17 per cent for SCs and 8.50 per cent for STs. Thus, both groups continue to suffer from under-representation in central and state legislatures. Another issue relates to the quality of representation afforded by the SC/ST representatives in the legislative bodies. Of course, it cannot be denied that political reservation does provide substantial quantitative presence of the SC/STs in the legislative bodies, which would otherwise have been completely nil, if not for political reservations. Nonetheless, the activities of SC/ST representatives are presumably microscopic and concentrated on matters that affect these groups only. Also, their effectiveness in representing the interests of the marginalised groups is most evident in their dealings on matters directly related to their welfare. However, there have been studies that have made the observation that there is a problem of low participation, less articulation, less assertiveness and less independence of SC/ST representatives than their colleagues belonging to high castes. To the extent that the problem of quality of representation exists, it may be attributed to the "structural constraints imposed by the arrangement for reserved seats or the method of election under reservation" (Galanter, 1991). Often, a legislator elected through reserved seat, especially a SC, is responsible to and dependent upon a constituency made up overwhelmingly of non-members (or high caste members). To the extent that the legislator is dependent on high caste vote and is thus, obliged to support them; thus a SC legislative candidate suffers from the limitation of not being able to represent fully the interests of SC/STs, who themselves happen to be a minority in most of the reserved constituencies. This arrangement acts as a filter in keeping the divergent interests of these groups from unifying and checks direct and forceful expression of their grievances and interests. It is precisely because of this limitation of political reservation that Ambedkar had suggested an alternative arrangement or method of election of SC/ST representatives, namely 'separate electorate' as against reservation of seats. The separate electorate would have ensured the representation of more independent and representative legislature of SC/STs in legislature.

Reservation in Private Sector – Affirmative Action Policy

One of the general worries about public sector reservation policy in employment and admission to educational Institutions is that it applies to a tiny government and government supported sectors and excludes a large private sector. For instance, in employment, the reservation policy excludes private employment where more than 90 per cent of the SC/ST workforce is engaged; with the result that there is lack of protection against practices of exclusion and discrimination in the private sector. There is notable exclusion in the following sectors – private industrial, services and agricultural. Similarly, the entire private owned educational institutions are excluded from the provision of reservation policy. It is only after the introduction of policy of privatisation and back-door de-reservation of government employment in the early 1990s that the demand for reservation in private sector has picked up. Government should develop a consensus between the government and the private sector for adoption of Affirmative Action Policy for private sector. The informal type of affirmative action policy in the private sector, with a group target approach, has helped the SC/STs to some extent.[22]

Human Development of the Scheduled Castes and Scheduled Tribes

There has been a positive improvement in the human development of SC/STs due to formal and informal affirmative action policies. The positive changes are reflected in the aggregate indicators of human development – income level, employment, social needs like education and health, and ultimately, in poverty. During 1983/84 and 1999/2000, we observed an improvement in the monthly per capita consumption expenditure (proxy indicator for income), literacy rate and incidence of poverty of SC/STs. As mentioned earlier, the share of SC/ST employees in government sector has significantly improved and apparently, it had positive multiplier effects on the social and economic situation of these two disadvantaged groups.

Although there has been some improvement, but it needs to be recognised that the disparities between SC/STs and non-SC/ST have not been reduced substantially so as to bridge the gap to a reasonable level. Consequently, the socially marginalised groups of SC/STs lag behind the non-SC/ST section of the Indian population with respect to attaining the desirable level in human development. For instance, in 2000, the infant mortality rate was higher among the SC/ STs as compared to non-SC/ST. Similarly, compared with non-SC/ST, the literacy rate among the SC/STs is lower by 14 per cent and 21 per cent, respectively. The SC/STs' monthly per capita expenditure is less by about 25 per cent and 34 per cent respectively, as compared with consumption expenditure of non-SC/ST. Again compared with non-SC/ST, the incidence of aggregate poverty is 70 per cent and about 100 per cent higher among the SC/STs respectively. The percentage of under-nourished children among the SC/STs is higher by 23 per cent and 27 per cent, respectively. Finally, the SC/STs' access to public health services, compared with non-SC/ST, is less by 23 per cent and 44 per cent. Thus, despite an improvement at the level of individual indicators, the level of human development among the SC/STs as compared to non-SC/ST in 2000 is relatively lower.

Much has changed for the better after independence and introduction of the constitution as well as reservation policy. Dalit's participation in national polity has increased at a revolutionary level. The election of K. R. Narayanan, a Dalit, as the President of the nation, the election of Mayawati as Chief Minister of most populous state Uttar Pradesh for four terms and a plethora of Dalits elected to cabinets of all federal and state governments, is the evidence of more than symbolic change.

Negative Consequences of Reservations

Some high caste opponents, intellectuals as well as some liberal Dalit supporters also consider that there are some negative effects of reservation policy to the progress of dalits and others.

1. Some people believe that the reservation for minor communities has left India more socially divided than ever. Of course, the reservation exists due to a division between people, but its opponents claim that it deepens the crack of social and economic division.
2. Another demerit of reservation is that, while most of the minor communities have already been secured, new minor communities emerge every waking day. As of now, some cattle-breeding and pastoral communities have been demanding reservation in public job sector and educational institutes.
3. Reservation creates an accommodation of and rewards the sub-maximal efforts by Dalits who enter various competitions.
4. The people who get positions due to reservation are stereotyped as inferior by their colleagues and thereby always are assigned superficial duties which further thwart their personal growth and possible future promotions.
5. The future generations of dalits, or at least those who are relatively free from oppression do not see any examples of in order to emulate. This prevents development of self-confidence and deepens the inferiority complex.

6. The reservations create a mindset in dalits which prefers studies in non-scientific subjects to prepare them for clerical and non-technical jobs which disables them from competing in commerce, growing market of technology and advance crafts. This can only exaggerate their inabilities to participate in the globalised and privatised economy.
7. The reservation, by its potential to promote inefficiency, retards national growth in general. In turn, the inefficient and poor economy can only increase real impoverishment which dalits shoulder the most. As Kuldip Nayer a noted liberal journalist and Member of Parliament says, "Without increasing the total wealth of nation, socialistic system of redistribution despite its apparent fairness, can only distribute poverty and nothing more".
8. Both opponents and supporters of reservations point out that main reason of religious conversion is the search for self-respect and human dignity. The reservations are now available to those who have discarded Hinduism and have become neo-Buddhists, or Sikhs, as long as they declare themselves as scheduled castes on applications. The attraction of reservations keeps this segment of Dalits enslaved to the old identities and also gives extra life to the heinous system of Varna and caste. In the end, ironically, the reservation becomes the hindrance in achieving personal freedom and dignity through religious conversion.
9. Due to new economic policy of privatisation, liberalisation, the governments' ability to provide employment has declined significantly. No one disagrees that this phenomenon will only grow with far greater speed. As a result, Dalit ability to depend on state to provide jobs will suffer a great setback leading to more frustration and discontent along with increased unemployment. Thus, the opponents of reservations believe, that staking future on reservation, dalit will waste precious time without self-development on dangerous and deceptive false hopes.
10. The economic globalisation has changed the rules of competition and success in international sphere. The policy

of government of preferential treatment based on caste will have no authority to compel globally competing companies to adopt any policy that can appear as threat to their competitive edge. Therefore the opponents contend that indefinite dependence on reservation by dalits will create a slippery slide backwards.

11. Reservation policy sends the message to young dalit generation that they really do not have to aim as high as their non-dalit counterparts. This breeds a culture of submaximal goals and compromised efforts. This not only impacts the current generation but also the future ones by limiting their ambitions and inspiration. The opponents rightfully point out that if the culture of merit and excellence is not allowed to grow amongst dalits, many future generations will be lost to inferior performance and mediocre achievements.
12. The occurrence shows the fact that there is severe backlash to the preferential treatment given to dalits. There has been dangerous polarisation of communities in almost all states of the nation. The opponents also believe that if the system of reservations extends further and every caste and community (Muslims and Christians, etc.) claims the share according to their proportion of population, the national integration process will suffer greatly. India, they say, will remain a conglomeration of nations based on caste and ethnic identities.
13. It is very disheartening that our politicians are bent upon creating disharmony among people with the singular motive of sustaining vote-banks. Caste-based reservation in education as well as in jobs is an utterly illogical provision. It is irrational to continue to provide subsidies, age relaxation benefits and career promotions even after the completion of graduation. Rather than achieve equality among all citizens, the prevailing system has ironically created resentment in the minds of lakhs of deserving candidates against the privileged, purportedly 'socially backward classes'. The fact is that reservations based on a system of meritocracy will rankle no one and benefit all in the long run.

Therefore, we can conclude that although the helicopter of empowerment of the minors is flying high and steady, it leaves behind a dusty contrail of social division, stunted development and angry citizens. Theories have proved that although reservation for minorities is a great way to eliminate poverty and discrimination, the excessive number of reservations has led to stunted development of India. While the founding fathers of the Constitution brought in the concept of reservation for a limited period with the noble motive of uplifting those who were discriminated against, thereby providing equality of opportunity, subsequently, politicians watered it down as a means to win elections. The proof of this comes in the form of even more castes and communities clamouring to be classified as BC/SC/ST/minorities. Therefore, the two major national parties must initiate an honest and bold discussion on whether existing reservation policies have been able to achieve their intended purpose. The time has come to revamp the reservation system.

But one should understand why SC/ST need reservation. Even in today's India, outside cities, a SC/ST person is not able to get basic facilities easily. People refuse to rent houses for SC/ST. Racial discrimination is abundant in college hostels and even in schools, leading to suicides/dropouts in many cases. The grandparents of the people of my generation were not even allowed to wear shirt, enter temple, and pass through upper caste people's roads. Without reservation, their quality of life would not have changed one bit. We should not look at the city-born SC/ST people who have misused the reservation who are a minor number compared to the plight of the SC/STs all throughout the nation, especially those who do not live in the cities.

Creamy layer is a debatable topic; I do not have strong opinions on it. However, I will not agree to the total fall of standards because of SC/ST reservation, as depicted by anti-reservation campaigns. In fact every year, the quality of the candidates coming in through reservation is increasing. Look at the minimum cutoff mark level going up every year for SC/STs for example in Tamil Nadu medical entrance exams. However, I believe OBC reservation is purely for votebank politics. People who were the ruler classes and merchant classes should never be allowed to avail benefits as suppressed people.

We can add more regulations to SC/ST reservations by bringing in constraints like that they should not immigrate out of India for the next 10 years as a moral repayment to the society or add creamy-layer etc. Again all these points are debatable. But getting away with the caste (SC/ST) based reservation totally is wrong.

The Hindu social system is liable for the growth and evolution by the policy of reservation. Hindu social system divided into various classes and castes i.e. the upper castes and the lower castes. As a matter of fact, the Hindu social system denied the education to the women, Scheduled Castes and Scheduled Tribes. The education of the women and Scheduled Castes and Scheduled Tribes begun only during the British period with the efforts of Dr B.R. Ambedkar and other social reformers.

The policy of reservation is special preferential treatment, it is very much necessary to bring equality among unequal. The special provisions have been made for the uplift of women, Scheduled Castes and Scheduled Tribes, who are gradually able to compete with the more advanced section of the society. Dr B.R. Ambedkar incorporated the special provisions in the Constitution of India for the advancement of the said classes. Further, Dr B.R. Ambedkar fought against the social injustice and struggled a lot to improve the conditions of women and Scheduled Castes and Scheduled Tribes. These sections of society who were suffering from atrocities, exploitations and injustices since centuries have no doubt benefiftted from the reservation system, yet it would take a long time to bring about a genuine social change, because of compartmentalised caste system and lack of economic equality and social democracy. In addition to it, the society seems to be divided into pro-reservationists and anti-reservationists, which has accentuated the caste consciousness, making caste the biggest hurdle towards social transformation. Further, the corporate sector is raising its voice against reservation in the private sector. However, it must be kept in mind the reservations to SCs/STs is not a charity, it is a national necessity for ensuring equitable development of the nation and to bring about social assimilation as early as possible. To sum up, SCs / STs reservation and subsequent OBC reservation should be understood in socio-economic perspective free from all narrow and sectarian outlook.

Reservations and Nation-Building

Despite certain flaws in the policy of reservations, its greatest utility lies in the building of a healthy nation. It is often said that the state is an organism, as a whole which is more important than its parts. The best state is that which seeks to provide ways and means for the development of its various parts. The happiness of the state does not lie in the happiness of its few rich or privileged sections; but the proper nourishment and growth of all the parts or sections of the society. A state which neglects the development of its weaker or underprivileged classes, would soon find that with a vast majority of its people living as imbeciles, the task of nation-building would soon cripple. As such, it is the duty of the state to see that the progress and development, especially of the weaker classes of the society, lies in providing proper opportunities to them so that they may take active part in the processes of nation-building. The reservations aim to weaken *Varna* system and caste loyalties, so that in the long run social and psychological oneness may develop among the people at all levels. In the absence of social and psychological oneness, the foundations of nation-building would be weak, frail and easily-broken. The policy of reservations is meant to develop a cohesive society. It is a step towards the creation of an egalitarian society. It is the only way to provide social justice to the depressed or marginalised classes. It compels the caste-Hindus to treat the disadvantaged classes on equal footing so that the nation may prosperously organise. The ultimate aim of reservations is to end all types of exploitation and create a reason-oriented social order. The untouchables remaining as untouchables in practice would mean a diseased social order; and a diseased social order is antithetical to nation-building.

The policy of reservations remind us that the state is still an organism, and the whole is greater than the parts. If each part of the body is fresh, the whole is active; and when the whole is active, the natural outcome is a strong nation. The policy of reservations is a clear proclamation stating that the whole is necessarily more significant and hence each part must be well-developed. The depressed must not feel a sense of shame; they must be elevated and uplifted in order to promote the cause of nation-building.

The reservations provide an opportunity to the weaker section of the society to develop their human excellence. It introduces justice into the political system. Human excellence is helpful towards the cultivation of nation-building. The reservations give a chance to men with very different capacities to direct their energies to the task of nation-building.

The state is a moral and legal institution; it must seek the welfare of all, including the suppressed classes. The state must provide for the fulfilment of all men, not mearly of some men. The reservations are meant to bring the depressed classes into the mainstream of the society, building them active and conscious citizens; thus making nation-building a living and sustaining force.

The depressed classes for centuries had lived in pain and servitude. Their servitude was more worse than the slaves of ancient Greece and Rome. Servitude had killed even their spirit of survival. Neglected and exploited by caste-Hindus, the suppressed classes had no meaningful existence. The idea of nation was alien to them. It is for the first time in the history of India that untouchability has been abolished and reservations have been provided to SCs/STs in the fields of education, services and legislatures, thereby an effort is made to assimilate them in the society, despite certain hurdles that still exist. The reservations have given them a new sense of pride and dignity, which is helpful towards nation-building.

In a heterogeneous society with diverse creeds and castes, often antagonistic to each other, what is essential is social change or social revolution. No nation-building is possible without social revolution, aiming towards the realisation of equality and social justice. A ramshackled society, where caste rancours prevail, cannot create a genuine nation; its ills have to be removed through a peaceful social revolution; and to bring into existence a new Man, having a sense of dignity. The policy of reservations for the weaker sections in this sense is a landmark; it is a silent revolution to enhance the cause of human dignity and social justice, thereby to strengthen the forces of nation-building.

The notion of graded inequality or the destruction of equality among the members of the society is dangerous for the growth of nation-building. All along in the history of India, the usurpations by the rich, robbery by the higher castes, and unbridled passions of the caste Hindus, had filled the untouchables with anger, avarice and hatred against them. The centuries old social order had brought the untouchables to the brink of ruin. The new-born social revolution aiming towards the creation of an egalitarian society is slowly, but surely, changing the mental outlook of the caste-Hindus. The policy of reservations for SCs/ STs is a part of this new social revolution, whereby a process of amalgamation between the high and low is proceeding smoothly. The reservations are meant to end the wretched situation of the weaker sections, restore their dignity, give boost to their talents, to end inequality, and to provide them opportunities to mingle with others, thus to usher in a healthy process of nation-building. In reality the reservations are a means to make the depressed one a social Man, living constantly outside himself and to awaken the consciousness of his own existence. The consciousness of his own existence and nation-building are both complimentary and supplementary to each other.

The reservations give primacy to social justice. It is, in fact, meant to remove the deep-rooted evil in our social order. Evil is inequality, social injustice. The task of reservation is therefore the triumph of good over evil. It is identified with the transformation of society – indeed a profound and radical transformation of untouchables whole perspective on their existence. Its purpose is to break the exploitative form of society and to replace it by the free form of ethical and egalitarian community. It is a step where the untouchables can show their full potential in social life.

Though the reservation alone cannot end all ailments and deformities of the social order; it is at least a step – a welcome step – towards the upliftment of 'wretched Man' to the status of 'Social Man'; thus removing, to some extent, the social and psychological barriers that impede nation - building.

References

1. Mulchand, S. Rana : *Reservations in India : Myths and Realities* (New Delhi, Concept Publishing House, 2008), p. 389.
2. Rahul Deeparkar: '*Regervation vs. Reservation: A Dalit Struggle in India*' in Mohammad Shabbir (ed.) Ambedkar on Law, Constitutin, and Social Justice (Jaipur, Rawat Publicatins, 2011), p. 53.

3. P. B. Shalunkhe : (ed) *Chatrapati Shahu the Pillar of Social Democracy*, (Bombay, The Education Department Government of Maharashtra Publication, 1994,) p.144.
4. Ghurye, G.S: *Caste and Race in India*, (Mumbai, Popular Prakashan, 2008) p. 287.
5. P.B. Shalunkhe, p. 151.
6. V. A. Pai Panandiker (ed.): *The Politics of Backwardness: Reservation Policy in India* (New Delhi, Konark Publishers Pvt. Ltd, 1997), p. 94.
7. Vinay Chandra Mishra (ed.): *Reservation Crisis in India*, (New Delhi, The Bar Council of India Trust, 1991) p. 276.
8. Report of the Committee on Untouchability, Economic and Educational Development of the Scheduled Castes and Connected Documents (1969), (Department of Social Welfare, Government of India), p. 3.
9. Mulchand, S. Rana: *Reservations in India: Myths and Realities*, (New Delhi, Concept Publishing Company, 2008) pp. 18-19.
10. K. S. Pandya and Jayashree Mahapatra: *Reservation Policy in India* (New Delhi, Ashish Publishing House, 1988) p. 18.
11. Shyamlal and K. S. Sexena (eds.): *Ambedkar and Nation Building* (Jaipur, Rawat Publishers 1998).
12. V. T. Rajshekar: *Separate Electorate and Separate settlement* (Bangalore, Dalit Sahitya Academy, 1996), p. 5.
13. S. K. Singh and A. K. Singh: *OBC, Woman Status and Educational Empowerment*, (New Delhi, Icon Publisher, 1995) p. 20.
14. K. S. Pandya on Jayashree Mahapatra, p. 19.
15. V. T. Rajshekar : *Separate Electorate and Separate Settlement*, p. 18.
16. D. R. Jatava : *Ambedkar : The Prime Mover*, (Jaipur, ABD Publisher, 2004), p. 32.
17. Shyamlal and K.S. Sexena , p. 66.
18. Mulchand S. Rana, p. 19.
19. *Ibid.*
20. Sukhadeo Thorat and Chittaranjan Senapati: *Reservation in Employment, Education and Legislature – Status and Emerging Issues*, (Working Paper Series, Indian Institute of Dalit Studies, Vol. II, 2007), p. 5.
21. *Ibid.*, p. 11.
22. *Ibid.*, 22.

CHAPTER–7

Gandhi, Nehru and Ambedkar

The twentieth century India had produced a luminous band of leaders whose contributions in the freedom struggle of the country and nation-building activities had been of a high order. The striking thing about modern India had been that the men who made its history also wrote most authoritatively about it. The country's leading politicians were its leading political thinkers. This was especially true of the trinity of Mohandas K. Gandhi, Jawaharlal Nehru and B. R. Ambedkar. Ramachandra Guha states:

> 'The first was the father of Indian nationalism who, between the 1920s and 1940s, forged a popular, countrywide movement against British Colonial rule. The second was the architect of the modern Indian nation-state serving as Prime Minister from the nation's birth in August 1947 until his death in May 1964. The third was the great leader of the country's oppressed castes who also oversaw, as the country's first Law Minister, the drafting of the Indian Constitution, which came into effect on 26 January 1950. But even as they fought and struggled, led and governed, Gandhi, Nehru and Ambedkar wrote at great length about the world they saw and shaped.'[1]

Despite certain dissimilarities in their ideas, outlook and approaches to the various issues, problems and challenges that confronted the country during the period, they were undoubtedly great patriots and men of integrity. Gandhi wore a loin-cloth but was bare-bodied, chest upwards; Nehru wore tightly buttoned-up *Achkan* decorated with a rose flower, and a tight-fitting trousers, and a Gandhi cap on his head; and Dr Ambedkar wore a suit and clasped a book in his hand. Mahatma Gandhi was called as the Father of the Nation; whereas Nehru and Dr Ambedkar were regarded as architects of modern India. Together they brought a nation to freedom and laid the underpinnings for the world's largest democracy.

Nehru venerated Gandhi, and Gandhi showered great affection on him. The two men differed in temperament and attitudes to modernity. Nehru was indifferent to religion; Gandhi believed deeply in his own version of God. Nehru believed that industrialisation was the only solution to the endemic poverty of India; Gandhi called instead for the renewal of the village economy. Nehru had great faith in the powers of the modern state to uplift and reform society; Gandhi was sceptical of State power, trusting instead the conscience and will of individuals and communities.[2]

Ambedkar, like his great rival, Gandhi, had multiple agendas as well as multiple careers. He was, at various times, a lawyer, teacher, legislator, educational organiser, party builder and cabinet minister. Through all these roles and assignments he continued to be a prolific writer. He published important books on many topics, including federation, theology and philosophy, finance, language, constitutionalism and, not least, the sociology, politics and history of the caste system.[3] Moral vision, political skill, legal acumen: these were all brought together by him in the framing of the Indian Constitution. This was a coming together of what Granville Austin has called the 'national' and 'social' revolutions, respectively. The national revolution focused on democracy and liberty; whereas the social revolution focused on emancipation and equality, which tradition the scriptures had withheld from women and low castes.[4]

Mahatma Gandhi

Mahatma Gandhi (1869-1948) was an inspired teacher and a prophet. He was a Hindu of the *vaisya* caste – neither high nor low –who had been partly educated in England. He had not lost his Hindu personality because of his western education. On the one hand, he could talk to westernised nationalists in their own political language, and on the other, he could be seen to be the expression of Hindu traditional values. He was 'idealistic, quirky, quixotic and determined, a cross between a saint and a ward politician; like the best crossbreeds, he managed to distill the qualities of both and yet transcend their contradictions.' His way of thinking was neither Hobbesian nor Comtean; it was more akin to Socrates and Buddha, and he developed his ideas on the basis of observation, experimentation and situatedness. His deepest feelings were relentlessly directed towards the search and realisation of truth. The gospel of truth and creative non-violence were central in the thought of Mahatma Gandhi. His was a fusion of the teachings of *Gita* and Buddhism, with the teachings of Thoreau, Ruskin and Tolstoy – thus he had tried to cultivate a cultural synthesis of the East and the West. He accepted a naive, but deeply profound concept of theological determinism of history, but it was not a mere fatalism. He refused to submit to a fatalistic attitude. Being an ardent advocate of the activism of the *Gita,* he combined an unwavering faith in the supremacy of God with the insistence on constant actions. His unique method of resistance through civil disobedience, allied to a talent for organisation, gave the Indian nationalist movement both a saint and a strategist.

To a century fraught with violence, Gandhi had offered an alternative, his doctrine of *Ahimsa* or non-violence. God-obsessed Gandhi had recognised in his frail silhouette, in the instinctive brilliance of his acts, the promise of a Mahatma – a Great Soul – and had led the movement of liberation. He was capable of rallying all the warring elements in Indian nationalism. He was a man who exercised almost hypnotic influence upon the diverse of characters, and his main effect on them was to drain away any revolutionary fervour they have had. He was an unerringly shrewd judge of men and events. He was indisputably one of the galvanic figures of his century. To his followers, he was a saint. To the British bureaucrats he was a conniving politician. He was a strange blend of great moral principles and quirky obsessions. The three great aims of his life were Indian freedom, the unity of his people – Hindus and Muslims – and the betterment of the lot of the untouchables. For these three goals, he was willing to suffer and die.

Gandhi's seminal book is 'Hind Swaraj' written in 1908, during his return voyage from London. This concise book teaches the gospel of love in place of hate. It replaces violence with self-sacrifice. It pits soul force against brute force. It is a severe condemnation of modern civilisation. It expounds the twin principles of truth and non-violence. Gandhi believed that 'if India adopted the doctrine of love as an active part of her religion and introduced it in her politics; Swaraj would descent upon India from heaven. But I am painfully aware that that event is far off as yet.'[5]

Gandhi's advice to the new ministers was offered in short sentences:

> 'Be humble. Be forbearing. Now you will be tested through and through. Beware of power; power corrupts. Do not let yourselves be entrapped by its pomp and pageantry. Remember, you are in office to serve the poor in India's villages.'[6]

Gandhi, indeed, was 'a century's conscience,' who led India to liberty. He was the 'discoverer of satyagraha', the one wanting to remove every tear from every eye. He was the pioneer of religious pluralism and dissenter from modernity.

Jawaharlal Nehru

Jawaharlal Nehru (1889-1964) was a moody, idealistic intellectual who felt an almost mystical empathy for the toiling peasant masses; an aristocrat who had passionate socialist convictions, and a product of Harrow and Cambridge where he studied for seven years, including the years at Inner Temple in London. He had imbibed most of the prejudices of Harrow and Cambridge, and in his likes and dislikes he was perhaps more an Englishman than an Indian. He was a queer mixture of East and West, out of place everywhere, at home nowhere. During his stay in England, he had imbibed the traditions of British humanist liberalism. He subscribed to the general philosophical ethos whose protagonists were J. S. Mill, Gladstone and Lord Morley. He was influenced by the writings of Bernard Shaw and Bertrand Russell. With his gentle charm, elegant manners, rapidly expanding culture, he had enjoyed an extraordinary social success wherever he went. He moved easily through the drawing-rooms of English society absorbing with the sponge of his still malleable personality the values and mannerisms he found there. So complete was the transformation wreaked by those seven years in England that, on his return to Allahabad, his family and friends found him completely de-Indianised.

Although a man of action, he had the capacity for some kind of philosophic detachment and like a thinking introvert he had often been tormented by doubts and quests. He was one of the chief figures who brought the independence struggle to a successful termination. Among Gandhi's great lieutenants in the struggle for freedom, Nehru occupied a pre-eminent place.

An idealist immersed in the doctrines of social revolution, Nehru dreamed of reconciling on the soil of India his two political passions: the parliamentary democracy of England and the economic socialism of Karl Marx. Under the cotton *khadi* he wore in deference to the dictates of Congress, he remained the quintessential English gentleman. In a land of mystics, he was a cool rationalist. He was a publicly declared agnostic in the most intensely spiritual land, and he never ceased to proclaim the horror the word 'religion' inspired in him. Nehru despised India's priests, her 'Sadhus', her chanting monks and pious Sheikhs. They had only served, he felt, to impede her progress, deepen her divisions and ease the task of her foreign rulers. He was a superb orator and writer, a man who treasured words as a courtesan jewels. His cool, pragmatic mind had rejected almost all of Gandhi's great moves: Civil disobedience, the Salt March, Quit India; but his heart had told him to follow the Mahatma and his heart, he later admitted, had been right. The Mahatma had made it clear that it was on his shoulders that he wished his mantle to fall.

M. J. Akbar has called Nehru 'the agnostic visionary of modern India', and further states:

> 'He was an idealist, and his ideas commanded an empire far larger than the India he ruled for eighteen years. He liked being called a philosopher-statesman in the Platonic mould, though he would hasten to add that his advice to philosophers was to cease philosophising and get down to work. But behind whatever Jawaharlal did was an ideology, a pattern of ideas which he believed were in the best interests of not just his nation but also the world... Nehru's heart was filled with old-fashioned love; it was a vast reservoir of emotion for his country and its people, which burst often into words, actions, reactions. And Nehru's mind was steeped in new ideas – in science, in political theory and in a secular interpretation of history.'[7]

Nehru was a proponent of westernisation and modernisation, but at the same time he was careful to preserve the past heritage and diverse cultures of the country. He made science and technology the handmaiden of economic progress. He had a great regard for the institutions fundamental to a democratic system, such as, the Parliament, the judiciary, the press and the Opposition. His biographer, Michael Brecher, writes:

> 'Nehru has provided a Symbol of unity at a time of great stress. He has laid the foundations of a working parliamentary democracy. He has fashioned the machinery for planning. He provided the philosophy for India's new Constitution with its emphasis on individual rights and the ideal of a secular and equalitarian society... And he has begun the task of social reform.'[8]

Dr B.R. Ambedkar

Dr B.R. Ambedkar (1891-1956) had studied at the Columbia University, London School of Economics, Bonn University and the Inner Temple. In his school and college education in India, he had experienced the frustrations and humiliations of being born in the untouchable caste – the Mahar community. His advanced education was in the field of economics. His writings on Indian sociology touching upon the problems of Shudras, the untouchables, the Hindu social order, etc. breathe a note of deep realism and are characterised by bitter denunciation of the old ancient law-givers. The concept of God, the immortality of the soul, the metaphysical spiritual monism of the Upanishad, the four-fold Varna system, the Vedantic metaphysics and the cry of 'Go back to the Vedas', all appeared to Dr Ambedkar as a worthless cant. Based on 'graded inequality', the Vedantic metaphysics had been an invitation to decay and disintegration of the Hindu society. The philosophy of Hindu spirituality, revival of old scriptures, and the romantic longing for the spirit of the past, were regarded by Dr Ambedkar as unreasonable and ridiculous. The highest reality for him was neither a metaphysical unknowable nor a transcendental vision. To him there was only one naked truth, that is Man is supreme. He propounded a philosophy of humanism, whose roots were not in dogma and renunciation, but in rationalism and empiricism. He held that a true religion should have its roots in the problems of life; its theories should operate as instruments of reconstructing society; and it should emanate from the nature and challenges of human society. The key feature of his ideology is social humanism, aiming to bring down the walls of exclusivity and meant to promote more open, liberal and fraternal values. A pragmatic and practical man, he dedicated his life to the service and emancipation of the downtrodden. He belonged to the galaxy of prophets, who showed the courage of the heart, the strength of the mind, and the reason of the conscience for the happiness and interest of the many, and of the aspirations and claims to equality of the so-called untouchables.

Through the liberation movements, such as Mahad *Satyagraha* (1927) and Kalaram temple-entry struggle (1930), Ambedkar attempted to change the Hindu mindset. The aim of Mahad S*atyagraha* was to unfurl 'the banner of equality' and to smash the 'steel frames of the caste system.' He consigned *Manusmriti* to flames on December 25, 1927, which act was a symbolic protest against the unjust social order. It was a revolt against graded inequality which nurtured the spirit of social segregation and separation.

In the early twenties of the twentieth century, Dr Ambedkar emerged as a promising leader to break the centuries old shackles and liberate the untouchables from the age-old bondage of the Hindu society. He did never deter from his noble goal of liberating his fellowmen from slavery and misery. He was a symbol of revolt against all the oppressive features of Hindu society. He brought a new awakening and a sense of social significance and confidence among the deprived and dispossessed section of the society, who regarded him as their saviour.

Historical Sociology

Gandhi, Nehru and Ambedkar differed in their views on the concept of historical sociology.

Gandhi accepted theological determinism. He said, 'Nothing can happen but by His will expressed in His eternal, changeless law which is He.' God signifies an unchanging and living law. The great prophets through their austerities provide to mankind a faint glimpse of that law. He believed that 'not a leaf moves without sanction from the divine.' But divine determinism in Gandhi never degenerated into fatalism because he was a strong advocate of the strenuous activism and energies of the Gita. His whole life was full of ceaseless actions; all inspired by the vision of a spiritual whole which imparted a higher meaning to his diverse actions as a social worker, a political leader and a moral prophet. Thus, Gandhi 'combined a faith in the supremacy of God with the insistence on constant actions."[9]

Nehru rejected Gandhi's concept of divine determinism of history. He wrote: "A belief in an absolute determinism seems to me to lead inevitably to complete inaction, to death in life." As such, the spiritual or divine interpretation of history was contrary to Nehru's philosophy. He recognised the role of objective forces, the economic and situational factors in his concept of historical sociology. His concept of historical sociology was thus rooted in science. In addition to, he recognised the role of heroes in history and gave instances of the creative role of men in history like Gandhi and Lenin.

Ambedkar had studied theories of history, analysed them, and formulated his concept that 'history is the biography of great man.' He rejected the notion of spiritual determinism or the manifestation of a divine teleology. He regarded the theological interpretation of history as unreasonable. Almost entirely, it was an indirect way to glorify Vedic Hinduism, of which Ambedkar was a staunch opponent.

Ambedkar had studied the concepts of Gobineau, Buckle, Spengler, Rousseau and Karl Marx on history. The principles of race, environment, culture, anthropology and conflict of classes expounded by the said thinkers, respectively, contained some element of truth, but that was not the whole truth, argued Ambedkar. He pointed out that there was a basic flaw in these theories of history. They emphasised the role of impersonal forces and considered such forces as everything and thereby neglected a vital factor of Man that had been the prime mover in history.

Instead of Gandhian concept of divine determinism, Ambedkar upheld that Man is the pre-eminent and the most dominant factor in the making of history. Even the effects of impersonal forces depend on Man. The deciding agent of history is Man, not God. He writes: "Flint may not exist everywhere. But where it does exist, it needs man to strike flint against flint to make fire."[9]

Ambedkar's notion of history thus stood in marked contrast to Gandhi. He discarded the Gandhian concept of theological determinism of history and, in its place put the notion of Man, who is the primary factor in the shaping and moulding of history. Man alone acts for, manages and manipulates history; and his role is crucial and decisive.

Untouchability

There were some ideological differences between Ambedkar and Mahatma Gandhi regarding their approach to the problem of the untouchables. For Ambedkar the cause of the untouchables was the first and foremost as he had taken a vow "to try his utmost to do away with the abominable thraldom and inhuman injustice under which the class, into which he was born, had been groaning". But, for Gandhi it was only one of the problems.

Ambedkar was of the opinion that the problem of the depressed classes was a political problem. On 20th November 1930, while emphasising this point in the Round Table Conference, he said:

> 'We are often reminded that the problem of the depressed classes is a social problem and that its solution lies elsewhere than in politics. We take strong exception to this view. We hold that the problem of the depressed classes will never be solved unless they get political power in their hands. If this is true, and I do not think that the contrary can be maintained then the problem of the depressed classes is, I submit, a political problem and must be treated as such.'[11]

Gandhi, like Ambedkar, abhorred untouchability. He considered it 'the greatest blot on Hinduism', and found it repugnant to reason and to the instinct of pity or love. While Gandhi wanted complete eradication of untouchability for emotional integration of Hindu society, Ambedkar was for abolition of *Varna* structure of the Hindu social order.[12]

During the first Round Table Conference, Ambedkar favoured separate electorate for the oppressed classes; while Gandhi (Second R.T.C) strongly opposed it on the plea that the move would disintegrate the Hindu society. Gandhi went for an indefinite hunger strike from September 20, 1932, against the decision of the then British Prime Minister, J. Ramsay MacDonald, granting Communal award to the depressed classes in the Constitution for governance of British India. In view of the mass upsurge generated in the country to save the life of Gandhi, Ambedkar was compelled to soften his stand. The result was the Poona Pact (September 24, 1932) wherein the principle of reservation of seats for the depressed classes and the joint electorates were agreed upon by Gandhi and Ambedkar both.

Like Gandhi, Nehru also believed that the hearts of the majority caste Hindus should be changed through education. The attitudes and actions of the caste Hindus towards the depressed classes should slowly change. Education would lead to increased awareness and social consciousness among the caste Hindus and the depressed classes. His educating process, like Gandhi, emphasised love and fellowship among the Indians.

Ambedkar was not satisfied with the efforts made by Mahatma Gandhi to remove untouchability. On 8th August, 1930, he declared at Nagpur:

> 'Great as has been his (Gandhi) moral support he has contrived to translate very little of it into practice, having regard to his personal influence and his pecuniary resources. Every year he goes on a tour to make collections for his spinners. Has he ever set out on a crusade against untouchability.'[13]

Ambedkar thus found a gap between the theory and practice of Gandhian ideas so far as the abolition of untouchability was concerned. He held that Gandhi made no genuine effort to remove the stigma of untouchability.

Further, Ambedkar believed that it would take years to abolish untouchability in practice. Speaking on the Third Report of the SC/ST Commissioner in the Rajya Sabha on 6 September 1954, he said:

> 'What is untouchability? Let us understand it very carefully. Untouchability, so far as I understand it, is a kind of a mental disease of Hindus...It is a mental twist; every Hindu believes that to observe untouchability is the right thing.... I cannot see how you blame the Hindus. For thousands of years, by the teaching of this dirty law they have got inculcated in their mind the doctrine that untouchability is a most sacred thing... He must not touch this, he must not touch that, he must not eat this, he must not eat

> that, etc....That is the position and all that we can do is to see that untouchability which, as I said, is a mental twist of the Hindus does not protrude so much into public life as to involve the civil liberties of the people.'[14]

Dr Ambedkar therefore thought that the evil itself would take years and years to vanish, for it was a question of 'mental twist'. But 'there was no reason why we should not strongly agitate for seeing, whether untouchability goes or not, that the social, economic, political and constitutional rights of the Scheduled Castes are fully protected.'

Being a deeply religious person Gandhi did not use the expression mental twist but called it a sin embedded in the inner core of a Hindu. The two expressions signified the same thing. He knew eradication of this evil was not alone a matter of some constitutional or socio-economic measures. The analysis and the solution of both Gandhi and Ambedkar were similar.[15]

The appraisal of both of them differed from the opinion of Gandhi's close intellectual colleague, Jawaharlal Nehru, with his pre-occupation with the concept of 'the foundation of economic relations and superstructure based on it.' That close colleague of Gandhi, Nehru had as late as 1952 grandly declared.

> 'I do not recognise that there is such a problem as that of the untouchables. There is a general problem of the economically poor and the problem of the untouchables is a part of that problem. It will take its place and receive its attention along with the other problems. There is no occasion, no purpose in bestowing any special thought upon it.'[16]

Non-violence

Non-violence was the sum and substance, the supreme creed of Gandhi's life. It was the symbol of moral and spiritual strength for him. He wrote:

> 'Non-violence is the first article of my faith. It is also the last article of my creed.'

Gandhi regarded non-violence as the imperative duty of the *satyagrahi* to make endless endeavours for the realisation of truth.

He considered non-violence as the strongest force known. It was a force of the subtlest kind. It was the mighty force that could be used against the most powerful government.

However, Nehru did not go as far as Gandhi in the acceptance of the creed of *Ahimsa*. Even in the days of the freedom struggle, he accepted non-violence only as a policy and never as a creed. But he supported non-violence on pragmatic considerations. He stated that violence could not provide any real solution to the problems of man; it only provided the semblance of solution. He hoped that a lasting solution could be brought about only by the methods of persuasion, conciliation, tolerance and negotiations. This belief in the potency of the techniques of peace was indicative of the subtle but deep influence of Gandhi on Nehru.

Ambedkar, too, believed in non-violent agitation. His temple entry *satyagraha* in 1930, in the historic town of Nasik, was totally non-violent. He also upheld non-violent, peaceful social change. But non-violence was neither the first article of his faith nor the last article of his creed as it was with Mahatma Gandhi. Gandhi had raised the concept of non-violence to lofty heights, but for Ambedkar it was more a realistic technique than a creed.

Modern Civilisation

The views of Gandhi and Ambedkar on modern or western civilisation were antithetical to each other. Gandhi challenged the foundations of modern civilisation. He disliked the technological, materialistic and lustful aspects of modern western civilisation. Apart from being exploitative of the weaker sections; it was equivalent to darkness and disease. He prophesied the doom of western civilisation and firmly held that non-violence could provide a healing tonic to modern civilisation. He opposed large-scale industrialism and mechanisation, and preferred small-scale industries. He had no love for giant machinery. Gandhi loved Indian civilisation. He wrote:

> 'The tendency of the Indian civilisation is to elevate the moral being, that of the Western civilisation is to propagate immorality. The latter is godless; the former is based on a belief in God. So understanding and so believing, it behoves every lover of India to

> cling to the old Indian civilisation, even as a child clings to the mother's breast.' [17]

Gandhi believed that the civilisation that India has evolved is not to be beaten in the world. He said:

> 'Nothing can equal the seeds sown by our ancestors. Rome went, Greece shared the same fate; the might of the Pharaohs was broken; Japan has become westernised; of China nothing can be said; but India is still, somehow or other, sound at the foundation…and that is her glory.'[18]

In contrast to Gandhi, Ambedkar thought that machinery and modern civilisation were indispensable for emancipating man from leading the life of a brute, and for providing him with leisure and making a life of culture possible. He proclaimed:

> 'The slogan of a democratic society must be machinery and more machinery, civilisation and more civilisation.'[19]

Nehru and Gandhi differed in temperament and attitudes to modern civilisation. Ramchandra Guha writes:

> 'Nehru thought that industrialisation was the only solution to the endemic poverty of India; Gandhi called instead for the renewal of village economy. Nehru had great faith in the powers of the modern state to uplift and reform society; Gandhi was sceptical of state power, trusting instead the conscience and will of individuals and communities.'[20]

Like Gandhi, the influence of Indian civilisation was there upon Nehru, despite his western education. He preferred social change not through violent or repressive means, but through peaceful and democratic means without sacrificing the roots of the Indian traditions. In a broadcast to the nation on 3 June 1947, Nehru acknowledged:

> 'The India of geography, of history and tradition, the India of our minds and hearts, cannot change.'[21]

In his Azad memorial Lectures delivered in February 1959 in Delhi, Nehru reiterated:

> 'I have often wondered that if our race forgot the Buddha, the Upanishads and the great epics, what then will it be like? It would

be uprooted and would lose the basic characteristics which have clung to it and given it distinction throughout these long ages. India would then cease to be India.'[22]

Nehru believed that the tradition of India had always been one of synthesis – a singular ability to absorb the culture of others and assimilate it without losing her own identity. But Ambedkar was critical of Vedic traditions because it was based on *Varna* system and graded inequality.

Ambedkar had opted for Buddhism because it was built on the foundations of liberty, equality, fraternity, morality and professed scientific, rational and humanistic outlook; but he while selecting a religion for himself and his followers chose 'the least harmful way for the country.' He chose Buddhism because it was a part and parcel of *Bhartiya* culture. He said: "I have taken care that conversion will not harm the traditions, the culture and history of this land."

Religion

Since Gandhi believed in truth and non-violence, he accepted the creative force of religion in human history. He accepted the spiritual and moral essence of Hinduism which according to him was the essence of all the great religions of mankind. True religion implied an emphasis on the moral values of man as spirit. As soon as the moral basis was lost one ceased to be religious. He did not identify religion with any creedal, dogmatic theology. To him, it meant a recovery of divine faith. It implied the cooperative adherence to the laws of God by the members of the society. Hence Gandhi said: "To try to root out religion itself from society is a wild-goose chase. And were such an attempt to succeed, it would mean the destruction of society."

Religion provided the dynamic impetus to Gandhi's actions and life. He was essentially a religious man in quest of *Moksha* – redemption and emancipation of the soul from the clutches of *Maya*. He wished to cultivate a true religious attitude in the spirit of the *Gita*. He pursued the path of *Karmayoga*, meaning the disinterested pursuit of one's obligations and duties, signifying a cosmic and spiritual awareness. He considered religion essential to tame the savage and brute instincts of man and thereby bind man to God and man to man. That is why Gandhi talked of the religious basis of political. It was this concept of religion as dynamic altruism that Gandhi wanted to make the basis of transformed social and political action.

Ambedkar too regarded religion as essential in man's life. But he did not accept the spiritual and moral essence of Hinduism, because it contained the system of rank and gradation, thereby upholding the principle of inequality. He wrote:

> 'A new life cannot enter a body that is dead. New life can enter only in a new body. The old body must die before a new body can come into existence and a new life can enter into it. To put it simply, the old must cease to be operative before the new can begin to enliven and to pulsate. This is what I meant when I said you must discard the authority of the *Shastras* and destroy the religion of the *Shastras*.'[23]

Ambedkar wanted religion but did not want hypocrisy in the name of religion. He considered religion an influence or force suffused through the life of each individual moulding his character, determining his actions and reactions, his likes and dislikes. He proclaimed that 'religion is for man and not man for religion.' Religion, for him, was a matter of principles only, not a matter of rules. At the moment 'religion degenerates into rules it ceases to be religion, as it kills responsibility which is the essence of a truly religious act.' He upheld that religion must be judged by social standards based on social ethics. No other standard would have any meaning if religion is held to be a necessary good for the wellbeing of the people. He wrote:

> 'Man cannot live by bread alone. He has a mind which needs food for thought. Religion instils hope in man and drives him to activity.'[24]

Ambedkar held that 'religion and slavery are incompatible.' Religion if it is to function must be in accord with reason which is merely another name for science. It must recognise the fundamental tenets of liberty, equality and fraternity. Unless a religion recognises these three fundamental principles of social life, religion will be doomed.

Gandhi regarded morality and adherence to the laws of God as the essence of religion; whereas Ambedkar believed that 'as a matter of truth, morality has no place in religion.' Morality comes in only wherein man comes in relation to man. He wrote:

> 'Every religion preaches morality but morality in not the root of religion. It is a wagon attached to it. It is attached and detached as the occasion requires. The action of morality in the functioning of religion is therefore, casual and occasional.'[25]

Religion, according to Ambedkar, other than Buddhism concentrated on the problems of the Souls, of worship, but they forgot man. He added that the Buddha alone when pressed for his views on the souls, said, "Such discussions are unprofitable. Nobody can prove the existence of the souls. I am concerned with man. I am concerned with establishing righteousness between man and man."[26]

Ambedkar rejected casteism and religious fanaticism. He pondered over the questions: What is religion for? Why is it necessary? According to him, the true definition of religion, meaningful and agreeable to all is: 'That which governs people is Religion? Accepting this definition, he stated that religion means the rules imposed for the maintence of society. But what should be the nature of rules which govern a society. He regarded this question more important than that of definition. Because the question which is religion and which is not religion, does not depend on its definition but on the motive and nature of the rules that bind and govern a society. What should be the nature of real religion? What should be the relation between a man and society? Ambedkar stated that the modern social philosophers have postulated three answers to this question. Some have said that the ultimate goal of society is to achieve happiness for the individual. Some say the society exists for development of the inherent qualities and energies of man and help him to develop his self. However, some claim that the chief object of social organisation is not the development or happiness of the individual but the creation of an ideal society. The concept of Hindu religion, he said, is however, very different from all these concepts. There is no place for an individual in Hindu religion. The Hindu religion is constituted on a class-concept. Hindu religion does not teach how an individual should behave with another individual. He stated:

> 'A religion which does not recognise the individual is not personally acceptable to me. Although society is necessary for the individual,

mere social welfare cannot be the ultimate goal of religion. According to me, individual welfare and progress (individual development) should be the real aim of the religion… A religion in which an individual has no importance is not acceptable to me. The Hinduism does not recognise the importance of an individual, and therefore it is not acceptable to me.'[27]

Ambedkar was unwilling to accept a religion in which one class alone has a right to gain knowledge, another has only a right to use arms, the third one to trade and the fourth, only to serve. He said:

'Everyone needs knowledge. Everybody needs arms. Everyone wants money. The religion, which forgets this, and with an intention to educate a few, keeps the rest in darkness, is not a religion but a conspiracy to keep the people in mental slavery.'[28]

As such, for Ambedkar Hindu religion, which is based on *Chaturvarna* is not beneficial for the untouchables. He stated that the basic idea underlying religion is to create an atmosphere for the spiritual development of an individual. A true religion is meant for the uplift of an individual; it must be based on sympathy, equality and liberty.

Nehru was agnostic. He was a Hindu, but not a temple going Hindu. He had great faith in secularism. Secularism was, indeed, an idea that underlay the very foundation of his thought. He insisted that the multiple faiths of India can and must co-exist peaceably in a free nation. The French writer Andre Malraux once asked Jawaharlal Nehru what had been his 'greatest difficulty since independence.' Nehru replied: "Creating a just state by just means." Then he added, "Perhaps, too, creating a secular state in a religious country."[29]

Ramachandra Guha writes:

'Nehru was indifferent to religion; Gandhi believed deeply in his own version of God.'[30]

Democracy

Gandhi was a critic of western democratic politics. It was full of contradictions. It believed in limitless expansion of capitalism and this resulted in exploitation of the weaker peoples.

Gandhi stressed that non-violence alone could lead to true democracy. Democracy and violence could not be reconciled. He wanted India to evolve 'True Democracy.' His true democracy meant: (i) complete non-violence; (ii) scrupulous exactness in dealing with opponents; (iii) removal of economic inequalities so that the weakest should have the same opportunity as the strongest; (iv) growth of village industries; (v) removal of untouchability; (vi) communal harmony; (vii) compulsory primary education; and (ix) decentralisation of power.

For Gandhi, 'true democracy is not inconsistent with a few persons representing the spirit, the hope and the aspirations of those whom they claim to represent.' The claim to represent should not sound undemocratic. He meant that the claim to represent was no more than the right to serve and to suffer for the common good.

Like Gandhi, Ambedkar was equally concerned for democracy, but his emphasis was that democracy should be in form as well as in fact. He wrote that political democracy would be meaningless in the absence of economic and social democracy. He laid down certain conditions for the success of democracy: (i) glaring inequalities to be removed; (ii) the existence of strong opposition; (iii) equality before law and in administration; (iv) observance of constitutional morality; (v) functioning of moral order in society; and (vi) the requirement of public conscience.

Ambedkar held the view that if the above conditions remain unfulfilled democracy would remain a top-dressing in our country. He considered that democracy was not a form of government; it was essentially a form of society. The social organisation must be free from rigid social barriers. To this aspect of social democracy, Ambedkar gave the highest priority. Social or economic evils, if not removed in a democracy, it is likely to meet revolution or decay.

Nehru was in favour of democracy. He pleaded that for the success of political democracy, economic democracy is essential. Though he accepted democracy as the best form of government, but still wondered whether:

> 'The quality of men who are selected by these modern democratic methods of adult franchise gradually deteriorates because of lack

> of thinking and the noise of propaganda.... He (the voter) reacts to sound and to the din, he reacts to repetition and he produces either a dictator or a dumb politician who is insensitive. Such a politician can stand all the din in the world and still remain standing on his two feet and, therefore, he gets selected in the end because the others have collapsed because of the din.'[31]

Socialism

Gandhian's theory of socialism was idealistic; whereas Ambedkar theory was realistic. Gandhi advocated equality of wages, the trusteeship and spiritual socialism. In his concept of socialism, the prince and the peasant, the poor and the rich, the employer and employee were to be treated equally. But this socialism was not to be attained by conquest of political power by an organised party. It would be attained through individual purification and non-violent means.

Ambedkar had no illusions. Realism was the keynote of his socialism. He advocated State socialism in the field of industry and also ownership in agriculture with a collectivised method of cultivation. He preferred nationalisation of insurance. He wanted revolutionary changes in tenancy laws. About his two-point plan of socialism, Ambedkar wrote:

> 'One is that it proposes state socialism in important fields of economic life. The second special feature of the plan is that it does not leave establishment of state socialism to the will of the legislature, it establishes state socialism by the law of the constitution, and thus, makes it unalterable by any act of the legislature and the executive.'[32]

Nehru's mission was to create a new society based on democracy and socialism. He believed that democracy alone could nurture the creative spirit of human beings. But if democracy could not bring about a release from poverty of large masses of human beings, then the creative spirit would only function in a few. If poverty and low standards continued then democracy, for all its fine institutions and ideals, would cease to be a liberating force. He believed that political democracy was not enough. It must develop into economic democracy also.

To achieve the above aims and to usher in a new society, Nehru implemented the policy of nationalisation of key industries, mixed economy and state-controlled undertakings. The private sector continued to have an important place, but he put the major industries in the public sector.

Nehru's policy of mixed economy formed the core of the Five Year Plans which were formulated during his period. He placed defense and the key industries and public utilities in the public sector. He tried to regulate the scope and activity of private enterprise in the overall national interest. He put his economic socialism in practice. The abolition of landlordism, introduction of cooperatives led by the peasantry, a socialised system of credit, efficient utilisation of natural resources, etc. were the main features of his economic socialism.

Nehru implemented his mission through Five Year Plans. These plans laid the foundations of an industrialised economy and brought about a tremendous expansion in transport and communication, in education and health services, and the numerous dams, factories and scientific laboratories during the Nehru era in the public sector. They stand as vivid memorials to the achievements of Nehru.

Gandhi and Ambedkar

Here an attempt is made to point out the similarities and dissimilarities between Gandhi and Ambedkar.

So far as similarities were concerned, Gandhi and Ambedkar both believed in non-violence and the protection of interests of the minorities. Both believed in the abolition of untouchability, though their ways were slightly different. Both upheld a casteless society and ending of discriminations and exploitation in all their forms. Both were symbols of simplicity, devotion and strength. Both carefully maintained the simple standards of life. Both believed that a healthy democracy depends upon a healthy political culture. The democratic code requires social habits and temperaments on the part of the *Netas* and the people alike in the absence of which the democratic ideals would be hurt in their vitals. Both were inspired by Buddhism; Gandhi by its concepts of non-violence and Ambedkar converted himself to Buddhism and pleaded its *Dhamma*. Both professed to work for the uplift of the hungry, the naked and the depressed. Both were crusaders for the rights of the downtrodden and weaker sections of the society. Both advocated social justice and resolved to undo the indignities heaped on the untouchables for the past many centuries. Both believed in peaceful social revolution towards the transformation of society. Both indeed were great nation-builders.

There were many dissimilarity between Gandhi and Ambedkar regarding their ideas and approaches. Gandhi was a theist; whereas Ambedkar an atheist. Gandhi experimented with his formulas of truth and truth to him was God; whereas for Ambedkar truth was rationalism. Perhaps here he was influenced by Hegel who, said: 'what is real is rational and what is rational is real?' Gandhi was a critic of western civilisation; Ambedkar was not. Gandhi appreciated the spirit of the Hindu scriptures and the *Varna* system; whereas Ambedkar questioned the infallibility of the Vedas, even burnt *Manusmriti* because it was the Bible of graded inequality and exploitation of the depressed.

Sometimes Gandhi appeared as another Plato vindicating the cause of the spiritual and moral approach to political problems; whereas Ambedkar was akin to John Dewey's pragmatism – thus Gandhi to some extent was idealist and Ambedkar a realist. Ambedkar stood for separate electorate for the untouchables; whereas Gandhi pleaded joint electorate with reservation of seats for the oppressed. Gandhi was the *satyagrahi* on the pilgrimage to Swaraj; Ambedkar was a social rebel on the pilgrimage to abolish untouchability.

Gandhi had a great faith in God, soul and its transmigration; Ambedkar refuted all such metaphysical concepts. Gandhi introduced saintly politics; Ambedkar advocated pragmatic politics. The methods of Gandhi were non-cooperation, satyagraha and civil disobedience; whereas Ambedkar believed in extending cooperation to the British in order to achieve his aim regarding the abolition of untouchability. He also had a great faith in constitutional methods rather than civil disobedience. Gandhi believed in trusteeship; whereas Ambedkar was the supporter of socialism. Gandhi was an advocate of village republics; whereas Ambedkar regarded the village as dens of localism. He said:

> 'I hold that these village republics have been the ruination of India. What is the village but a sink of localism, a den of ignorance, narrow-mindedness and communalism?'

Gandhi was a mass leader; whereas Ambedkar a leader of the depressed. Gandhi's voice was the voice of the Nation; whereas Ambedkar's voice was that of the untouchables. Gandhi laid more emphasis on economic democracy; whereas Ambedkar's emphasis was on social democracy. He believed that political and economic democracy must be accompanied by social democracy; otherwise democracy would remain a top-dressing on the Indian soil which is essentially undemocratic. He believed that democracy in form was not enough; it must exist in fact.

Interpreting religion in a broad way, Gandhi regarded it as the elixir of life. Ambedkar too considered religion as essential in man's life, but it should be a true religion based on liberty, equality, fraternity and the dignity of man. Gandhi was a religious warrior; Ambedkar was the warrior of a true religion based on rationality and fraternity.

Gandhi's ideology was heavily coated with traditional symbolism; whereas Ambedkar's ideology was vehemently against the traditions of an antique society, it was more akin to the ideals of the age of enlightenment, the key features of which were Man and rationality.

Gandhi's message was spiritual. His favourite was '*Raghupati Raghava Raja Ram*,' Vaishnav *Bhajans* and devotional songs. Ambedkar's favourite message to the untouchables was organise, educate, struggle and capture power. To capture political power was essential for the uplift of untouchables and to accelerate social change. To Gandhi power had no allurement. Ambedkar advised his followers to capture power, which is essential for social change.

Gandhi's culture was *Charka, Gita*, *dhoti* and stick. Ambedkar's culture was a light blue suit, a tie, a book and simple living and high thinking. He often quoted Edmund Burke's sentence that "large empires and little minds go ill together."

Gandhi, like Gokhale, believed in the spiritualisation of politics. Ambedkar emphasised the development of constitutional morality both among the leaders and the people in the absence of which no democracy in the long run could succeed.

Gandhi's sole aim was not to inflict harm upon another, but to practice self-sacrifice and perform acts of pure renunciation in order to endure liberation. Ambedkar's sole aim was to abolish untouchability, and to destroy the Hindu scriptures that had justified and rationalised untouchability so long. He made a merciless attack upon the *Varna* system and pleaded to uproot it thoroughly so that a new society based on social humanism could usher in. He had no malice against Hinduism, but wanted to reform its outdated taboos and exploitative nature of its scriptures. Gandhi upheld spiritualisation and said:

> 'If Rama dwells in your hearts, it is easy to shake the foundations of not one but twenty empires more powerful than this one.'

Ambedkar had no fascination either for Rama or God. He believed that for centuries Rama has not been able to liberate the untouchables. At the Round Table Conference, he emphatically said:

> 'Our wrongs have remained as open sores and they have not been righted although 150 years of British rule have rolled away.'

He did not accuse the British but found that they were quite incompetent to tackle the problem of depressed classes because of the fear of resistance from upper castes and landed aristocracy.

The fundamental basis of Gandhian ideology is the conception of God, or an omnipresent fundamental spiritual reality, 'an all-embracing Living Light', which in plain words is called Truth. Gandhi was a metaphysical idealist who believed in a God who is kind and responsive to the prayers of the devotee. He regarded faith in the omnipotent God an essential requirement for the Satyagraha. "The only weapon of the Satyagrahi is God.' He was in search of spiritual truth which could be realised not by dialectical skill or conceptual cognition but by spiritual experience based on pure and holy life and persistent endeavour to concretize the norm of *Ahimsa* in one's actions and motivation. But Gandhi did not negate rational arguments and practical observation. He constantly experimented with truth and tried to make his propositions sounder by repeated observations.

Ambedkar stood in total contrast to Gandhi in this respect. The metaphysical idealism of Gandhi did not appeal to him. He had little or no faith either in spiritualism or God. He discarded the concept of soul and its transmigration. Except *Ahimsa* which he acquired from Buddhism, he rejected the supernatural and spiritual values. Spiritualism, he thought, was the creation of the Hindu scriptures; and beneath its mask the upper castes had tried to rationalise the *Varna* system in order to keep the depressed in perpetual bondage. The justification of things pertaining to social order under the shield of God was a spiritless argument.

Ambedkar was a pragmatist to the core. He considered that the Indian history and social evolution had been disfigured by false Hindu scriptures, and unless rationality is not employed in interpreting them, it would be difficult to search a unifying principle by which the whole society could be woven in one thread. His attachment to intellectual truth was as great as his faith in reason. His faith in rational discussion was immense. Instead of divine approach, he adopted rationalistic method to understand the problems of society. In addition to rationality, his ideology centres on Man. The fundamental basis of his ideology has been Man, society, reason and scientific spirit. In his ideology Man alone emerges triumphant, not god. In short, his methodology was rationalism, not god; and his concern was Man, not spiritualism.

Gandhi gave precedence to political reform in comparison to social reform, whereas Ambedkar gave precedence to social reform. Ambedkar was also critical of the Congress and Gandhi. He said:

> 'The Congress is largely composed of men who are by design political radicals and social Tories. Their chant is that the social and the political are two distinct things having no bearing on each other. To them the social and the political are two suits and can be worn one at a time as the season demands.'[33]

References

1. Ramachandra Guha (ed.) : *Makers of Modern India* (New Delhi, Penguin Books India Pvt. Ltd. , 2010), p.1.
2. *Ibid.,* p. 327.
3. *Ibid.,* p. 207.
4. Ramchandra Guha : *India After Gandhi* (London, Picador, 2007) p. 107.
5. M. K. Gandhi: *Hind Swaraj* (Ahmedabed, Navajivan Publishing House, 1938), p. 16.
6. Op. cit. Rajmohan Gandhi : *Mohandas : A True Story of a Man, his People and an Empire* (New Delhi, Penguin Books, 2006), p. 632.
7. M. J. Akbar: *Nehru: The Making of India* (New Delhi, Roli Books, 2002), pp. ix-x.

8. *Nehru: A Political Biography* (Bombay, Jaico Publishing House, 1969), pp. 306, 07.
9. V. P. Varma*: Modern Indian Political Thought* (Agra, Lakshmi Narain Agarwal, 1978), p. 345.
10. *Dr Babasaheb Ambedkar Writings and Speeches*, Vol. 1, p. 212.
11. *Op. cit.* D. C. Ahir: *The Legacy of Dr Ambedkar* (Delhi, B. R. Publishing Corporation, 1990), p. 26.
12. Vijay K. Srivastava: *Ambedkar, Dalit Politics and Inclusion* (Delhi, Swastik Publications, 2012), p. 51.
13. *Dr Babasaheb Ambedkar Writings and Speeches*, Vol. 17, Part Three, p. 55.
14. op. cit. Madhu Limaya : *Manu, Gandhi and Ambedkar and other Essays* (Delhi, Gian Publishing House, 2008), p. 18.
15. *Ibid.,* p.19.
16. *Ibid.,* p. 20.
17. *Hind Swaraj*, p. 55.
18. *Ibid,* pp. 52-53.
19. Op. cit. D. C. Ahir, p. 297.
20. *Maker of Modern India*. pp. 326-27.
21. Op. cit. Reg Wright: *Nehru A Life* (Madras, Orient Longman Ltd, 1923), p. 42.
22. Op. cit. S. Gopal: *Jawaharlal Nehru : An Anthology* (New Delhi, Oxford University Press, 1983), p. 230.
23. *Dr Babasaheb Ambedkar Writings and Speeches*, Vol. 1, pp. 77-78.
24. Op. cit. D. C. Ahir, p. 301.
25. *Ibid,* p. 302.
26. *Dr Babasaheb Ambedkar Writings and Speeches*, vol. 17, Part Three, p. 493.
27. *Ibid.,* pp. 122-23.
28. *Ibid.,* p. 123.
29. Op. cit., *India After Gandhi* (London Picador, 2007), p. 226.
30. *Makers of Modern India*, p. 326.
31. Op. cit., *India After Gandhi* , p. 148.
32. Op. cit. I. S. Vidyasagar : *Concept of Humanism of Dr Ambedkar* (Jaipur, ABD Publishers, 2005), p. 123.
33. *Dr Babasaheb Ambedkar Writings and Speeches*, Vol. 1, p. 263.

CHAPTER–8

Ambedkar's Vision of Nation-Building

Ambedkar was one of the most important thinker-activists of modern India. His struggles for the emancipation of the untouchables, his goal of national unity and fraternal relationship amongst the countrymen, and his method of constitutional rule of law and justice made him a great nation-builder. His vision of nation-building was both negative and positive.

Negatively speaking, he disliked the philosophy based on the triple qualities of *Sankhya* school and Hindu social philosophy as described in *Bhagavat Gita*. Because according to him, *Sankhya* philosophy is a merciless distortion of Kapil's philosophy, and that is why the caste system and graded inequality had become the fundamental rule of Hindu life. The abolition of untouchability, the annihilation of caste system, the ending of *Varna* System and graded inequality are significant features of Ambedkar's model of just society or nation.

Positively speaking, Ambedkar's ideal vision of nation-building could be materialised in three words – liberty, equality and fraternity, which he borrowed from Buddhism, and not from the French revolution.

In Ambedkar's Vision of nation-building Man occupies the central place. In the models of some of his contemporaries God is placed above man, that is, Man is below God. The communists and atheists have no faith in God and for them Man is equal to man. Buddhism has faith in man who is placed above God, that is, man is supreme.[1]

Therefore, Ambedkar's model which is derived from Buddhism excels all other models of social change and social solidarity. What is significant in Ambedkar's model is that it breaks divine fetters and tells man to be his own lord. Man must solve his problems here and now.

In Ambedkar's vision of nation-building, one must not forget, the pivotal role is that of Man and the principle of rationality. All sorts of problems must be judged from the angle of reason or rationality. Supremacy of reason is, what Ambedkar pleads, in nation-building. In a speech broadcast on Air India, Delhi, on 3rd October, 1954, Ambedkar said:

> 'Today the Indian person is under the sway of different idealistic stands. One is the idealism indicated in the preamble of the Constitution and the other is the social idealism incorporated in religion. One who has understanding may know that those are the two contradictory idealism. Political idealism recognised values of life in respect of liberty, equality and fraternity. However, the prevailing social idealism of *Sanatani* attitude has rejected those principles in practice. How long such contradictory life is going to run? There is no other way out than submission of one to the other. I am sure enough and so I hope that what is the Indian political idealism of the majority today will become the social idealism of all.'[2]

In simple words, the Indian political idealism of the majority would become the social idealism of all, if the standards used for judging are Man and Rationality. Both these elements are central in Ambedkar's vision of nation-building.

Ambedkar's vision of nation-building is not an idealistic or utopian model. It is a practical model, evolved out of experience, knowledge and struggles. It aims towards the creation of national unity through social amalgamation, which is attainable through universal education. Denial of education had thrown the depressed classes into the morass of ignorance, a slough of despond, perpetual bondage and eternal deprivation. Ambedkar therefore asserts that education is not only the birthright of every human being but also a significant weapon of social change.

An attempt is made in this chapter to indicate the basic characteristics of Ambedkar's vision of nation-building or a just society.

Casteless Society

The first characteristic of Ambedkar's vision of nation-building is casteless society. His views on the caste system are contained in the address that he prepared to be delivered at the 1936 annual conference of the Jat-Pat-Todak Mandal of Lahore. This address was not delivered owing to the cancellation of the Conference by the Reception Committee on the ground that the views expressed in the speech would be unbearable to the Conference.

Ambedkar gave precedence to social reform over political reform. He was critical of Socialists who were seeking to apply the economic interpretation of history to the facts of India. They gave priority to economic reform over every other kind of reform. Ambedkar asked the Socialists:

> 'Can you have economic reform without first bringing about a reform of the social order?... If Socialism is a practical programme and is not merely an ideal, distant and far off, the question for a Socialist is not whether he believes in equality. The question for him is whether he minds one class ill-treating and suppressing another class as a matter of system, as a matter of principle and thus allow tyranny and oppression to continue to divide one class from another...If the Socialists wish to make socialism a definite reality then they must recognise that the problem of social reform is fundamental and that for them there is no escape from it.'[3]

The social order prevalent in India, argued Ambedkar, was a matter which a Socialist ought to have dealt with. He must take into account the monster of caste. He said:

> *'A socialist cannot have political reform; he cannot have economic reform, unless he kills the monster of caste.'*[4]

Ambedkar fully exposed the weaknesses of the caste system which is hindering the process of nation-building. Caste in the hands of the orthodox has been a powerful weapon for killing all reform. He wrote:

'The effect of caste on the ethics of the Hindus is simply deplorable. Caste has killed public spirit. Caste has destroyed the sense of public charity. Caste has made public opinion impossible. A Hindu's public is his caste. His responsibility is only to his caste. Virtue has become caste-ridden and morality has become caste-bound. There is no sympathy to the deserving. There is no appreciation of the meritorious. There is no charity to the needy. Suffering as such calls for no response. There is charity but it begins with the caste and ends with the caste. There is sympathy but not for men of other caste.'[5]

Ambedkar argued that a Hindu would not acknowledge and follow the leadership of a great and good man. Generally, he would follow a leader if he is a man of his caste. The capacity to appreciate merits in a man apart from his caste does not exist in a Hindu. There is appreciation of virtue but only when the man is a fellow caste-man. The whole morality is as bad as tribal morality. The Hindus thus, according to Ambedkar, have committed treason against their country in the interests of their caste.

Ambedkar, therefore, pleaded for change in social order by doing away with caste. There was no doubt, in his opinion, that:

'Unless you change your social order you can achieve little by way of progress. You cannot mobilise the community either for defense or for offence. You cannot build anything on the foundations of caste. You cannot build up a nation; you cannot build up a morality. Anything that you will build on the foundations of caste will crack and will never be a whole.'[6]

To build an ideal society, Ambedkar wanted to abolish caste. This was a question of supreme importance for him. He was convinced that the real remedy is inter-marriage. Fusion of blood can alone create the feeling of being kith and kin and unless this feeling of kinship, of being kindred, becomes paramount the separatist feeling – the feeling of being aliens – created by caste will not vanish. As such, Ambedkar wrote: "The real remedy for breaking caste in inter-marriage. Nothing else will serve as the solvent of caste."

Ambedkar, therefore, pleaded that caste must be uprooted in order to create an ideal society based on liberty, equality and fraternity.

That alone would be a correct approach to nation-building. Casteless society is essential for nation-building or ideal way of living. He wrote:

> 'An ideal society should be mobile, should be full of channels for conveying a change taking place in one part to other parts. In an ideal society there should be many interests consciously communicated and shared. There should be varied and free points of contact with other modes of association. In other words there must be social endosmosis.'[7]

To uproot caste and to create a casteless society, according to Ambedkar, was a national cause. He wrote:

> 'Caste is no doubt primarily the breath of the Hindus. But the Hindus have fouled the air all over and everybody is infected – Sikh, Muslim and Christian. You, therefore, deserve the support of all those who are suffering from this infection, Sikh, Muslim and Christian. Yours is more difficult than the other national cause, namely Swaraj…There is no use having Swaraj, if you cannot defend it. More important than the question of defending Swaraj is the question of defending the Hindu under the Swaraj. In my opinion, only when the Hindu society becomes a casteless society that it can hope to have strength enough to defend itself. Without such internal strength, Swaraj for Hindus may turn out to be only a step towards slavery.'[8]

Thus, Ambedkar believed that no healthy nation-building is possible unless caste is abolished, and a casteless society is created.

Methods of Social Change

The second characteristic is the emphasis on peaceful social change. The broad objectives of nation-building are very much reflected in the 'preamble' of the Indian Constitution. Ambedkar held the view that to maintain democracy not merely in form, but also in fact, what is required is to hold fast to constitutional methods of achieving our social and economic objectives. It means the bloody methods of revolution are to be abandoned. It means the methods of civil disobedience; non-cooperation and *satyagraha* are to be abandoned. When there is no way left for constitutional methods for achieving economic and social objectives, there is a great deal of justification for unconstitutional methods. But where constitutional methods are open, there is no justification for these unconstitutional methods. These methods are nothing but 'the grammar of anarchy' and the sooner they are abandoned, the better it would be for nation-building. Revolution, on the face of it, appeared to be an anathema to Ambedkar. He detested revolutionary violence. He did not like the methods of rebellion, revolt, insurrection and violence. He appeared to be sceptical of the justness of revolutions as they invariably represent the triumph of the collective over to individual.

Ambedkar, thus, believed in the peaceful and constitutional methods for realising the social and economic objectives enshrined in our Constitution. The Constitutional methods are better towards building a sense of social cohesion and nationhood.

Unity of the Country

The third feature is the unity of the country. Ambedkar was greatly concerned about the unity of the country. These feelings were demonstrated by him in the maiden speech that he delivered in the Constituent Assembly on 17th December, 1946, when Prime Minister Nehru's 'Objectives Resolution' was under discussion. Nehru had moved this Resolution in the Assembly on 13th December. M.R. Jayakar had moved an amendment to Nehru's resolution seeking postponement of the passing of the Resolution. The President of the Assembly unexpectedly asked Ambedkar to speak.

After expressing his dissatisfaction with paragraphs 5 to 7 of the Resolution in which objectives of the future constitution were set out, Ambedkar turned to Jayakar's amendment. He supported the mover's plea for postponement of the passing of the Resolution, but for different reasons altogether. He pleaded for postponement because he considered it necessary in the interest of the unity of the country. Ambedkar said:

> 'Now, Sir, I have got not the slightest doubt in my mind as to the future evolution and the ultimate shape of the social, political and economic structure of this great country. I know today we are divided politically, socially and economically. We are a group of warring camps and I may go even to the extent of confessing that

> I am probably one of the leaders of such a camp. But, Sir, with all this, I am quite convinced that given time and circumstances nothing in the world will prevent this from becoming one. With all our castes and creeds, I have not the slightest hesitation that we shall in some form be a united people. I have no hesitation in saying that notwithstanding the agitation of the Muslim League for the partition of India some day enough light would dawn upon the Muslims themselves and they too will begin to think that a United India is better even for them.'[9]

So far as the ultimate goal was concerned, Ambedkar thought none of the members of the Assembly need have any apprehensions or doubts. He said:

> 'Our difficulty is not about the ultimate future. Our difficulty is how to make the heterogeneous mass that we have today take a decision in common and march on the way which leads us to unity. Our difficulty is not with regard to the ultimate; our difficulty is with regard to the beginning. Mr. Chairman, therefore, I should have thought that in order to make us willing friends, in order to induce every party, every section in this country to take on to road it would be an act of greatest statesmanship for the majority party even to make a concession to the prejudices of people who are not prepared to march together and it is for that, that I propose to make this appeal. Let us leave aside slogans, let us leave aside words which frighten people. Let us even make a concession to the prejudices of our opponents, bring them in, so that they may willingly join with us on marching upon that road, which as I said, if we walk long enough, must necessarily lead us to unity. If I, therefore, from this place support Dr Jayakar's amendment, it is because I want all of us to realise that whether we are right or wrong whether the position that we take is in consonance with our legal rights, whether that agrees with the statement of May 16 or December 6, leave all that aside. This is too big a question to be treated as a matter of legal rights. It is not a legal question at all. We should leave aside all legal considerations and make some attempt, whereby those who are not prepared to come, will come. Let us make it possible for them to come, that is my appeal.'[10]

Continuing the theme, Ambedkar said:

> 'Sir, I like to put the matter in a some-what different way. The way I like to put it, is this: I am not asking you to consider whether you have the right to pass this Resolution straightaway or not. It may be that you have the right to do so. The question I am asking is this: Is it prudent for you to do so? Is it wise for you to do so? Power is one thing; wisdom is quite a different thing and I want this House to consider this matter from that point of view, not of what authority is vested in this Constituent Assembly. I want this House to consider the matter from another point of view, namely, whether it would be wise, whether it would be prudent to do so at this stage? The answer that I give is that it would not be prudent, it would not be wise. I suggest that another attempt may be made to bring about a solution of the dispute between the Congress and the Muslim League. The subject is so vital, so important that I am sure it could never be decided on the mere basis of the dignity of one or the other party. In deciding the destinies of people, the dignity of the leaders or men or parties ought to count for nothing. As Burke said, 'it is easy to give power, but difficult to give wisdom.' Let us prove by one conduct that we have not only the power but also the wisdom to carry with us all sections of the country which is bound to lead us to unity.'[11]

Dr Ambedkar's forthright declaration of his firm faith in the ultimate unity of the country greatly impressed all the members of the Constituent Assembly. Commenting on this historic speech, N. V. Gadgil, who was an eye-witness to this event, wrote:

> 'His (Ambedkar's) speech was so statesmanlike, so devoid of bitterness and so earnestly challenging that the whole of Assembly listened to it in rapt silence. His main points were that the Constitution must be framed in the interest of the nation as a whole and that it should unify the country. The speech was greeted with a tremendous ovation and he was smothered with congratulations in the lobby.'[12]

Further, when the Constituent Assembly had finished its task of the framing of the Constitution, Ambedkar in his concluding speech had stated:

> 'Will history repeat itself? It is this thought which fills me with anxiety. This anxiety is deepened by the realisation of the fact that in addition to our old enemies in the form of castes and creeds we are going to have many political parties with diverse and opposing political creeds. Will Indians place the country above their creed or will they place creed above country? I do not know. But this much is certain that if the parties place creed above country, our independence will be put in jeopardy a second time and probably be lost forever. This eventuality we must all resolutely guard against. We must be determined to defend our independence with the last drop of our blood.'[13]

Safeguards to Minorities

The fourth characteristic is to protect the interests of minorities. Ambedkar believed that for nation-building it is essential to provide safeguards to minorities. He had no doubt that the Constituent Assembly had done wisely in providing such safeguards for minorities. In India, both the minorities and the majorities had followed a wrong path. It was wrong for the majority to deny the existence of minorities. It was equally wrong for the minorities to perpetuate themselves. A solution must be found which will serve a double purpose. He said:

> 'It must recognise the existence of the minorities to start with. It must also be such that it will enable majorities and minorities to merge someday into one. The solution proposed by the Constituent Assembly is to be welcomed because it is a solution which serves this two-fold purpose.'[14]

To the diehards who had developed a kind of fanaticism against minority protection, Ambedkar said two things. One was that minorities were an explosive force which, if it erupted, could blow up the whole fabric of the state. The history of Europe bore ample and appalling testimony to this fact. The other was that the minorities in India had agreed to place their existence in the hands of the majority. Ambedkar said:

> 'They (minorities) have loyally accepted the rule of the majority which is basically a communal majority and not a political majority. It is for the majority to realise its duty not to discriminate

against minorities. Whether the minorities will continue or will vanish must depend upon this habit of the majority. The moment the majority loses the habit of discriminating against the minority, the minorities can have no ground to exist. They will vanish.'[15]

Thus, according to Ambedkar, a safeguard to minorities is essential for nation-building.

Linguistic States

The fifth relates to linguistic States. In a memorandum submitted in 1948 to the Linguistic Provinces Commission, Dr Ambedkar had expressed his views on the re-organisation of States on linguistic basis. While acknowledging the danger to the unity of India inherent in the creation of linguistic provinces with their pride in race, language and literature developing into mentalities of being separate nations; Ambedkar saw certain definite political advantages in the reconstitution of provinces on linguistic basis.

On receipt of the report of the States Reorganisation Commission, he found it necessary to modify his view to some extent, and penned his final view on the formation of linguistic States in the book titled 'Thoughts on Linguistic States' which was published in 1955. Ambedkar favoured formation of unilingual states as against multi-lingual states as, according to him, the former fosters the fellow-feeling which is the foundation of a stable and democratic state; while the later with its enforced juxtaposition of two different linguistic groups leads to faction fights for leadership and discrimination in administration – factors which are incompatible with democracy. He, however, qualified his support for unilingual states by the condition that its official language shall be Hindi and until India becomes fit for this purpose, English shall continue. He also mentioned the dangers of a linguistic state:

'A linguistic state with its regional language as its official language may easily develop into an independent nationality. The road between an independent nationality and an independent state is very narrow. If this happens, India will cease to be a Modern India we have and will become the medieval India consisting of a variety of states indulging in rivalry and warfare.'[16]

This danger is of course inherent on the creation of linguistic States. There is equal danger in not having linguistic states. Ambedkar wrote:

> 'The former danger a wise and firm statesman can avert. But the dangers of a mixed state are greater and beyond the control of a statesman however eminent.'[17]

How can this danger be met? The only way Ambedkar could think of meeting the danger was to provide in the Constitution that the regional language shall not be the official language of the state. The official language of the state shall be Hindi and until India becomes fit for this purpose English. He asked: Will Indians accept this? If they do not, linguistic states may easily become a peril, or a great hindrance in the path of nation-building.

State Socialism

The sixth characteristic is state socialism. Ambedkar believed that the nation-building should be on the lines of Fabian socialism. He did not favour capitalism because it promoted caste discrimination and inhuman exploitation of workers. He was quite aware of the exploitative potential of capital and hence he had declared, 'capitalism and Brahminism as the twin enemy of his movement.'[18] However, he did not develop any systematic theory about capitalism or imperialism. He regarded British imperialism and Indian feudalism as the two leaches that clung to Indian people.

About Ambedkar's socialistic antecedents there was no doubt. Despite his reservations about the emphasis on the economic dimension of socialism, he broadly remained a socialist. Speaking on Nehru's 'Objectives Resolution' in the Constituent Assembly on 16th December, 1946, Ambedkar said;

> 'If this Resolution has a reality behind it and a sincerity, of which I have not the least doubt, coming as it does from the Mover of the Resolution, I should have expected some provision whereby it would have been possible for the State to make economic, social and political justice a reality and I should have from that point of view expected the Resolution to state in most explicit terms that in order that there may be social and economic justice in the country,

that there would be nationalisation of industry and nationalisation of land; I do not understand how it could be possible for any future government which believes in doing justice socially, economically and politically, unless its economy is a socialistic economy.'[19]

The main provisions of Ambedkar's socialistic programme were: (i) all important industries and services to belong to the nation; (ii) insurance industry to be in public sector and insurance be compulsory for every citizen; (iii) private sector to have a role in the economy but not a dominating one; and (iv) nationalisation of land and promotion of cooperative farming on a collective principle.

Ambedkar had no systematic theory of socialism. His socialistic learnings and ideas were more akin to Fabian socialism. He believed that the ideal society could materialise only through State socialism and change in the economic structure of the society.

Ambedkar held the view that the soul of democracy is the doctrine of one man, one value. Unfortunately democracy has attempted to give effect to this doctrine only so far as the political structure is concerned by adopting the role of one man, one vote which is supposed to translate into fact the doctrine of one man, one value. It has left the economic structure to take the shape given to it by those who are in a position to mould it. The constitutional lawyers dominated by the antiquated conception never go beyond adult suffrage and fundamental rights, because they believed that the scope and function of constitutional law was to prescribe the shape and form of the political structure of society. Ambedkar said:

> 'They never realised that it was equally essential to prescribe the shape and form of the economic structure of society, if democracy is to live up to its principle of one man, one value. Time has come to take a bold step and define both the economic structure as well as the political structure of society by the Law of the Constitution.'[20]

It meant that Ambedkar wished to prescribe the shape and form of the economic structure of society, and to give it equal importance with the political structure. His was an attempt to establish State socialism without abrogating parliamentary democracy and without leaving its establishment to the will of a parliamentary democracy. He wished to make State socialism a part of the constitutional law of the land. He did not want to leave it to the legislature to bring it into being by the ordinary process of law. He said:

> 'Those who want the economic structure of society to be modelled on State socialism must realise that they cannot leave the fulfilment of so fundamental a purpose to the exigencies of ordinary law which simple majorities – whose political fortunes are never determined by rational causes – have a right to make and unmake. For these reasons political democracy seems to be unsuited for the purpose.'[21]

What is significant in Ambedkar is that he wanted State socialism within the framework of parliamentary democracy because individual freedom is best protected in a free society! He, therefore, stated:

> 'The problem therefore is to have state socialism without dictatorship, to have state socialism with parliamentary democracy. The way out seems to be to retain parliamentary democracy and to prescribe state socialism by the law of the Constitution so that it will be beyond the reach of a parliamentary majority to suspend, amend or abrogate it. It is only by this that one can achieve the triple object, namely, to establish socialism, retain parliamentary democracy and avoid dictatorship.'[22]

So in Ambedkar's ideal society or nation-building State socialism or the form and shape of the economic structure of society occupied an important place. Any constitution which merely prescribes the form of the political structure of the society, leaving the economic structure untouched, is not a complete document.

Path of Devotion or Hero-Worship

The seventh characteristic is to avoid the path of devotion. Ambedkar cautioned all those who are interested in the maintenance of democracy, not 'to lay their liberties at the feet of even a great man, or to trust him with powers which enable him to subvert their institutions.' There is nothing wrong in being grateful to great men who have rendered life-long services to the country. But there are limits to gratefulness.

Ambedkar agreed with the words of the Irish patriot, Daniel O, Connel, who said, "no man can be grateful at the cost of his honour, no woman can be grateful at the cost of her chastity, and no nation can be grateful at the cost of its liberty." He believed that this caution is far more necessary in the case of India than in the case of any other country, for in India, *Bhakti* or what may be called the path of devotion or hero-worship, plays a part in its politics unequalled in magnitude by the part it plays in the politics of any other country in the world. *Bhakti* in religion may be a road to the salvation of the soul. But in politics, *Bhakti* or hero-worship is a sure road to degradation and to eventual dictatorship.[23]

Social Democracy

The eighth characteristic is social democracy. Ambedkar held the view that mere political democracy is not enough; and for building a nation, what is essential is social democracy. He, therefore, said:

> 'Political democracy cannot last unless there lies at the base of it social democracy. What does social democracy mean? It means a way of life which recognises liberty, equality and fraternity as the principles of life.'[24]

He held that these principles of liberty, equality and fraternity are not to be treated as separate items in a trinity. They form a union of trinity in the sense that to divorce one from the other is to defect the very purpose of democracy. He stated:

> 'Liberty cannot be divorced from equality; equality cannot be divorced from liberty. Nor can liberty and equality be divorced from fraternity. Without equality, liberty would produce the supremacy of the few over the many. Equality without liberty would kill individual initiative. Without fraternity, liberty and equality could not become a natural course of things. It would require a constable to enforce them.'[25]

Ambedkar considered that there is complete absence of two things in Indian society. One of these is equality. On the social plane, we have in India a society based on the principle of graded inequality which means elevation for some and degradation for others. On the economic plane, we have a society in which there are some who have immense wealth as against many who live in abject poverty. He, therefore, uttered a warning:

> 'On the 26th of January, 1950, we are going to enter into a life of contradictions. In politics we will have equality and in social and economic life we will have inequality. In politics will be recognising the principle of one man one vote and one vote one value. In our social and economic life, we shall, by reason of our social and economic structure, continue to deny the principle of one man one value. How long shall we continue to live this life of contradictions? How long shall we continue to deny equality in our social and economic life? If we continue to deny it for long, we will do so only by putting our political democracy in peril. We must remove this contradiction at the earliest possible moment or else those who suffer from inequality will blow up the structure of political democracy which this Assembly has so laboriously built up.'[26]

The main thrust of his argument is that no nation-building is possible merely by creating the structure of political democracy. Political democracy unless it is not accompanied by economic and social democracy would be hollow and meaningless. As such, both the social and economic democracy are necessary for nation-building. The relationship between the two has been summarised by Ambedkar in the following words:

> 'Today the Indian person is under the sway of different idealistic stands. One is the idealism indicated in the preamble of the Constitution and the other is the social idealism incorporated in religion. One who has understanding may know that those are the two contradictory idealisma. Political idealism recognised values of life in respect of liberty, equality and fraternity. However, the prevailing social idealism of *Sanatani* attitude has rejected those principles in practice. How long such contradictory life is going to run? There is no other way out than submission of one to the other. I am sure enough and so I hope that what is the Indian political idealism of the majority will become the social idealism of all.'[27]

Social Cleavages

The ninth characteristic is that social cleavages and frictions be reduced or minimised. Social cleavages are a great hindrance in the path of nation-building. Ambedkar was aware of it. He often stated that 'there must lie no glaring inequalities in the society? A society, which does not preach equality between man and man, woman and man, is opposed to the principle of social justice. There must not be an oppressed class. There must not be a suppressed class. There must not be a class which has got all the privileges and a class which has got all the burdens to carry. Such a thing, such a division, such an organisation of a society has within itself the germs of a bloody revolution, and perhaps it would be impossible for the democracy to cure them.[28]

Lincoln once said, although people have not understood his meaning, in the Gatisburg's speech that 'a house divided against itself cannot stand.' He was of course referring to the conflict between the Southern States and the Northern States. He said, "If you of the Southern States and we of the Northern States are divided, we shall not be able to stand together when a foreign enemy comes." That was probably the meaning that he wanted to convey when he said that the house divided cannot stand. But Ambedkar thought that phrase of his or sentence of his was pregnant with much deeper meaning, and to him, it meant:

> 'That the deep cleavages between class and class are going to be one of the greatest hindrances in the success of democracy.'[29]

The question is what happens to nation-building through the mechanism of democracy. In democracy, everybody, even the oppressed, the suppressed, those who are deprived of their rights and those who carry the burden, they have the right to vote in the same way as those who have all the privileges, and probably those who are privileged are fewer than those who are unprivileged and since we adopt a majority rule as the rule of decision, it is quite possible that if the privileged few will not willingly and voluntarily surrender their privileges, then the distance between them and the lower orders will destroy democracy and bring into existence something quite different.

Although in theory the distinction between the privileged and the suppressed has been abolished by the Constitution, in practice the marks are present to a great extent, because of glaring economic inequalities. There is, therefore, no doubt that one of the causes for the breakdown of a just society in the existence of these social cleavages. Social cleavages weaken the cause of nation-building. Unless and until, the social cleavages are not removed, both in theory and practice, our endeavour towards nation-building would not be a success. Social cleavages make the society hollow; they sap its vitality and create inner contradictions of great magnitude. As such, social cleavages harm the growth of nation-building.

Social Amalgamation

The tenth characteristic is that, while discussing Ambedkar's vision of nation-building, one should not forget the importance that he attached to social amalgamation. On 5th February, 1940, he had clearly stated:

> 'I do not agree with Mr. Gandhi and the Congress when they say that India is a nation. I do not agree either with the foreign relations Committee of the Muslim League when they say that Hindus and Muslims could not be welded together into a nation. My belief is that we are not a nation. But my confident hope is that we can be a nation provided proper processes of social amalgamation are set forth.'[30]

Thus, Ambedkar's belief was that India can become a nation provided proper processes of social amalgamation are initiated and implemented.

Individual Liberty[31]

The eleventh characteristic relates to individual liberty on which Ambedkar laid great emphasis. No society or the nation can progress if individual liberty is curtailed.

Liberty falls under two classes. There is civil liberty and there is political liberty. Civil liberty refers to (i) liberty of movement which is another name for freedom from arrest without due process of law; (ii) liberty of speech (which of course includes liberty of thought, liberty of reading, writing and discussion); and (iii) liberty of action.

The first kind of liberty is of course fundamental. Not only fundamental, it is also most essential. About its value, there can be no manner of doubt. The second kind of liberty which may be called freedom of opinion is important for many reasons. It is a necessary condition of all progress: intellectual, moral, political and social. Where it does not exist the status-quo becomes stereotyped and all originality even the most necessary is discouraged. Liberty of action means doing what one likes to do. It is not enough that liberty of action should be formal. It must be real. So understood, liberty of action means effective power to do specific things. There is no freedom where there are no means of taking advantage of it. Real liberty of action exists only where exploitation has been annihilated, where no suppression of one class by another exists, where there is no unemployment, no poverty and where a person is free from the fear of losing his job, his home, and his food as a consequence of his action.

Political liberty consists in the right of the individual to share in the framing of laws and in the making and unmaking of governments.

So, according to Ambedkar, an ideal society must be based on civil liberty and political liberty, though difficult to state their limitations and boundaries. In the words of Ambedkar:

> 'There is a place for liberty in my philosophy of life. This I have to tell you insistently. However, this too is to be told that there is no place for unbridled liberty in it. For, the unbridled liberty is detrimental to equality. In my philosophy the place of equality is superior to that of liberty. Even then there is no scope whatsoever for absolute equality in it. Because unlimited equality comes in the way of existence of liberty and there is a need for a scope of liberty.'[32]

Fraternity

The twelfth characteristic is fraternity. Ambedkar laid great emphasis on the principle of fraternity in the absence of which nation-building is not possible. What does fraternity mean? Fraternity means a sense of common brotherhood of all Indians. Indians should become one people. It is this principle which gives unity and solidarity to social life. It is a difficult thing to achieve. How difficult it is, can be realised from the story related by James Bryce in his volume on

'American Commonwealth' about the United States of America. The story is as given below.

> 'Some years ago the American Protestant Episcopal Church was occupied in its triennial convention in revising its liturgy. It was thought desirable to introduce among the short sentence prayers a prayer for the whole people, and an eminent New England divine proposed the words 'O Lords, bless our nation'. Accepted one afternoon on the spur of the moment, the sentence was brought up next day for reconsideration; When so many objections were raised by the laity to the word 'nation' as importing too definite a recognition of national unity, that it was dropped, and instead there were adopted the words 'O Lord, bless these United States.'[33]

There was so little solidarity in the USA at the time when this incident occurred that the people of America did not think that they were a nation, if the people of the United States could not feel that they were a nation, how difficult it is for Indians to think that they are a nation.

The concept of fraternity occupies a significant place in Ambedkar's ideal or just society. In his essay on 'Philosophy of Hinduism' he gives the meaning of fraternity as stated under:

> 'There are two forces prevalent in society – individualism and fraternity. Individualism is ever present. Every individual is ever asking, 'I and my neighbours, are we all brothers, are we even fifteenth cousins, am I their keeper, why should I do right to them' and under the pressure of his own particular interests acting as though he was an end to himself, thereby developing a non-social and even an anti-social self. Fraternity is a force of opposite character. Fraternity is another name for fellow feeling. It consists in a sentiment which leads an individual to identify himself with the goods of others whereby the good of others becomes to him a thing naturally and necessarily to be attended to like any of the physical conditions of our existence.'[34]

In his other essay on 'The Hindu Social Order: Its Essential Principles', Ambedkar explains the importance of fraternity in a 'free social order':

> 'Fraternity is the name for the disposition of an individual to treat men as the object of reverence and love and the desire to be in unity with the fellow beings. This statement is well expressed by Paul, when he said 'of one blood are all nations of men. There is neither Jew nor Greek, neither bond nor free, neither male nor female; for yet all are one in Christ Jesus.' Equally well was it expressed when the Pilgrim Fathers on their landing at Plymouth said: 'We are knit together as a body in the most sacred covenant of the Lord....by virtue of which we hold ourselves tied to all care of each others' good and of the whole.' These sentiments are of essence of fraternity. Fraternity strengthens socialites and gives to each individual a stronger personal interest in practically consulting the welfare of others.'[35]

So fraternity is essentially an attitude of respect and reverence towards fellowmen and that should be the aim of an ideal society or nation-building.

Ambedkar remembered the days when politically-minded Indians resented the expression 'the people of India.' They preferred the expression 'the Indian nation.' He was of opinion that in believing that we are a nation, we are cherishing a great delusion. He said:

> 'How can people divided into several thousands of castes be a nation? The sooner we realise that we are not as yet a nation in the social and psychological sense of the word, the better for us. For then only we shall realise the necessity of becoming a nation and seriously think of ways and means of realising the goal. The realisation of this goal is going to be very difficult – far more difficult than it has been in the United States.'[36]

Ambedkar stated that the United States had no caste problem. In India there are castes. The castes are anti-national. They are anti-national because they bring about separation in social life, and they generate jealousy and antipathy between caste and caste. But, said Ambedkar, that 'we must overcome all these difficulties if we wish to become a nation in reality.' For fraternity can be a fact only when there is a nation. Without fraternity, equality and liberty will be no deeper than coats of paint.

After the framing of the Constitution, Ambedkar stated that the tasks ahead are difficult, even they may not be pleasant to some, because political power in India had too long been the monopoly of a few and the many were not only beast of burden, but also beasts of prey. This monopoly had not merely deprived them of their chance of betterment; it had sapped them of what might be called the significance of life. These downtrodden classes were tired of being governed; they were impatient to govern themselves. This urge for self-realisation in the downtrodden classes must not be allowed to develop into a class struggle. That would indeed be a day of disaster. He said:

> 'Therefore, the sooner room is made for the realisation of their aspiration, the better for the few, the better for the country, the better for the maintenance for its independence and the better for the continuance of its democratic structure. This can only be done by the establishment of equality and fraternity in all spheres of life.'[37]

That is why Ambedkar laid so much stress on fraternity towards nation-building and democracy. Fraternity is another name for democracy. Democracy is not merely a form of government. It is primarily a mode of associated living, of conjoint communicated experience. It is essentially an attitude of respect and reverence towards one's fellow men.[38] Fraternity is the cornerstone of the whole democratic civilisation; it is sacred which everybody must respect; and it helps to sustain the moral order among men. Recognising its importance, Ambedkar said:

> 'I would like to hold fraternity as supreme because in the event of liberty and equality being disobeyed the very fraternity itself would prove to be the protector indeed.'[39]

A True Religion

The thirteenth relates to a true religion. Ambedkar was a religious man; he was not in favour of destruction of religion, he wanted that for an ideal society or healthy nation-building, what is required is a true religion. He condemned a religion of rules and wished that its place be taken by a religion of principles. A religion of principles alone is a true religion.

He drew a distinction between rules and principles. Rules are practical; they are habitual ways of doing things according to prescription. But principles are intellectual; they are useful methods of judging things. Rules seek to tell an agent just what course of action to pursue. Principles do not prescribe a specific course of action. He, therefore, stated:

> 'Religion must mainly be a matter of principles only. It cannot be a matter of rules. The moment it degenerates into rules it ceases to be Religion, as it kills responsibility which is the essence of a truly religious act. What is this Hindu religion? Is it a set of principles or is it a code of rules?'[40]

Ambedkar argued that the Hindu religion, as contained in the Vedas and the Smritis, is nothing but a mass of sacrificial, social, political and sanitary rules and regulations, all mixed up. What is called religion by the Hindus is nothing but a multitude of commands and prohibitions. Religion, in the sense of spiritual principles, truly universal, applicable to all races, to all countries, to all times, is not to be found in them, and if it is so, it does not form the governing part of a Hindu life. The Hindu religion is nothing but a set of rules, or a multitude of commands and prohibitions. It is at best 'legalised class-ethics.' Ambedkar refused to call the Hindu Code of ordinances as religion. This code of ordinances has many evils. It tends to deprive moral life of freedom and spontaneity. It imposes servile conformity to externally imposed rules. There is no loyalty to ideals; there is only conformity to commands. They are iniquitous in that they are not the same for one class as for another. This iniquity is made perpetual in that they are prescribed to be the same for all generations. Further, this Code has been invested with the character of finality and fixity. That being the case, said Ambedkar, how can humanity endure this Code of eternal laws, without being cramped and without being crippled?

He frankly stated:

> 'I have, therefore, no hesitations in saying that such a religion must be destroyed and I say, there is nothing irreligious in working for the destruction of such a religion. Indeed I had that it is your bounden duty to tear the mask, to remove the

> misrepresentation that as caused by misnaming this Law as Religion.'[41]

Ambedkar only condemned a religion of rules. He did not question the necessity for a religion. He believed that a true religion is the foundation of society or nation or a true civil government. He urged that these ancient rules of life or religion be annulled, and its place be taken by a religion of principles, which alone can lay claim to being a true religion. He was so convinced of the necessity of religion that he outlined what he regarded as necessary items in this religious reform. He suggested cardinal items in this reform, such as, one and only one standard book of Hindu religion; priesthood among Hindus be abolished; no ceremony should be performed by a priest who does not hold a *sanad;* a priest should be a servant of the state and; the number of priests should be limited.

Ambedkar believed that a true religion is that which is based on principles. A new doctrinal basis should be given to Hindu religion, that is, it should be in consonance with liberty, equality and fraternity or in short, with democracy. In simple words, the nation-building should be based on religious principles as would be in consonance with liberty, equality and fraternity enshrined in Buddhism. He wrote:

> 'It means a complete change in outlook and in attitude towards men and things. It means conversion, but if you do not like the word, I will say, it means new life. But a new life cannot enter a body that is dead. New life can enter only in a new body. The old body must die before a new body can come into existence and a new life can enter into it. To put it simply, the old must cease to be operative before the new can begin to enliven and to pulsate.'[42]

This is what Ambedkar meant when he advocated to discard a religion of rules, or to discard the authority of the *Shastras* and destroy the religion of the *Shastras*. To create a new life, a new society, and a new nation, Ambedkar pleaded for a true religion or a religion of principles.

The basic problem, argued Ambedkar, was whether Hindus should conserve the whole of their social heritage (a religion of rules), or select what is helpful and transmit to future generations only that much and no more. He quoted with approval the following words of his teacher, John Dewey:

> 'Every society gets encumbered with what is trivial, with dead wood from the past, and with what is positively perverse…. As a society becomes more enlightened, it realises that it is responsible not to conserve and transmit the whole of it existing achievements, but only such as make for a better future society.'[43]

Ambedkar thus advised the Hindus not to adhere to a religion of rules, but to adopt the means of some change towards the building of a religion of principles. He wrote:

> 'The Hindus must consider whether the time has not come for them to recognise that there is nothing fixed, nothing eternal, nothing *sanatan*; that everything is changing, that change is the law of life for individuals as well as for society. In a changing society, there must be a constant revolution of old values and the Hindus must realise that if there must be standards to measure the acts of men there must also be a readiness to revise those standards.'[44]

Thus, a religion of rules is archaic and outdated; there must be a true religion or a religion of principles to build a better future society.

Empowerment of Women

The fourteenth characteristic is the empowerment of women. Ambedkar believed in the dignity and empowerment of women. He was keen to ameliorate the condition of women who had been the target of Manu's wrath. The *Manusmriti* had sown contempt for women, degraded them as slaves, denied them the right of education and the right to property. Being India's first Law Minister and Chairman of the Drafting Committee of the Constituent Assembly, Ambedkar thought it appropriate, to free women from the age-old thraldom by reforming the Hindu social laws created by Manu. He, therefore, took initiative to draft and introduce the Hindu Code Bill in the Constituent Assembly. The Hindu Code Bill, the most formidable legislative measure of modern India, sought among other reforms, to put an end to a variety of marriage systems prevailing in India and legalise only monogamous marriages. The Code also sought to confer on women the right of property and adoption which had been denied to them. It put men and women on an equal level in all legal matters.

Indicating the importance of the Code Bill, Ambedkar said in the Con-Assembly:

> 'I should like to draw the attention of the House to one important fact. The great political philosophers Burke who wrote his great book against the French Revolution said that those who want to conserve must be ready to repair. And all I am asking this House is: If you want to maintain the Hindu system, Hindu culture and Hindu society, do not hesitate to repair where repair is necessary. This Bill asks for nothing more than to repair those parts of the Hindu system which have become dilapidated.'[45]

The efforts of Ambedkar to unify the Hindu Code, to make it progressive and in tune with the modern thought were laudable. But there was a stiff opposition to the Code Bill both inside and outside the Con-Assembly. The orthodox elements were unwilling to change the social structure of the Hindu society. His efforts to codify and liberalise the Hindu social law were virtually wrecked by the protagonists of orthodoxy and in the face of growing opposition; Prime Minister Nehru lost the grip and decided to drop the Bill. Dr Ambedkar, therefore, resigned in September, 1951.

The Hindu Code Bill was later split into four Bills, and the same were put on the Statute Book by Parliament. The Hindu Marriage Act, 1955; the Hindu Succession Act, 1956; the Hindu Minority and Guardianship Act 1956; and the Hindu Adoption and Maintenance Act, 1956, are the four enactments which incorporated the ideas and principles of the Hindu Code Bill formulated by Ambedkar. They give independent status to women and endow them with the right of adoption, succession and property, so completely denied by *Manusmriti*. Therefore, it is true to say that in the task of nation-building, according to Ambedkar, the empowerment of women and giving them an independent status, through change in Hindu social laws, was essential.

Precedence for Social Reform

In his address titled, 'Ranada, Gandhi and Jinnah,' delivered on the 101st birthday of the late Justice Mahadev Govind Ranada which fell on the 18th January 1940, Ambedkar gave precedence to social reform over political reform. He held that in this respect Ranada was correct who upheld the priority of social reform. The thesis that political reform was to have precedence over social reform appeared basically wrong to Ambedkar. The cry of political reform was meant to block the path of social reform. Giving precedence to social reform, Ambedkar said:

> 'The thesis of political reform is unsupportable, and I have no doubt that the opponents of Ranada were wrong and in pursuing it did not serve the best interests of the country...The thesis that political reform should precede social reform becomes on the face of it an absurd proposition, unless the idea is that the government is to protect those who have vested rights and to penalise those who have none.'[46]

According to Ambedkar, Ranada gave precedence to social reform over political reform. Ranada argued that there were no rights in the Hindu society which the moral sense of man could recognise. There were privileges and disabilities, privileges for a few and disabilities for a vast majority. Ranada struggled to create rights. He wanted to vitalise the conscience of the Hindu society which had become moribund as well morbid. He aimed to create a real social democracy, without which there could be no sure and stable politics. The conflict was between two opposing points of view and it centred round the question which is more important for the survival of a nation, political freedom or strong moral fibre. Ranada took the view that moral stamina was more important than political freedom.

Ambedkar assert that 'Ranada was not only wise but he was also logical? Ranada told his opponents against playing the part of political radicals and social tories. In clear terms Ranada warned them saying:

> 'You cannot be liberal by halves. You cannot be liberal in politics and conservative in religion. The heart and the head must go together. You cannot cultivate your intellect, enrich your mind, enlarge the sphere of your political rights and privileges, and at the same time keep your hearts closed and cramped. It is an idle dream to expect men to remain enchained and enshackled in their own superstition and social evils, while they are struggling hard to

> win rights and privileges from their rulers. Before long these vain dreamers will find their dreams lost.'[47]

Ambedkar believed that the above words of Ranada have been true, even prophetic. He said:

> 'Let those who deny this consider: Where are we today in politics and why are we where we are? It is now 50 years since the National Congress was born.... Where does this country stand today at the end of 50 years of political marching? What is the cause of this deadlock?'[48]

According to Ambedkar, the answer is simple. The cause of deadlock is the absence of communal settlement. The communal settlement is necessary for political settlement. The answer to the question is to be found in the wrong social system, which is too undemocratic, too overweighed in favour of the classes and against the masses, too class conscious and too communally minded. Ambedkar said:

> 'Political democracy would become a complete travesty if it were built upon its foundations. That is why nobody except the high caste Hindus will agree to make it the case of a political democracy without serious adjustments...People likes to entertain thoughts which sooth them and which throw responsibility on others. This is the psychology of escapism. But it cannot alter the fact that it is the defects of social system which has given rise to the communal problem and which has stood in the way of India getting political power.'[49]

Ambedkar was thus trying to emphasise the precedence of social reform over political reform. He wished to cleanse the old order in order to build a new one. The advocates of political reform had failed to see the virtue of social reform. Ambedkar thus recognised the necessity of social reform first in order to improve the moral tone of the society. Ambedkar wrote:

> 'For I regard social reform more fundamental than political reform....The ardour for social reform has cooled down. The craze for politics has held the Indian public in its grip. Politics has become an appetizer – a mastic the more one tastes it the more one craves it.'[50]

Thus, the precedence of social reform over political reform was categorically recognised by Ambedkar.

Ambedkar's Last Message

And the last was Ambedkar's message to his brethren. He had struggled throughout his life for the emancipation of the untouchables, and finally the untouchability was abolished by the enactment of the Constitution. He not only secured the socio-economic and political justice for the suffering millions but enshrined their rights in the Constitution. But the liberator and emancipator of the downtrodden people was not satisfied with his achievements. As a matter of fact, towards the fag end of his life he was sad, depressed and worried as to what would happen to his people after his death. When questioned about this mood of despondency by his honorary private secretary, Ambedkar on 30th July, 1956, responded as given below:

> 'You people do not know, what is troubling me and what makes me sad. I feel sad because I have not been able to fulfill my mission to the extent I wanted. I wanted to make my people a governing class in my life. I can now almost crippled and prostrated by illness. Whatever, I have been able to achieve is being enjoyed by educated few who have proved to be the worst lot; with no sympathy for their poor ignorant brethren. It is a pity that the vast illiterate masses in the villages have remained unchanged economically.'[51]

Ambedkar further said:

> 'I also wanted someone from my lieutenants to come forward and make the movement more effective to achieve the results for the attainments of which I have suffered and struggled hard throughout my life. But alas! My lieutenants on whom I had full trust and confidence that they will run the movement are fighting among themselves for leadership and power; unmindful of the heavy responsibility that is to devolve upon them after me.'[52]

After this, Ambedkar paused a little, then with a glow in his eyes and raising his voice a bit, he told Nanak Chand Rattu, his honorary private secretary, the following words:

> 'Tell my people, whatever I have done; I have been able to do after passing through crushing miseries and endless troubles all my life and fighting with my opponents all my life. With great difficulty I have brought this caravan where it is seen today. Let the caravan march on despite the hurdles that may come in its way. If my lieutenants are not able to take the caravan ahead, they should leave it there, but under no circumstances should they allow the caravan to go back. This is the message to my people.'[53]

The whole point that Ambedkar emphasised seems to be that the mere abolition of untouchability legally in not enough; what is important is to bring about an end to their economic disparities and social inequalities that exist in practice. That would probably lead to a healthy nation-building.

Final Reflections

Thus, the basic features or characteristics of Ambedkar' vision of nation-building can be grouped into two distinct parts.

The first part consists of destroying the social laws or practices that weaken nation-building. In it the emancipation of the untouchables, the abolition of untouchability, and annihilation of caste and the demolition of *Varna* System or graded inequality are significant.

The second part is a constructive one, aiming towards the building-up of a healthy nation or society. Keeping faith in the unity of the country, Ambedkar's vision of nation-building revolves around secularism, socialism, safeguarding minority interests, linguistic states, hero-worship, social democracy, empowerment of women, individual liberty, fraternity, a true religion, social amalgamation and so on.

Thus, Ambedkar's vision of nation-building is a holistic one – eliminating or destroying what is undesirable and building or developing or reforming tendencies which can promote nation-building. In a nutshell, Ambedkar believed that social democracy, social amalgamation, social justice and social harmony are fundamental for nation-building, especially in the social and psychological sense. The stamina of nation-building lies in a real social democracy, without which there could be no sure and stable politics. The foundation of a Nation's strength and prosperity is laid in pure domestic life, in a high standard of moral worth, and of public spirit, in simple habits, in courage, uprightness, and a certain soundness and moderation of judgment which springs quite as much from character as from intellect, from social democracy as from social amalgamation.

Dr Ambedkar's vision of nation-building is highly useful, and his observations in matters social, economic and political are coming true. Today, what we witness is that social tension and caste conflicts are continuously on the increase. Ambedkar's thoughts and his vision of nation-building have, therefore, assured more relevance today.

References

1. C. D. Naik: *Ambedkar's Perspective on Buddhism and Other Religions* (Delhi, Kalpaz Publications, 2009), p. 354.
2. Op. cit. C. D. Naik: *Thoughts and Philosophy of Dr B. R. Ambedkar* (New Delhi, Sarup and Sons, 2003), pp. 2-3.
3. *Dr Babasaheb Ambedkar Writings and Speeches*, Vol. 1, pp. 46-47.
4. *Ibid.,* p. 47.
5. *Ibid.,* pp. 56-57.
6. *Ibid.,* p. 66.
7. *Ibid.,* p. 57.
8. *Ibid.,* p. 80.
9. *Dr Babasaheb Ambedkar Writings and Speeches*, Vol. 13, p. 9.
10. *Ibid.,* p. 10.
11. *Ibid.,* p. 12.
12. Op. cit. D. C. Ahir: *The Legacy of Dr Ambedkar* (Delhi, B. R. publishing Corporation, 1990), p. 68.
13. *Dr Babasaheb Ambedkar Writings and Speeches*, Vol. 13, p. 1214.
14. *Ibid.,* p. 62.
15. *Ibid.,* pp. 62-63.
16. *Dr Babasaheb Ambedkar Writings and Speeches*, Vol. 1, p. 145.
17. *Ibid.*
18. Sadhana Thakur: *Thoughts and Philosophy of Dr B. R. Ambedkar* (New Delhi, Anmol Publications, 2014), p. 3.
19. *Dr Babasaheb Ambedkar Writings and Speeches*, Vol. 13, p.9.
20. *Ibid.,* Vol. 1, p. 412.
21. *Ibid.,* p. 411.
22. *Ibid.,* pp. 411-12
23. *Ibid.,* Vol. 13, pp. 1215-16.

24. *Ibid,* p. 1216.
25. *Ibid.*
26. *Ibid.*
27. Op. cit. C. D. Naik: *Thoughts and Philosophy of Dr Ambedkar*, pp. 2-3.
28. Kanta Kataria : *Relevance of Ambedkar's Ideology*, (Jaipur, Rawat Publications, 2015), p. 142.
29. *Dr Babasaheb Ambedkar Writings and Speeches*, Vol. 13, p. 476.
30. *Ibid,* Vol. 17, Part-Two, p. 318.
31. D. C. Ahir, p. 296.
32. Op. cit. C. D. Naik : *Thoughts and Philosophy of Dr Ambedkar*, p. 2.
33. *Dr Babasaheb Ambedkar Writings and Speeches*, Vol. 1, p. 1217.
34. Op. cit. Mohammed Shabbier (ed): *Ambedkar on Law, Constitution and Social Justice* (Jaipur, Rawat Publications, 2011), p. 161.
35. *Ibid.*, p. 162.
36. *Dr Babasaheb Ambedkar Writings and Speeches*, Vol. 13, p. 1217.
37. *Ibid.*, p.1218.
38. Y. K. Singh : *B. R. Ambedkar* (New Delhi, APH Publishing Corporation, 2013), p. 172.
39. Op. cit. C. D. Naik, p. 2.
40. *Dr Babasaheb Ambedkar Writings and Speeches*, Vol. 1, p. 75.
41. *Ibid.*, p. 76.
42. *Ibid.*, p. 78.
43. *Ibid.*, p. 79.
44. *Ibid.*, pp. 79-80.
45. Op. cit. D. C. Ahir, p.131.
46. *Dr Babasaheb Ambedkar Writings and Speeches*, Vol. 1, p. 221.
47. *Ibid.*, p. 223.
48. *Ibid.*, p. 224.
49. *Ibid.*
50. *Ibid.*, p. 226.
51. D. C. Ahir, p. 212.
52. *Ibid.*
53. *Ibid.*

Appendices

Appendix – I

Ambedkar's Selective Quotes

Justice has always evoked ideas of equality, of proportion of compensation. Equity signifies equality. Rules and regulations, right and righteousness are concerned with equality in value. If all men are equal, then all men are of the same essence, and the common essence entitles them of the same fundamental rights and equal liberty...In short justice is another name of liberty, equality and fraternity.

Slavery does not merely mean a legalised form of subjection. It means a state of society in which some men are forced to accept from others the purposes which control their conduct.

I measure the progress of a community by the degree of progress which women have achieved.

If you ask me, my ideal would be the society based on liberty, equality and fraternity. An ideal society should be mobile and full of channels of conveying a change taking place in one part to other parts.

Why does a human body become deceased? The reason is that as long as the human body is not free from suffering, mind cannot be happy. If a man lacks enthusiasm, either his body or mind is in a deceased condition....Now what saps the enthusiasm in man? If there is no enthusiasm, life becomes drudgery - a mere burden to be dragged. Nothing can be achieved if there is no enthusiasm. The main reason for this lack of enthusiasm on the part of a man is that an individual looses the hope of getting an opportunity to elevate himself.

Hopelessness leads to lack of enthusiasm. The mind in such cases becomes deceased....When is enthusiasm created? When one breaths an atmosphere where one is sure of getting the legitimate reward for one's labour, only then one feels enriched by enthusiasm and inspiration.

To idealise the real which more often than not is full of inequities is a very selfish thing to do. It is only when a person finds a personal advantage in things, as they are that he tries to idealise the real. To proceed to make such an ideal real is nothing short of criminal. It means perpetuating inequity on the ground that whatever is settled is settled for all times. Such a view is opposed to all morality. No society with ideal conscience has ever accepted it. On the contrary whatever progress in improving the terms of associated life between individuals and classes has been made in the course of history is due entirely to the recognition of the ethical doctrine that whatever is wrongly settled is never settled and must be resettled.

In every country the intellectual class is the most influential class. This is the class which can foresee, advise and lead. In no country does the mass of the people live the life for intelligent thought and action. It is largely imitative and follows the intellectual class. There is no exaggeration in saying that the entire destination of the country depends upon its intellectual class. If the intellectual class is honest and independent, it can be trusted to take the initiative and give a proper lead when a crisis arises. It is true that the intellect by itself is no virtue. It is only a means and the use of a means depends upon the ends which an intellectual person pursues. An intellectual man can be a good man but he may easily be a rogue. Similarly an intellectual class may be a band of high-souled persons, ready to help, ready to emancipate erring humanity or it may easily be a gang of crooks or a body of advocates of narrow clique from which it draws its support.

My final words of advice to you are educate, agitate and organise; have faith in yourself. With justice on our side I do not see how we can loose our battle. The battle to me is a matter of joy. The battle is in the fullest sense spiritual. There is nothing material or social in it. For ours is a battle not for wealth or for power. It is battle for freedom. It is the battle of reclamation of human personality.

You must abolish your slavery yourselves. Do not depend for its abolition upon god or a superman. Remember that it is not enough that a people are numerically in the majority. They must be always watchful, strong and self-respecting to attain and maintain success. We must shape our course ourselves and by ourselves.

Untouchability shuts all doors of opportunities for betterment in life for Untouchables. It does not offer an Untouchable any opportunity to move freely in society; it compels him to live in dungeons and seclusion; it prevents him from educating himself and following a profession of his choice.

Untouchability has ruined the Untouchables, the Hindus and ultimately the nation as well. If the depressed classes gained their self-respect and freedom, they would contribute not only to their own progress and prosperity but by their industry, intellect and courage would contribute also to the strength and prosperity of the nation. If the tremendous energy Untouchables are at present required to fritter away in combating the stigma of Untouchability had been saved them, it would have been applied by them to the promotion of education and development of resources of their nation as a whole.

There have been many Mahatmas in India whose sole object was to remove Untouchability and to elevate and absorb the depressed classes, but everyone has failed in their mission. Mahatmas have come, Mahatmas have gone but the Untouchables have remained as Untouchables.

From the point of view of annihilation of caste, the struggle of the saints did not have any effects on society. The value of a man is axiomatic and self-evident; it does not come to him from the gilding of Bhakti. The saints did not struggle to establish this point. On the contrary, their struggle had very unhealthy effect on the depressed classes. It provided the Brahmins with an excuse to silence them by telling them that they would be respected if they attained the status of Chokhamela.

It is mischievously propagated by Hindu scriptures that by serving the upper classes the Shudras achieve salvation. Untouchability is another appellation of slavery. No race can be raised by destroying its self-respect. So if you really want to uplift the Untouchables, you must treat them in the social order as free citizens, free to carve out their destiny.

Some people think that religion is not essential to the society. I do not hold this view. I consider the foundations of religion are essential to the society. At the roots of Hindu social system lies a Dharma as prescribed in the Manusmriti. Such being the case I do not think it is possible to abolish the inequality in the Hindu society unless a foundation of the Smriti-religion is removed and a better one laid in its place. I however, despair of Hindu society, being able to reconstruct itself on such a better foundation.

My religious conversion is not inspired by any material motive. This is hardly anything I cannot achieve even while remaining an Untouchable. There is no other feeling than that of a spiritual feeling underlying my religious conversion. Hinduism does not appeal to my conscience. My self-respect cannot assimilate Hinduism. In your case change of religion is imperative for worldly as well as spiritual ends. Do not care for the opinion of those who foolishly ridicule the idea of conversion for material ends. Why should you live under the fold of that religion which has deprived you of honour, money, food and shelter?

I tell you, religion is for man and not man for religion. If you want to organise, consolidate and be successful in this world, change this religion. The religion that does not recognise you as a human being, or give you water to drink, or allow you to enter in temples is not worthy to be called a religion. The religion that forbids you to receive education and comes in the way of your material advancement is not worthy of the appellation 'religion'. The religion that does not teach its followers to show humanity in dealing with its co-religionists is nothing but a display of a force. The religion that teaches its followers to suffer the touch of animals but not the touch of human beings is not a religion but a mockery. The religion that compels the ignorant to be ignorant and the poor to be poor is not a religion but a visitation!

The basic idea underlying religion is to create an atmosphere for the spiritual development of the individual. This being the situation, it is clear that you cannot develop your personality at all in Hinduism. In Hinduism, conscience, reason and independent thinking have no scope for development.

It is your claim to equality which hurts them. They want to maintain the status quo. If you continue to accept your lowly status ungrudgingly, continue to remain dirty, filthy, backward, ignorant, poor and disunited, they will allow you to live in peace. The moment you start to raise your level, the conflict starts. Untouchability is not transitory or temporary feature; it is eternal, it is lasting. Frankly it can be said that the struggle between the Hindus and the Untouchables is a never-ending conflict. It is eternal because the religion which assigns you the lowest status in society is itself divine and eternal according to the belief of the so-called high caste Hindus. No change warranted by change of time and circumstances is possible.

Every man must have a philosophy of life, for everyone must have a standard by which to measure his conduct. And philosophy is nothing but a standard by which to measure.

Freedom of mind is the real freedom. A person whose mind is not free though he may not be in chains, is a slave, not a free man. One whose mind is not free, though he may not be in prison, is a prisoner and not a free man. One whose mind is not free though alive, is no better than dead. Freedom of mind is the proof of one's existence.

What is the proof to judge that the flame of mental freedom is not extinguished in the mind of person? To whom can we say that his mind is free. I call him free who with his conscience awake realises his rights, responsibilities and duties. He who is not a slave of circumstances and is always ready and striving to change them in his flavour, I call him free. One who is not a slave of usage, customs, of meaningless rituals and ceremonies, of superstitions and traditions; whose flame of reason has not been extinguished, I call him a free man. He who has not surrendered his free will and abdicated his intelligence and independent thinking, who does not blindly act on the teachings of others, who does not blindly accept anything without critically analysing and examining its veracity and usefulness, who is always prepared to protect his rights, who is not afraid of ridicule and unjust public criticism, who has a sound conscience and self-respect so as not become a tool in the hands of others, I call him a free man. He who does not lead his life under the direction of others, who sets his own goal of life according to his own reasoning and decides for himself as to how and in what way life should be lead, is a free man. In short, who is a master of his own free will, him alone I call a free man.

Why does a human body become deceased? The reason is that as long as the human body is not free from suffering, mind cannot be happy. If a man lacks enthusiasm, either his body or mind is in a deceased condition....Now what saps the enthusiasm in man? If there is no enthusiasm, life becomes drudgery - a mere burden to be dragged. Nothing can be achieved if there is no enthusiasm. The main reason for this lack of enthusiasm on the part of a man is that an individual looses the hope of getting an opportunity to elevate himself. Hopelessness leads to lack of enthusiasm. The mind in such cases becomes deceased.... When is enthusiasm created? When one breaths an atmosphere where one is sure of getting the legitimate reward for one's labour, only then one feels enriched by enthusiasm and inspiration.

The fundamental principle of Buddhism is equality... Buddhism was called the religion of Shudras. There was only one man who raised his voice against separatism and Untouchability and that was Lord Buddha.

Religion must mainly be a matter of principles only. It cannot be a matter of rules. The moment it degenerates into rules, it ceases to be a religion, as it kills responsibility which is an essence of the true religious act.

We must begin by acknowledging that there is a complete absence of two things in Indian Society. One of these is equality. On the social plane we have an India based on the principles of graded inequality, which means elevation for some and degradation for others. On the economic plane we have a society in which there are some who have immense wealth as against many who live in abject poverty.

The second thing we are wanting in is the recognition of the principle of fraternity. What does fraternity mean? Fraternity means a sense of common brotherhood of all Indians, all Indians being one people. It is a principle that gives solidarity to social life. It is difficult thing to achieve. It seems to me that there lies a heavy duty to see that democracy does not vanish from the earth as a governing principle of human relationship. If we believe in it, we must both be true and loyal to it. We must not only be staunch in our faith in democracy but we must resolve to see that whatever we do, we do not help the enemies of democracy to uproot the principles of liberty, equality and fraternity. It follows that we must strive along with other democratic countries to maintain the basis of democratic civilisation. If democracy lives we are sure to reap the benefit of it. If democracy dies it will be our doom. On that there can be no doubt.

Justice has always evoked ideas of equality, of proportion of compensation. Equity signifies equality. Rules and regulations, right and righteousness are concerned with equality in value. If all men are equal, then all men are of the same essence, and the common essence entitles them of the same fundamental rights and equal liberty... In short justice is another name of liberty, equality and fraternity.

I hate injustice, tyranny, pompousness and humbug, and my hatred embraces all those who are guilty of them. I want to tell my critics that I regard my feelings of hatred as a real force. They are only the reflexes of love I bear for the causes I believe in and I am in no wise ashamed of it.

India is a peculiar country and her nationalists and patriots are a peculiar people. A patriot and a nationalist in India is one who sees with open eyes his fellow men treated as being less than man. But his humanity does not rise in protest. He knows that men and women for no cause are denied their rights. But it does not prick his civil sense of helpful action. He finds a whole class of people shut out from public employment. But it does not rouse his sense of justice and fair play. Hundreds of evil practices that injure man and society are perceived by him. But they do not sicken him with disgust. The patriot's one cry is power for him and his class. I am glad I do not belong to that class of patriots. I belong to that class which takes its stand on democracy and which seeks to destroy monopoly in every form. Our aim is to realise in practice our ideal of one man one value in all walks of life - political, economical and social.

There is no nation of Indians in the real sense of the world, it is yet to be created. In believing we are a nation, we are cherishing a great delusion. How can people divided into thousand of castes be a nation? The sooner we realise that we are not yet a nation, in a social and psychological sense of the world, the better for us.

A democratic form of government presupposes a democratic form of a society; the formal framework of democracy is of no value and would indeed be a misfit if there was no social democracy. It may not be necessary for a democratic society to be marked by unity, by community of purpose, by loyalty to public ends and by mutuality of sympathy. But it does unmistakably involve two things. The first is an attitude of mind, and attitude of respect and equality towards their fellows. The second is a social organisation free from rigid social barriers. Democracy is incompatible and inconsistent with isolation and exclusiveness resulting in the distinction between the privileged and the unprivileged.

What we must do is not to content ourselves with mere political democracy. We must make our political democracy a social democracy as well. Political democracy cannot last unless there is at the base of it, a social democracy. What does social democracy mean? It means a way of life which recognises liberty, equality and fraternity as the principles of life. These principles of liberty, equality and fraternity are not to be treated as separate items. They form a union in the sense that, to divorce one from the other is to defeat the very purpose of democracy. Liberty cannot be divorced from equality, nor can liberty and equality be divorced from fraternity.

Without social union, political unity is difficult to be achieved. If achieved, it would be as precarious as a summer sapling, liable to be uprooted by the gust of wind. With mere political unity, India may be a state. But to be a state is not to be a nation and a state which is not a nation has small prospects of survival in the struggle of existence. This is especially true where nationalism - the most dynamic force of modern times, is seeking everywhere to free itself by the destruction and disruption of all mixed states. The danger to a mixed and composite state therefore lies not so much in external aggression as in the internal resurgence of nationalities which are fragmented, entrapped, suppressed and held against their will.

On the 26th January 1950, we are going to enter into a life of contradictions. In politics we will have equality and in social and economic life we will have inequality. In politics we will be recognising the principle of one man one vote and one vote one value. In our social and economic life, we shall by reason of our social and economic structure, continue to deny the principle of one man one value. How long shall we continue to live this life of contradictions? How long shall we continue to deny equality in our social and economic life? If we continue to deny it for long, we will do so only by putting our political democracy in peril. We must remove this contradiction at the earliest possible moment else those who suffer from inequality will blow up the structure of democracy which this Constituent Assembly has so laboriously built up.

The monopoly has not merely deprived them of their chance of betterment; it has sapped them of what may be called the significance of life. Those downtrodden classes are tired of being governed. They are impatient to govern themselves. This urge of self-realisation in the downtrodden must not be allowed to devolve into class struggle or class war. It would lead to the division of the House. That would indeed be a day of disaster. For, as has been well-said by Abraham Lincoln: "A house divided against cannot stand very long". Therefore the sooner room is made for realisation of their aspiration, the better for the few, the better for the country, the better for the independence and the better for the continuance of its democratic structure. This can only be done by the establishment of equality and fraternity in all walks of life.

My social philosophy may be said to be enshrined in three words: liberty, equality and fraternity. My philosophy has roots in religion and not in political science. I have derived them from the teachings of my master, the Buddha.

An ideal society should be mobile, should be full of channels for conveying a change taking place in one part to other parts. In an ideal society there should be many interests consciously communicated and shared.

The strength of a society depends upon the presence of points of contacts, possibilities of interaction between different groups that exist in it. These are what Carlyle calls "Organic filaments", i.e. the elastic threads which helps to bring the disintegrating elements together and to reunite them.

Law and religion are two forces which govern the conduct of men. At times they act as handmaids to each other. At other times they act as check and counter-check. Of the two forces, Law is personal while religion is impersonal. Law being personal it is capable of being unjust and iniquitous. But religion being impersonal, it can be impartial, it is capable of defeating the inequity committed by law. Religion is believed to ennoble man and not degrade him. Hinduism is an exception.

APPENDIX - II

Excerpts from the Constituent Assembly speech by Dr B.R. Ambedkar on Friday, the 25th November, 1949.

…I feel, however good a Constitution may be, it is sure to turn out bad because those who are called to work it, happen to be a bad lot. However, bad a Constitution may be, it may turn out to be good if those who are called to work it, happen to be a good lot. The working of a Constitution does not depend wholly upon the nature of the Constitution. The Constitution can provide only the organs of State such as the Legislature, the Executive and the Judiciary. The factors on which the working of those organs of the State depend are the people and the political parties they will set up as their instruments to carry out their wishes and their politics. Who can say how the people of India and their purposes or will they prefer revolutionary methods of achieving them? If they adopt the revolutionary methods, however good the Constitution may be, it requires no prophet to say that it will fail. It is, therefore, futile to pass any judgement upon the Constitution without reference to the part which the people and their parties are likely to play.

... my mind is so full of the future of our country that I feel I ought to take this occasion to give expression to some of my reflections thereon. On 26th January 1950, India will be an independent country (*Cheers*). What would happen to her independence? Will she maintain her independence or will she lose it again? This is the first thought that comes to my mind. It is not that India was never an independent country. The point is that she once lost the independence she had. Will she lost it a second time? It is this thought which makes me most anxious for the future. What perturbs me greatly is the fact that not only India has once before lost her independence, but she lost it by the infidelity and treachery of some of her own people. In the invasion of Sind by Mahommed-Bin-Kasim, the military commanders of King Dahar accepted bribes from the agents of Mahommed-Bin-Kasim and refused to fight on the side of their King. It was Jaichand who invited Mahommed Gohri to invade India and fight against Prithvi Raj and promised him the help of himself and the Solanki Kings. When Shivaji was fighting for the liberation of Hindus, the other Maratha noblemen and the Rajput Kings were fighting the battle on the side of Moghul Emperors. When the British were trying to destroy the Sikh Rulers, Gulab Singh, their principal commander sat silent and did not help to save the Sikh Kingdom. In 1857, when a large part of India had declared a war of independence against the British, the Sikhs stood and watched the event as silent spectators.

Will history repeat itself? It is this thought which fills me with anxiety. This anxiety is deepened by the realisation of the fact that in addition to our old enemies in the form of castes and creeds we are going to have many political parties with diverse and opposing political creeds. Will Indians place the country above their creed or will they place creed above country? I do not know. But this much is certain that if the parties place creed above country, our independence will be put in jeopardy a second time and probably be lost for ever. This eventuality we must all resolutely guard against. We must be determined to defend our independence with the last drop of our blood. (*Cheers*)

On the 26th of January 1950, India would be a democratic country in the sense that India from that day would have a government of the people, by the people and for the people. The same thought comes to my mind. What would happen to her democratic Constitution? Will she be able to maintain it or will she lose it again. This is the second thought that comes to my mind and makes me as anxious as the first.

It is not that India did not know what Democracy is. There was a time when India was studded with republics, and even where there were monarchies, they were either elected or limited. They were never absolute. It is not that India did not know Parliaments or Parliamentary Procedure. A study of the Buddhist Bhikshu Sanghas discloses that not only there were Parliaments - for the Sanghas were nothing but Parliaments – but the Sanghas knew and observed all the rules of

Parliamentary Procedure known to modern times. They had rules regarding seating arrangements, rules regarding Motions, Resolutions, Quorum, Whip, Counting of Votes, Voting by Ballot, Censure Motion, Regularisation, *Res Judicata*, etc. Although these rules of Parliamentary Procedure were applied by the Buddha to the meetings of the Sanghas, he must have borrowed them from the rules of the Political Assemblies functioning in the country in his time.

This democratic system India lost. Will she lose it a second time? I do not know. But it is quite possible in a country like India – where democracy from its long disuse must be regarded as something quite new – there is danger of democracy giving place to dictatorship. It is quite possible for this new born democracy to retain its form but give place to dictatorship in fact. If there is a landslide, the danger of the second possibility becoming actuality is much greater.

If we wish to maintain democracy not merely in form, but also in fact, what must we do? The first thing in my judgement we must do is to hold fast to constitutional methods of achieving our social and economic objectives. It means we must abandon the bloody methods of revolution. It means that we must abandon the method of civil disobedience, non-cooperation and satyagraha. When there was no way left for constitutional methods for achieving economic and social objectives, there was a great deal of justification for unconstitutional methods. But where constitutional methods are open, there can be no justification for these unconstitutional methods. These methods are nothing but the Grammar of Anarchy and the sooner they are abandoned, the better for us.

The second thing we must do is to observe the caution which John Stuart Mill has given to all who are interested in the maintenance of democracy, namely, not "to lay their liberties at the feet of even a great man, or to trust him with power which enable him to subvert their institutions". There is nothing wrong in being grateful to great men who have rendered life-long services to the country. But there are limits to gratefulness. As has been well said by the Irish Patriot Daniel O'Connel, no man can be grateful at the cost of his honour, no woman can be grateful at the cost of her chastity and no nation can be grateful at the cost of its liberty. This caution is far more necessary in the case of India than in the case of any other country. For in India, Bhakti or what may be called the path of devotion or hero-worship, plays a part in its politics unequalled in magnitude by the part it plays in the politics of any other country in the world. Bhakti in religion may be a road to the salvation of the soul. But in politics, Bhakti or hero-worship is a sure road to degradation and to eventual dictatorship.

The third thing we must do is not to be content with mere political democracy. We must make our political democracy a social democracy as well. Political democracy cannot last unless there lies at the base of it social democracy. What does social democracy mean? It means a way of life which recognises liberty, equality and fraternity as the principles of life. These principles of liberty, equality and fraternity as the principles of life. These principles of liberty, equality and fraternity are not to be treated as separate items in a trinity. They form a union of trinity in the sense that to divorce one from the other is to defeat the very purpose of democracy. Liberty cannot be divorced from equality, equality cannot be divorced from liberty. Nor can liberty and equality be divorced from fraternity. Without equality, liberty would produce the supremacy of the few over the many. Equality without liberty would kill individual initiative. Without fraternity, liberty would produce the supremacy of the few over the many. Equality without liberty would kill individual initiative. Without fraternity, liberty and equality could not become a natural course of things. It would require a constable to enforce them. We must begin by acknowledging the fact that there is complete absence of two things in Indian Society. One of these is equality. On the social plane, we have in India a society based on the principle of graded inequality which we have a society in which there are some who have immense wealth as against many who live in abject poverty. On the 26th of January 1950, we are going to enter into a life of contradictions. In politics we will have equality and in social and economic life we will have inequality. In politics we will be recognising the principle of one man one vote and one vote one value. In our social and economic life, we shall, by reason of our social and economic structure, continue to deny the principle of one man one value. How long shall we continue to live this life of contradictions? How long shall we continue to deny equality in our social and economic life? If we continue to deny it for long, we will do so only by putting our political democracy in peril. We must remove this contradiction at the earliest possible moment or else those who suffer from inequality will blow up the structure of political democracy which is Assembly has to laboriously built up.

The second thing we are wanting in is recognition of the principle of fraternity. What does fraternity mean? Fraternity means a sense of common brotherhood of all Indians-of Indians being one people. It is the principle which gives unity and solidarity to social life. It is a difficult thing to achieve. How difficult it is, can be realised from the story related by James Bryce in his volume on American Commonwealth about the United States of America.

The story is –I propose to recount it in the words of Bryce himself- that –

"Some years ago the American Protestant Episcopal Church was occupied at its triennial Convention in revising its liturgy. It was thought desirable to introduce among the short sentence prayers a prayer for the whole people, and an eminent New England divine proposed the words 'O Lord, bless our nation'. Accepted one afternoon, on the spur of the moment, the sentence was brought up next day for reconsideration, when so many objections were raised by the laity to the word nation' as importing too definite a recognition of national unity, that it was dropped, and instead there were adopted the words 'O Lord, bless these United States'."

There was so little solidarity in the U.S.A. at the time when this incident occurred that the people of America did not think that they were a nation. If the people of the United States could not feel that they were a nation, how difficult it is for Indians to think that they are a nation. I remember the days when politically-minded Indians, resented the expression "the people of India". They preferred the expression "the Indian nation." I am of opinion that in believing that we are a nation, we are cherishing a great delusion. How can people divided into several thousands of castes be a nation? The sooner we realise that we are not as yet a nation in the social and psychological sense of the world, the better for us. For then only we shall realise the necessity of becoming a nation and seriously think of ways and means of realising the goal. The realisation of this goal is going to be very difficult – far more difficult than it has been in the

United States. The United States has no caste problem. In India, there are castes. The castes are anti-national. In the first place because they bring about separation in social life. They are anti-national also because they generate jealousy and antipathy between caste and caste. But we must overcome all these difficulties if we wish to become a nation in reality. For fraternity can be a fact only when there is a nation. Without fraternity equality and liberty will be no deeper than coats of paint.

These are my reflections about the tasks that lie ahead of us. They may not be very pleasant to some. But there can be no gainsaying that political power in this country has too long been the monopoly of a few and the many are only beasts of burden, but also beasts of prey. This monopoly has not merely deprived them of their chance of betterment; it has sapped them of what may be called the significance of life. These downtrodden classes are tired of being governed. They are impatient to govern themselves. This urge for self-realisation in the downtrodden classes must no be allowed to devolve into a class struggle or class war. It would lead to a division of the House. That would indeed be a day of disaster. For, as has been well said by Abraham Lincoln, a House divided against itself cannot stand very long. Therefore, the sooner room is made for the realisation of their aspiration, the better for the few, the better for the country, the better for the maintenance for its independence and the better for the continuance of its democratic structure. This can only be done by the establishment of equality and fraternity in all spheres of life. That is why I have laid so much stresses on them.

I do not wish to weary the House any further. Independence is no doubt a matter of joy. But let us not forget that this independence has thrown on us great responsibilities. By independence, we have lost the excuse of blaming the British for anything going wrong. If hereafter things go wrong, we will have nobody to blame except ourselves. There is great danger of things going wrong. Times are fast changing. People including our own are being moved by new ideologies. They are getting tired of government by the people. They are prepared to have governments for the people and are indifferent whether it is Government of the people and by the people. If we wish to preserve the Constitution in which we have sought to enshrine the principle of government of the people, for the people and by the people, let us resolve not to be tardy in the recognition of the evils that lie across our path and which induce people to prefer government for the people to government by the people, nor to be weak in our initiative to remove them. That is the only way to serve the country. I know of no better.

Selected Bibliography

Primary Sources

Dr Babasaheb Ambedkar Writings and Speeches

Government of Maharashtra, Bombay

Vol. 1 (1979)

Castes in India (1916)

Annihilation of Caste (1936)

Maharashtra as a Linguistic Province (1948)

Need for Checks and Balances (1953)

Thought on Linguistic States (1955)

Ranade, Gandhi and Jinnah (1943)

Evidence before the South borough Committee (1919)

Federation *versus* Freedom (1939)

Communal Deadlock and a Way to Solve It (1945)

States and Minorities (1947)

Small Holdings in India (1918)

Mr. Russell and the Reconstruction of Society (1918)

Vol. 2 (1982)

Dr Ambedkar in Bombay Legislature (1927-1939).

Dr Ambedkar with the Simon Commission (1927-28).

Dr Ambedkar at the Round Table Conferences (1930-1939).

Vol. 3 (1987)

Philosophy of Hinduism

India and the pre-requisites of Communism

Revolution and Counter-Revolution

Buddha or Karl Marx

Vol. 4 (1987)

Riddles in Hinduism

Vol. 5 (1989)

Essays on Untouchables and Untouchability

Vol. 6 (1989)

The Problem of the Rupee (1923)

Evolution of Provincial Finance in British India (1952)

Vol. 7 (1990)

Who were the Shudras?

The Untouchables

Vol. 8 (1990)

Pakistan or the Partition of India

Vol. 9 (1990)

What Congress and Gandhi have done to the Untouchables

Mr. Gandhi and the Emancipation of the Untouchables

Vol. 10 (1991)

Dr Ambedkar as Member of the Governor General's Executive Council, 1942-46

Vol. 11 (1992)

The Buddha and His Dhamma

Vol. 12 (1993)

Unpublished Writings; Ancient Indian Commerce; Notes on Laws; Waiting for a Visa, Miscellaneous Notes, etc

Vol. 13 (1994)

Dr Ambedkar as the Principal Architect of the Constitution of India

Vol. 14 (1994, Part-1)

Dr Ambedkar and The Hindu Code Bill

Vol. 15 (1995, Part-2)

Dr Ambedkar and The Hindu Code Bill

Vol. 16 (1997)

Dr Ambedkar as Free India's First Law Minister and Member of Opposition in Indian Parliament (1947-1956)

Vol. 17 (2003)

Dr B.R. Ambedkar and his Egalitarian Revolution – Struggle for Human Rights. Events Starting from March 1927 to 17 November 1956 in the Chronological Order (Part I)

Dr B.R. Ambedkar and his Egalitarian Revolution – Socio-Political and Religious Activities. Events Starting from November 1929 to 8 May 1956 in the Chronological Order. (Part II)

Dr B.R. Ambedkar and his Egalitarian Revolution – Speeches. Events Starting from 1 January to 20 November 1956 in the Chronological Order. (Part III)

II

- *Annihilation of Caste*, Bhim Patrika Prakashan, Jullundur, 1944.
- *Buddha or Karl Marx*, Anand Sahitya Sadan, Aligarh, U.P., 1989.
- *Evolution of Provincial Finance in British India*, P. S. King and Sons Ltd., London, 1925.
- *Federation versus Freedom*, Gokhale Institute of Politics and Economics 1939, R.K. Tatnis Bombay, 1939.
- *Gandhi and the Emancipation of the Untouchables*, Thacker and Co. Ltd., Bombay, 1943.
- *Gandhi and Gandhism,* Bhim Patrika Publications, Jullunder, 1970.
- *History of Indian Currency and Banking*, Bombay, Thacker & Co. 1946.
- *Pakistan or Partition of India*, Thacker and Co. Ltd., Bombay, 1946.
- *Ranade, Gandhi and Jinnah,* Bheem Patrika Publications, Jullundhar, 1964.
- *States and Minorities*, Thacker and Co. Ltd., Bombay, 1947.
- *States and Minorities, What are their Rights and How to secure them in the Constitution of Free India*, Babasaheb Ambedkar Memorial Society Hyderabad, 1970.
- *State Socialism*, Bheem Patrika Publications, Jalandhar, 1990.
- *The Untouchables*: Who were they and why they became Untouchables, Amrit Book Co., New Delhi, 1948.

- *The Problem of the Rupee: Its Origin and Its Solution*, P. S. King and Sons Ltd., London, 1923. Reprinted by Thacker and Co., Bombay, 1947, under the title History of Indian Currency and Banking.
- *Thoughts on Pakistan,* Thacker and Co. Ltd. Bombay, 1941.
- *Thoughts on Linguistic States*, published by B. R. Ambedkar, 26 Alipur Road, Civil Lines, Delhi, 1955.
- *The Buddha and His Dhamma,* Sidhartha College Publications, Bombay, 1957.
- *The Rise and Fall of Hindu Women*, Bheem Patrika, Jallundhar, 1980.
- *What Congress and Gandhi have done to the Untouchables*, Thacker and Co. Ltd., Bombay 1945.
- *Who were Shudra*? And how they came to be Fourth Varna in Indo-Aryan Society, Thacker and Co. Ltd., Bombay, 1946.
- *Communal Deadlock and a Way to Solve it,* Address on May 6, 1945, Bheem Patrika Prakashan Jullundur city.
- *On Poona Pact*, Bheem Patrika Prakashan, Jullundur.

III

Speeches and Articles of Dr Ambedkar

- Ambedkar's Presidential Address before All India Scheduled Caste Federation at Nagpur.
- Ambedkar's Pressidential Address at Ist Session of All India Depressed Classes Congress August, 8, 1930.
- Ambedkar's Memorandum entitled '*The Cabinet Mission and the Untouchables,* Ambedkar College, Mahad Librarian, 1962.
- *Annihilation of Caste: with a Reply to Mahatma Gandhi* – Undelivered address before the Annual Conference of the Jat Pat Todak Mandal of Lahore, 1936.
- *Castes in India: Their Genesis, Mechanism and Development* – a paper read by him before the Anthropology Seminar at Columbia University, New York, May 1916. Published in Indian Antiquary, Vol. XLI, May, 1917.

- *Communal Deadlock and Way to Solve it* – Address to the Annual Session of the All India Scheduled Castes Federation, Bombay, 1945.
- *Federation versus Freedom* - address delivered on 29th January 1939 (Kala Memorial Lecture) at the Annual Function of the Gokhale Institute of Politics and Economics, Poona.
- *Future of Parliamentary Democracy,* Speech on 28th October, 1951 in DAV College, Jullunder city.
- *Memorandum submitted to the Minorities Committee of RTC* dated 12th November, 1930 which obtained a scheme of political safeguards for the protection of Depressed Classes in the future Constitution of a self-governing India.
- *Memorandum placed before the Cabinet Mission*, New Delhi, 5th April, 1946.
- *Mr. Russell and Reconstruction of Society* – a review article published in the Journal of the Indian Economic Society, Vol. I, 1918.
- *On Parliamentary Democracy* – Speech delivered at Poona District Law Library, Poona, 1952.
- *Prospects of Parliamentary Democracy in India*, Talk for B.B.C. London, 20th May, 1956.
- *Ranade, Gandhi and Jinnah* – Address on the 101st Birth Celebration of M. G. Ranade at Poona of 10th January, 1943.
- *Small Holdings in India and Their Remedies* – an article published in the Journal of the Indian Economic Society, Vol. I, 1918.
- *Statement on Safeguard for Depressed Classes* submitted to the Simon Commission on behalf of Bahishkrit Hitkarini Sabha on May 29, 1928 (by Ambedkar).
- *The Buddha and the Future of His Religion*, The Maha Bodhi Journal, Calcutta, Vol. 58, April-May 1950.
- *The Rise and Fall of the Hindu Woman*, The Maha Bodhi Journal, Calcutta, June, 1951.
- *Thus Spoke Ambedkar,* Vol. I, Selected Speeches compiled by Bhagwan Das, Buddhist Publishing House, Jalandhar, 1963.
- *Thus Spoke Ambedkar*, Vol. II, Bhagwan Das, Buddhist Publishing House, Jalandhar, 1968.

- *Thus Spoke Ambedkar,* Vol. III, Bhagwan Das, Ambedkar Sahithya Prakashan, Bangalore, 1979.
- *Thus Spoke Ambedkar*, Vol. IV, Bhagwan Das, Ambedkar Sahithya Prakashan, Banglore, 1979.
- *Why Conversion* – Speech delivered in Marathi at the Mahar Parishad on 30-31May, 1936 in Bombay, Translated into English by Vasant Moon, Lokrajya, Bombay, 1981.

Secondary Sources

- Appadorai, *The Substance of Politics*, Oxford University Press, Delhi, 1965.
- Abarill Chandra, *Social and Political Ideas of B. R. Ambedkar*, Alekh Publishers, Jaipur, 1977.
- A.C. Banerjee, *Indian Constitutional Document*, Vol. III, Calcutta, A Mukerjee and Co. 1949.
- A.K. Vakil, *Gandhi Ambedkar Disputes: An Analytical Study*, Ashish Publishing House, New Delhi, 1991.
- A.K. Majumdar and Bhanwar Singh, *Ambedkar and Social Justice*, Radha Publications, New Delhi, 1997.
- A. M. Rajasekharaih, *Social Philosophy of Dr Ambedkar*, Dr Ambedkar Memorial Trust, Hyderabad, 1987.
- A.M. Rajasekhariah, *The Politics of Emancipation*, Sindhu Publications, Bombay, 1971.
- A.M. Rajasekhariah, *B. R. Ambedkar: The quest for Social Justice*, Uppal Publishing House, New Delhi, 1989.
- B. K. Ahluwalia and Shashi Ahluwalia (ed), *Dr Ambedkar and Human Rights,* Vivek Publishing Company, Delhi, 1981.
- C. B. Khairmody, *Bhimrao Ramji Ambedkar: A Biography,* Vol. i-iv, Bharat Bhushan Printing Press, Bombay, 1959.
- Chandra Bharill, *Social and Political Ideas of B. R. Ambedkar*, Aalekh Publishers, Jaipur, 1977.
- Christophe Jaffrelot, *Dr Ambedkar and Untouchability,* Permanent Black, New Delhi, 2005.
- C. L. Wayper, *Political Thought*, New Delhi, B. I. Publications, 1974.

- Constituent Assembly Debates I to XII, Lok Sabha Secretariat, New Delhi, 1985.
- David Thomson (ed), *Political Ideas*, Middlesex, Penguin Books, 1970.
- D. D. Basu (3rd ed), *Commentary on Constitution of India*, Calcutta, 1955.
- Devbrata Bose, *The Problems of Indian Society*, Popular Prakashan, Bombay, 1968.
- Dinkar Khabade, *Dr Ambedkar and Western Thinkers*, Pune, Usha Wagh, Sugava Prakashana, 1989.
- D. R. Jatava, *B. R. Ambedkar: A Vision of Man and Morals*, ABD Publishers, Jaipur, 1999.
- D. R. Jatava, *The Political Philosophy of Dr Ambedkar,* Phoenix Publishing Agency, Agra, 1965.
- D. R. Jatava, *The Social Philosophy of B. R. Ambedkar,* Phoenix Publishing House, Agra, 1965.
- D. R. Jatava, *The Critics of Dr Ambedkar,* Bhartiya Shoshit Jan Utthan Parishad, New Delhi, 1975.
- D. R. Jatava, *B.R. Ambedkar Study in Society and Politics,* National Publishing House, New Delhi, 1998.
- D. R. Jatava, *Ambedkar:The Prime Mover*, Jaipur, ABD Publishers, 2004.
- D. C. Ahir, *Buddhism and Ambedkar*, Ajay Prakashan, New Delhi, 1968.
- D. C. Ahir, *Gandhi and Ambedkar,* Ajay Prakashan, New Delhi, 1969.
- D. C. Ahir, *Dr Ambedkar and Indian Constitution*, Buddha Vihara, Lucknow, 1972.
- D. C. Ahir, *The Legacy of Dr Ambedkar,* B. R. Publishing Corporation, Delhi, 1990.
- D. C. Gupta, *Indian National Movement and Constitutional Development*, Vikas Publishing House, Delhi, 1970.
- Dhananjay Keer, *Dr Ambedkar: Life and Mission*, Popular Prakashan, Bombay, 1971.
- D. K. Baisantry, *Dr Ambedkar-A Pioneer of Labour Welfare*, Buddhist Publishing House, Jalandhar, 1990.

- D. N. Banerjee, *Some Aspects of the Indian Constitution*, World Press Pvt. Ltd., Calcutta, 1962.
- Donald E. Smith, *India as a Secular State*, Princeton University Press, London, 1963.
- E. Barker, *Plato and His Predecessors*, London, 1952.
- Edward Thompson, *Enlist India for Freedom*, Victor Gollanecz Ltd., London, 1940.
- Forsyth and Keens-Soper (ed), *A Guide to the Political Classics*, Oxford, Oxford University Press, 1988.
- G. Buhler, *The Laws of Manu*, Motilal Banarasidas, Delhi, 1964.
- Gian Singh, *Dr Ambedkar and Humanism*, Bheem Patrika Publication, Jalandhar, 1990.
- G. S. Loknande, *Bhimrao Ramji Ambedkar: A Study in Social Democracy*, Intellectual Publishing House, IIndRevised Edition, New Delhi, Intellectual Publishing House, 1982.
- G. S. Ghurye, *Caste and Class in India*, Popular Book Depot, Bombay, 1957.
- L. R. Balley (ed), *Thoughts on Ambedkar*, Bheem Patrika, Jullundhar, 1972.
- Hoti Lal Nim (complied), *Thoughts on Dr Ambedkar*, Siddharth Educational and Cultural Society, Agra, 1969.
- J. C. Johari, *Comparative Politics*, Sterling Publishing, New Delhi, 1976.
- J. H. Huttan, *Caste in India*, Oxford University Press, London, 1969.
- J. J. Shukla, *Dr B. R. Ambedkar on Hinduism*, Globe Books and Periodicals, Ahmedabad.
- Jeanette Robin, *Dr Ambedkar and His Movement,* Dr Ambedkar Publication Society, Hyderabad, 1964.
- J.S. Narayan Rao, A. Somasekhar, K. Audiseshaiah, *B. R. Ambedkar: His Relevance Today*, Gyan Publishing House, New Delhi, 2002.
- Kanta Kataria, *Relevance of Ambedkar's Ideology*, Jaipur, Rawat Publications, 2015.
- Kshirsagar Ramchandra Kamaji, *Political Thought of Dr Babasaheb Ambedkar,* Intellectual Publishing House, New Delhi, 1992.

- K. M. Munshi, *Indian Constitutional Documents*, Vol. I-II, Munshi Papers Bhartiys Vidya Bhawan, Bombay, 1967.
- K. M. Panikar, *The Foundation of New India*, George Allen and Unwin, London, 1963.
- K. S. Bharti, *Foundation of Ambedkar Thought,* Nagpur, Datta Son Publication, 1990.
- Kusum Sharma, *Ambedkar and Indian Constitution,* Ashish Publishing House, New Delhi, 1997.
- Leo Huberman, *Introduction to Socialism*, Progressive Book Depot, New Delhi, 1968.
- L. R. Balley (ed), *Thoughts on Ambedkar*, Bheem Patrika, Jullundhur, 1972.
- L. S. Rathore, *Formative Influence on B. R. Ambedkar*, keynote address, National Post Graduate College, Lucknow.
- L. S. Rathore, *Dr Ambedkar: His Works and Key Concepts*, keynote address, National Post Graduate College, Lucknow.
- L. S. Rathore, *Political and Social Philosophy of Dr Ambedkar,* keynote address, National Post Graduate College, Lucknow, May 26-27,2007.
- M. G. Chitkara, *Dr Ambedkar and Social Justice,* APH Publishing Corporation, New Delhi, 2002.
- Michael Curtis (ed), *The Great Political Theories*, New York, Avon Book Division, 1961.
- M. K. Dongre, *Economic Thoughts of Dr B. R. Ambedkar,* Ambedkar Samaj Publication, Nagpur, 1974.
- M. L. Ranga (ed), *B. R. Ambedkar, Life, Work and Relevance*, New Delhi, Manohar Publishers, 2000.
- Mohammad Shabbir, *Ambedkar on Law, Constitution and Social Justice,* Rawat Publication, New Delhi, 2005.
- N. Srinivasan, *Democratic Government in India,* Asia Publishing House, Delhi, 1954.
- O. P. Gauba, *Dimensions of Social Justice*, National Publishing House, New Delhi, 1983.
- Owen M Lynch, *The Politics of Untouchability*, National Publishing House, Delhi, 1974.

- P. Laxmi Narsu, *The Essence of Buddhism*, Thacker and Co., Bombay, 1948.
- Paul Carus, *The Gospel of Buddha*, National Book Trust, New Delhi, 1975.
- Aramanand Singh, *Equality, Reservation and Discrimination*, Deep and Deep Publication, New Delhi.
- Ramchandra Guha (ed), *Makers of Modern India*, New Delhi, Penguin Books India, 2010.
- Ramchandra Guha, *India After Gandhi*, London, Picador, 2008.
- Ramesh Chandra and Sangh Mittra, *The Ambedkar Era*, New Delhi, Commonwealth Publishers, 2003.
- Ramesh Chandra and Sangh Mittra, *Caste System in India*, New Delhi, Commonwealth Publishers, 2003.
- Sanjay Prakash Sharma, *Dr B. R. Ambedkar: A Crusader of Social Justice,* RBSA Publishers Jaipur, 2003.
- Shashi Ahaluwalia, *Founder of Modern India,* New Delhi, Mandi Publication, 1986.
- Sitamath Tattvabhushana, *The Philosophy of Brahmoism*, Madras, Higginbotham and Co., 1990.
- S. K. Ghosh, *Protection of Minorities and Scheduled Castes*, Ashish Publishing House, New Delhi, 1980.
- S. N. Mandal, *Dr Ambedkar: His Thought and Observation*, New Delhi, National Publishing House, 2004.
- S. R. Bakshi, *Political Ideology of B. R. Ambedka*r, Deep and Deep Publications Pvt. Ltd., New Delhi.
- S. R. Bhakshi (ed), *Social Ideology of B. R. Ambedkar*, New Delhi, Deep and Deep Publication, 2001.
- S. R. Sharma, *Life and Works of Dr Ambedkar*, Jaipur, Book Enclave, 2006.
- S. S. Shashi (ed.), *Ambedkar and Social Justice*, Vol. 1, Ministry of Information and Broadcasting, Government of India, Patiala House, New Delhi,1992.
- Shanti Deva and C. M. Wagh, *Dr Ambedkar and Conversion*, Dr Ambedkar Publications Society, Hyderabad, 1965.
- Sukhbir Singh, *History of Political Thought*, Vol. I, Meerut, Rastogi Publications, 2006.

- V. Chandra Mouli, *B. R. Ambedkar –Man and His Vision,* Sterling Publisher Pvt. Ltd., New Delhi, 1990.
- V. P. Gupta and Mohini Gupta (ed), *Makers of Modern India Series II, Dr Ambedkar,* Delhi, AMBE Books, 1998.
- V. P. Verma, *Modern Indian Political Thought,* Agra, Lakshmi Narain Agarwal, 1978.
- V. P. Menon, *Transfer of Power in India,* Orient Longmans, Bombay, 1957.
- V. P. Menon, *The Story of the Integration of Indian States*, Macmillan, New York, 1956.
- Ven Sangharakshita, *Ambedkar and Buddhism*, Windhorse Publications, Glasgow, England, 1986.
- W. N. Kuber, *Dr Ambedkar: A Critical Study*, New Delhi, People's Publishing House, 1973.
- W. N. Kuber, *Builders of Modern India, B. R. Ambedkar,* Publications Division, Ministry of Information and Broadcasting, Delhi, 1987.
- Yogesh Chandha, *Rediscovering Gandhi*, London, Arrow Books, 1980.
- Zelliot Eleanor, *Gandhi and Ambedkar*, Pune, Trailokya Boudh Mahasangh Sahayak Gana, 1983.

Index

B